Advanced Deep Learning
with Keras

Apply deep learning techniques, autoencoders, GANs,
variational autoencoders, deep reinforcement learning,
policy gradients, and more

Rowel Atienza

BIRMINGHAM - MUMBAI

Advanced Deep Learning with Keras

Acquisition Editor: Frank Pohlmann, Andrew Waldron, Suresh Jain

Content Development Editor: Alex Sorrentino

Technical Editor: Gaurav Gavas

Project Editor: Kishor Rit

Proofreader: Safis Editing

Indexers: Aishwarya Gangawane

Graphics: Tom Scaria

Production Coordinator: Sandip Tadge

First published: October 2018

Production reference: 1311018

Published by Packt Publishing Ltd.
Livery Place
35 Livery Street
Birmingham B3 2PB, UK.

ISBN 978-1-78862-941-6

www.packtpub.com

`mapt.io`

Mapt is an online digital library that gives you full access to over 5,000 books and videos, as well as industry leading tools to help you plan your personal development and advance your career. For more information, please visit our website.

Why subscribe?

- Spend less time learning and more time coding with practical eBooks and Videos from over 4,000 industry professionals

- Learn better with Skill Plans built especially for you

- Get a free eBook or video every month

- Mapt is fully searchable

- Copy and paste, print, and bookmark content

Packt.com

Did you know that Packt offers eBook versions of every book published, with PDF and ePub files available? You can upgrade to the eBook version at `www.Packt.com` and as a print book customer, you are entitled to a discount on the eBook copy. Get in touch with us at `customercare@packtpub.com` for more details.

At `www.Packt.com`, you can also read a collection of free technical articles, sign up for a range of free newsletters, and receive exclusive discounts and offers on Packt books and eBooks.

Contributors

About the author

Rowel Atienza is an Associate Professor at the Electrical and Electronics Engineering Institute of the University of the Philippines, Diliman. He holds the Dado and Maria Banatao Institute Professorial Chair in Artificial Intelligence. Rowel has been fascinated with intelligent robots since he graduated from the University of the Philippines. He received his MEng from the National University of Singapore for his work on an AI-enhanced four-legged robot. He finished his Ph.D. at The Australian National University for his contribution on the field of active gaze tracking for human-robot interaction. Rowel's current research work focuses on AI and computer vision. He dreams on building useful machines that can perceive, understand, and reason. To help make his dreams become real, Rowel has been supported by grants from the Department of Science and Technology (DOST), Samsung Research Philippines, and Commission on Higher Education-Philippine California Advanced Research Institutes (CHED-PCARI).

I would like to thank my family, Che, Diwa, and Jacob. They never cease to support my work.

I would like to thank my mother who instilled into me the value of education.

I would like to express my gratitude to the people of Packt and this book's technical reviewer, Frank, Kishor, Alex, and Valerio. They are inspiring and easy to work with.

I would like to thank the institutions who always support my teaching and research agenda, University of the Philippines, DOST, Samsung Research PH, and CHED-PCARI.

I would like to acknowledge my students. They have been patient as I develop my courses in AI.

About the reviewer

Valerio Maggio is currently a Post-Doc Data Scientist at Fondazione Bruno Kessler (FBK) in Trento, Italy, responsible for Machine Learning and Deep Learning in the MPBA lab (Predictive Models for Biomedicine and Environment). Valerio has a Ph.D. in Computational Science from the University of Naples "Federico II." His research interests are focused on Machine Learning and Deep Learning applied to Software Maintenance and Computational Biology. Valerio is very much involved in the scientific Python community, and he is an active speaker at many Python conference.

He is also the lead organiser of PyCon Italy/PyData Florence, and EuroSciPy. He uses Python as the mainstream language for his deep/machine learning code, making an intensive use of Python to analyse, visualise, and learn from data. In the context of Deep Learning, Valerio is the author of a quite popular Keras/TensorFlow tutorial, publicly available on his GitHub Profile – `github.com/leriomaggio/deep-learning-keras-tensorflow` – and presented in many conferences (EuroSciPy, PyData London, PySS) and University courses. Valerio is also passionate about (black) tea, and an "old-school" Magic The Gathering (MTG) player, who enjoys playing and teaching MTG to newbies.

Packt is Searching for Authors Like You

If you're interested in becoming an author for Packt, please visit `authors.packtpub.com` and apply today. We have worked with thousands of developers and tech professionals, just like you, to help them share their insight with the global tech community. You can make a general application, apply for a specific hot topic that we are recruiting an author for, or submit your own idea.

Table of Contents

Preface

In recent years, deep learning has made unprecedented success stories in difficult problems in vision, speech, natural language processing and understanding, and all other areas with abundance of data. The interest in this field by companies, universities, governments, and research organizations has accelerated the advances in the field. This book covers select important advances in deep learning. The advanced theories are explained by giving a background of the principles, digging into the intuition behind the concepts, implementing the equations and algorithms using Keras, and examining the results.

Artificial Intelligence (AI), as it stands today, is still far from being a well-understood field. Deep learning, as a sub field of AI, is in the same position. While it is far from being a mature field, many real-world applications such as vision-based detection and recognition, product recommendation, speech recognition and synthesis, energy conservation, drug discovery, finance, and marketing are already using deep learning algorithms. Many more applications will be discovered and built. The aim of this book is to explain advanced concepts, give sample implementations, and let the readers, as experts in their field, identify the target applications.

A field that is not completely mature is a double-edged sword. On one edge, it offers a lot of opportunities for discovery and exploitation. There are many unsolved problems in deep learning. This translates into opportunities to be the first to market – product development, publication, or recognition. The other edge is that it would be difficult to trust a not completely well-understood field in a mission-critical environment. We can safely say that if asked, very few machine learning engineers will ride an auto-pilot plane controlled by a deep learning system. There is a lot of work to be done to gain this level of trust. The advanced concepts that are discussed in this book have a high chance of playing a major role as the foundation in gaining this level of trust.

Every book in deep learning will not be able to completely cover the whole field. This book is not an exception. Given the time and space, we could have touched interesting areas such as detection, segmentation and recognition, visual understanding, probabilistic reasoning, natural language processing and understanding, speech synthesis, and automated machine learning. However, this book believes in choosing and explaining select areas so that readers can take up other fields that are not covered.

As the reader is about to read the rest of this book, they need to keep in mind that they chose an area that is exciting and can have a huge impact on the society. We are fortunate to have a job that we look forward to working on as we wake up in the morning.

Who this book is for

The book is intended for machine learning engineers and students who would like to gain a better understanding of advanced topics in deep learning. Each discussion is supplemented with code implementation in Keras. This book is for readers who would like to understand how to translate theory into a working code implementation in Keras. Apart from understanding theories, code implementation is usually one of the difficult tasks in applying machine learning to real-world problems.

What this book covers

Chapter 1, Introducing Advanced Deep Learning with Keras, covers the key concepts of deep learning such as optimization, regularization, loss functions, fundamental layers, and networks and their implementation in Keras. This chapter also serves as a review of both deep learning and Keras using sequential API.

Chapter 2, Deep Neural Networks, discusses the functional API of Keras. Two widely-used deep network architectures, ResNet and DenseNet, are examined and implemented in Keras, using functional API.

Chapter 3, Autoencoders, covers a common network structure called autoencoder that is used to discover the latent representation of the input data. Two example applications of autoencoders, denoising and colorization, are discussed and implemented in Keras.

Chapter 4, Generative Adversarial Networks (GANs), discusses one of the recent significant advances in deep learning. GAN is used to generate new synthetic data that appear real. This chapter explains the principles of GAN. Two examples of GAN, DCGAN and CGAN, are examined and implemented in Keras.

Chapter 5, Improved GANs, covers algorithms that improve the basic GAN. The algorithms address the difficulty in training GANs and improve the perceptual quality of synthetic data. WGAN, LSGAN, and ACGAN are discussed and implemented in Keras.

Chapter 6, Disentangled Representation GANs, discusses how to control the attributes of the synthetic data generated by GANs. The attributes can be controlled if the latent representations are disentangled. Two techniques in disentangling representations, InfoGAN and StackedGAN, are covered and implemented in Keras.

Chapter 7, Cross-Domain GANs, covers a practical application of GANs, translating images from one domain to another or commonly known as cross-domain transfer. CycleGAN, a widely used cross-domain GAN, is discussed and implemented in Keras. This chapter also demonstrates CycleGAN performing colorization and style transfer.

Chapter 8, Variational Autoencoders (VAEs), discusses another recent significant advance in deep learning. Similar to GAN, VAE is a generative model that is used to produce synthetic data. Unlike GAN, VAE focuses on decodable continuous latent space that is suitable for variational inference. VAE and its variations, CVAE and β-VAE, are covered and implemented in Keras.

Chapter 9, Deep Reinforcement Learning, explains the principles of reinforcement learning and Q-Learning. Two techniques in implementing Q-Learning for discrete action spaces are presented, Q Table update and Deep Q Network (DQN). Implementation of Q-Learning using Python and DQN in Keras are demonstrated in OpenAI gym environments.

Chapter 10, Policy Gradient Methods, explains how to use neural networks to learn the policy for decision making in reinforcement learning. Four methods are covered and implemented in Keras and OpenAI gym environment, REINFORCE, REINFORCE with Baseline, Actor-Critic, and Advantage Actor-Critic. The example presented in this chapter demonstrates policy gradient methods on a continuous action space.

To get the most out of this book

- **Deep learning and Python**: The reader should have a fundamental knowledge of deep learning and its implementation in Python. While previous experience in using Keras to implement deep learning algorithms is important, it is not required. *Chapter 1, Introducing Advanced Deep Learning with Keras* offers a review of deep learning concepts and their implementation in Keras.

- **Math**: The discussions in this book assume that the reader is familiar with calculus, linear algebra, statistics, and probability at the college level.

- **GPU**: Majority of the Keras implementations in this book require GPU. Without GPU, it is not practical to execute many of the code examples because of the time involved (many hours to days). The examples in this book use reasonable data size as much as possible in order to minimize the use of high-performance computers. The reader is expected to have access to at least NVIDIA GTX 1060.

- **Editor**: The code examples in this book were edited using `vim` in Ubuntu Linux 16.04 LTS, Ubuntu Linux 17.04, and macOS High Sierra. Any Python-aware text editor is acceptable.

- **Tensorflow**: Keras requires a backend. The code examples in this book were written in Keras with TensorFlow backend. Please ensure that the GPU driver and `tensorflow` are both installed properly.

- **GitHub**: We learn by example and experimentation. Please `git pull` or `fork` the code bundle for the book from its GitHub repository. After getting the code, examine it. Run it. Change it. Run it again. Do all creative experiments by tweaking the code examples. It is the only way to appreciate all the theories explained in the chapters. Giving a star on the book GitHub repository is also highly appreciated.

Download the example code files

The code bundle for the book is hosted on GitHub at

`https://github.com/PacktPublishing/Advanced-Deep-Learning-with-Keras`

We also have other code bundles from our rich catalog of books and videos available at `https://github.com/PacktPublishing/`. Check them out!

Download the color images

We also provide a PDF file that has color images of the screenshots/diagrams used in this book. You can download it here: `http://www.packtpub.com/sites/default/files/downloads/9781788629416_ColorImages.pdf`.

Conventions used

The code examples in this book are in Python. More specifically, `python3`. The color scheme is based on vim syntax highlighting. Consider the following example:

```
def encoder_layer(inputs,
                  filters=16,
                  kernel_size=3,
                  strides=2,
                  activation='relu',
                  instance_norm=True):
    """Builds a generic encoder layer made of Conv2D-IN-LeakyReLU
    IN is optional, LeakyReLU may be replaced by ReLU

    """

    conv = Conv2D(filters=filters,
                  kernel_size=kernel_size,
                  strides=strides,
                  padding='same')

    x = inputs
    if instance_norm:
        x = InstanceNormalization()(x)
    if activation == 'relu':
        x = Activation('relu')(x)
    else:
        x = LeakyReLU(alpha=0.2)(x)
    x = conv(x)
    return x
```

Whenever possible, docstring is included. At the very least, text comment is used
to minimize space usage.

Any command-line code execution is written as follows:

```
$ python3 dcgan-mnist-4.2.1.py
```

The example code file naming is: `algorithm-dataset-chapter.section.number.py`. The command-line example is DCGAN on MNIST dataset in Chapter 4, second section and first listing. In some cases, the explicit command line to execute is not written but it is assumed to be:

```
$ python3 name-of-the-file-in-listing
```

`The file name of the code example is included in the Listing caption.`

Get in touch

Feedback from our readers is always welcome.

General feedback: Email `feedback@packtpub.com`, and mention the book's title in the subject of your message. If you have questions about any aspect of this book, please email us at `questions@packtpub.com`.

Errata: Although we have taken every care to ensure the accuracy of our content, mistakes do happen. If you have found a mistake in this book we would be grateful if you would report this to us. Please visit, `http://www.packtpub.com/submit-errata`, selecting your book, clicking on the Errata Submission Form link, and entering the details.

Piracy: If you come across any illegal copies of our works in any form on the Internet, we would be grateful if you would provide us with the location address or website name. Please contact us at `copyright@packtpub.com` with a link to the material.

If you are interested in becoming an author: If there is a topic that you have expertise in and you are interested in either writing or contributing to a book, please visit `http://authors.packtpub.com`.

Reviews

Please leave a review. Once you have read and used this book, why not leave a review on the site that you purchased it from? Potential readers can then see and use your unbiased opinion to make purchase decisions, we at Packt can understand what you think about our products, and our authors can see your feedback on their book. Thank you!

For more information about Packt, please visit `packtpub.com`.

1
Introducing Advanced Deep Learning with Keras

In this first chapter, we will introduce the three deep learning artificial neural networks that we will be using throughout the book. These deep learning models are MLPs, CNNs, and RNNs, which are the building blocks to the advanced deep learning topics covered in this book, such as Autoencoders and GANs.

Together, we'll implement these deep learning models using the Keras library in this chapter. We'll start by looking at why Keras is an excellent choice as a tool for us. Next, we'll dig into the installation and implementation details within the three deep learning models.

This chapter will:

- Establish why the Keras library is a great choice to use for advanced deep learning

- Introduce MLPs, CNNs, and RNNs – the core building blocks of most advanced deep learning models, which we'll be using throughout this book

- Provide examples of how to implement MLPs, CNNs, and RNNs using Keras and TensorFlow

- Along the way, start to introduce important deep learning concepts, including optimization, regularization, and loss function

By the end of this chapter, we'll have the fundamental deep learning models implemented using Keras. In the next chapter, we'll get into the advanced deep learning topics that build on these foundations, such as Deep Networks, Autoencoders, and GANs.

Why is Keras the perfect deep learning library?

Keras [*Chollet, François. "Keras (2015)." (2017)*] is a popular deep learning library with over 250,000 developers at the time of writing, a number that is more than doubling every year. Over 600 contributors actively maintain it. Some of the examples we'll use in this book have been contributed to the official Keras GitHub repository. Google's **TensorFlow**, a popular open source deep learning library, uses Keras as a high-level API to its library. In the industry, Keras is used by major technology companies like Google, Netflix, Uber, and NVIDIA. In this chapter, we introduce how to use **Keras Sequential API**.

We have chosen Keras as our tool of choice to work within this book because Keras is a library dedicated to accelerating the implementation of deep learning models. This makes Keras ideal for when we want to be practical and hands-on, such as when we're exploring the advanced deep learning concepts in this book. Because Keras is intertwined with deep learning, it is essential to learn the key concepts of deep learning before someone can maximize the use of Keras libraries.

 All examples in this book can be found on GitHub at the following link: https://github.com/PacktPublishing/Advanced-Deep-Learning-with-Keras.

Keras is a deep learning library that enables us to build and train models efficiently. In the library, layers are connected to one another like pieces of Lego, resulting in a model that is clean and easy to understand. Model training is straightforward requiring only data, a number of epochs of training, and metrics to monitor. The end result is that most deep learning models can be implemented with a significantly smaller number of lines of code. By using Keras, we'll gain productivity by saving time in code implementation which can instead be spent on more critical tasks such as formulating better deep learning algorithms. We're combining Keras with deep learning, as it offers increased efficiency when introduced with the three deep learning networks that we will introduce in the following sections of this chapter.

Likewise, Keras is ideal for the rapid implementation of deep learning models, like the ones that we will be using in this book. Typical models can be built in few lines of code using the **Sequential Model API**. However, do not be misled by its simplicity. Keras can also build more advanced and complex models using its API and `Model` and `Layer` classes which can be customized to satisfy unique requirements. Functional API supports building graph-like models, layers reuse, and models that are behaving like Python functions. Meanwhile, `Model` and `Layer` classes provide a framework for implementing uncommon or experimental deep learning models and layers.

Installing Keras and TensorFlow

Keras is not an independent deep learning library. As shown in *Figure 1.1.1*, it is built on top of another deep learning library or backend. This could be Google's **TensorFlow**, MILA's **Theano** or Microsoft's **CNTK**. Support for Apache's **MXNet** is nearly completed. We'll be testing examples in this book on a **TensorFlow backend using Python 3**. This due to the popularity of TensorFlow, which makes it a common backend.

We can easily switch from one back-end to another by editing the Keras configuration file `.keras/keras.json` in Linux or macOS. Due to the differences in the way low-level algorithms are implemented, networks can often have different speeds on different backends.

On hardware, Keras runs on a CPU, GPU, and Google's TPU. In this book, we'll be testing on a CPU and NVIDIA GPUs (Specifically, the GTX 1060 and GTX 1080Ti models).

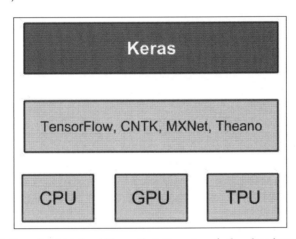

Figure 1.1.1: Keras is a high-level library that sits on top of other deep learning models.
Keras is supported on CPU, GPU, and TPU.

Before proceeding with the rest of the book, we need to ensure that Keras and TensorFlow are correctly installed. There are multiple ways to perform the installation; one example is installing using `pip3`:

```
$ sudo pip3 install tensorflow
```

If we have a supported NVIDIA GPU, with properly installed drivers, and both NVIDIA's **CUDA** Toolkit and **cuDNN Deep Neural Network library**, it is recommended that we install the GPU-enabled version since it can accelerate both training and prediction:

```
$ sudo pip3 install tensorflow-gpu
```

The next step for us is to then install Keras:

```
$ sudo pip3 install keras
```

The examples presented in this book will require additional packages, such as `pydot`, `pydot_ng`, `vizgraph`, `python3-tk` and `matplotlib`. We'll need to install these packages before proceeding beyond this chapter.

The following should not generate any error if both TensorFlow and Keras are installed along with their dependencies:

```
$ python3
>>> import tensorflow as tf
>>> message = tf.constant('Hello world!')
>>> session = tf.Session()
>>> session.run(message)
b'Hello world!'
>>> import keras.backend as K
Using TensorFlow backend.
>>> print(K.epsilon())
1e-07
```

The warning message about `SSE4.2 AVX AVX2 FMA`, which is similar to the one below can be safely ignored. To remove the warning message, you'll need to recompile and install the TensorFlow source code from `https://github.com/tensorflow/tensorflow`.

```
tensorflow/core/platform/cpu_feature_guard.cc:137] Your CPU supports
instructions that this TensorFlow binary was not compiled to use:
SSE4.2 AVX AVX2 FMA
```

This book does not cover the complete Keras API. We'll only be covering the materials needed to explain the advanced deep learning topics in this book. For further information, we can consult the official Keras documentation, which can be found at `https://keras.io`.

Implementing the core deep learning models - MLPs, CNNs, and RNNs

We've already mentioned that we'll be using three advanced deep learning models, they are:

- **MLPs**: Multilayer perceptrons

- **RNNs**: Recurrent neural networks
- **CNNs**: Convolutional neural networks

These are the three networks that we will be using throughout this book. Despite the three networks being separate, you'll find that they are often combined together in order to take advantage of the strength of each model.

In the following sections of this chapter, we'll discuss these building blocks one by one in more detail. In the following sections, MLPs are covered together with other important topics such as loss function, optimizer, and regularizer. Following on afterward, we'll cover both CNNs and RNNs.

The difference between MLPs, CNNs, and RNNs

Multilayer perceptrons or MLPs are a fully-connected network. You'll often find them referred to as either deep feedforward networks or feedforward neural networks in some literature. Understanding these networks in terms of known target applications will help us get insights about the underlying reasons for the design of the advanced deep learning models. MLPs are common in simple logistic and linear regression problems. However, MLPs are not optimal for processing sequential and multi-dimensional data patterns. By design, MLPs struggle to remember patterns in sequential data and requires a substantial number of parameters to process multi-dimensional data.

For sequential data input, RNNs are popular because the internal design allows the network to discover dependency in the history of data that is useful for prediction. For multi-dimensional data like images and videos, a CNN excels in extracting feature maps for classification, segmentation, generation, and other purposes. In some cases, a CNN in the form of a 1D convolution is also used for networks with sequential input data. However, in most deep learning models, MLPs, RNNs, and CNNs are combined to make the most out of each network.

MLPs, RNNs, and CNNs do not complete the whole picture of deep networks. There is a need to identify an *objective* or *loss function*, *an optimizer*, and a *regularizer*. The goal is to reduce the loss function value during training since it is a good guide that a model is learning. To minimize this value, the model employs an optimizer. This is an algorithm that determines how weights and biases should be adjusted at each training step. A trained model must work not only on the training data but also on a test or even on unforeseen input data. The role of the regularizer is to ensure that the trained model generalizes to new data.

Multilayer perceptrons (MLPs)

The first of the three networks we will be looking at is known as a **multilayer perceptrons or (MLPs)**. Let's suppose that the objective is to create a neural network for identifying numbers based on handwritten digits. For example, when the input to the network is an image of a handwritten number 8, the corresponding prediction must also be the digit 8. This is a classic job of classifier networks that can be trained using logistic regression. To both train and validate a classifier network, there must be a sufficiently large dataset of handwritten digits. The Modified National Institute of Standards and Technology dataset or MNIST [1] for short, is often considered as the *Hello World!* of deep learning and is a suitable dataset for handwritten digit classification.

Before we discuss the multilayer perceptron model, it's essential that we understand the MNIST dataset. A large number of the examples in this book use the MNIST dataset. MNIST is used to explain and validate deep learning theories because the 70,000 samples it contains are small, yet sufficiently rich in information:

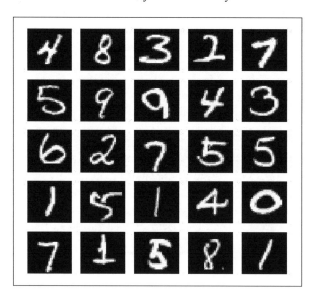

Figure 1.3.1: Example images from the MNIST dataset. Each image is 28 × 28-pixel grayscale.

MNIST dataset

MNIST is a collection of handwritten digits ranging from the number 0 to 9. It has a training set of 60,000 images, and 10,000 test images that are classified into corresponding categories or labels. In some literature, the term **target** or **ground truth** is also used to refer to the **label**.

In the preceding figure sample images of the MNIST digits, each being sized at 28 X 28-pixel grayscale, can be seen. To use the MNIST dataset in Keras, an API is provided to download and extract images and labels automatically. *Listing 1.3.1* demonstrates how to load the MNIST dataset in just one line, allowing us to both count the train and test labels and then plot random digit images.

Listing 1.3.1, `mnist-sampler-1.3.1.py`. Keras code showing how to access MNIST dataset, plot 25 random samples, and count the number of labels for train and test datasets:

```
import numpy as np
from keras.datasets import mnist
import matplotlib.pyplot as plt

# load dataset
(x_train, y_train), (x_test, y_test) = mnist.load_data()

# count the number of unique train labels
unique, counts = np.unique(y_train, return_counts=True)
print("Train labels: ", dict(zip(unique, counts)))

# count the number of unique test labels
unique, counts = np.unique(y_test, return_counts=True)
print("Test labels: ", dict(zip(unique, counts)))

# sample 25 mnist digits from train dataset
indexes = np.random.randint(0, x_train.shape[0], size=25)
images = x_train[indexes]
labels = y_train[indexes]

# plot the 25 mnist digits
plt.figure(figsize=(5,5))
for i in range(len(indexes)):
    plt.subplot(5, 5, i + 1)
    image = images[i]
    plt.imshow(image, cmap='gray')
    plt.axis('off')

plt.show()
plt.savefig("mnist-samples.png")
plt.close('all')
```

The `mnist.load_data()` method is convenient since there is no need to load all 70,000 images and labels individually and store them in arrays. Executing `python3 mnist-sampler-1.3.1.py` on command line prints the distribution of labels in the train and test datasets:

```
Train labels:  {0: 5923, 1: 6742, 2: 5958, 3: 6131, 4: 5842, 5: 5421, 6:
5918, 7: 6265, 8: 5851, 9: 5949}

Test labels:  {0: 980, 1: 1135, 2: 1032, 3: 1010, 4: 982, 5: 892, 6: 958,
7: 1028, 8: 974, 9: 1009}
```

Afterward, the code will plot 25 random digits as shown in the preceding figure, *Figure 1.3.1*.

Before discussing the multilayer perceptron classifier model, it is essential to keep in mind that while MNIST data are 2D tensors, they should be reshaped accordingly depending on the type of input layer. The following figure shows how a 3 × 3 grayscale image is reshaped for MLPs, CNNs, and RNNs input layers:

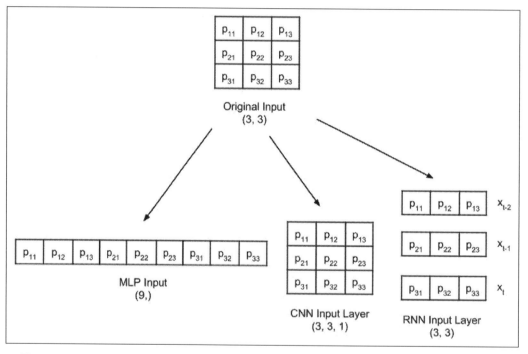

Figure 1.3.2: An input image similar to the MNIST data is reshaped depending on the type of input layer. For simplicity, reshaping of a 3 × 3 grayscale image is shown.

MNIST digits classifier model

The proposed MLP model shown in *Figure 1.3.3* can be used for MNIST digit classification. When the units or perceptrons are exposed, the MLP model is a fully connected network as shown in *Figure 1.3.4*. It will also be shown how the output of the perceptron is computed from inputs as a function of weights, w_i and bias, b_n for the nth unit. The corresponding Keras implementation is illustrated in *Listing 1.3.2*.

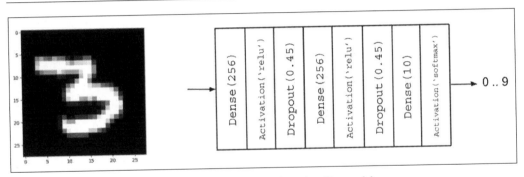

Figure 1.3.3: MLP MNIST digit classifier model

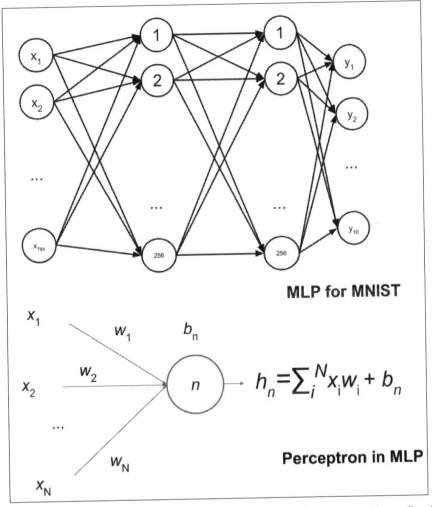

MLP for MNIST

$$h_n = \sum_i^N x_i w_i + b_n$$

Perceptron in MLP

Figure 1.3.4: The MLP MNIST digit classifier in Figure 1.3.3 is made up of fully connected layers. For simplicity, the activation and dropout are not shown. One unit or perceptron is also shown.

Listing 1.3.2, `mlp-mnist-1.3.2.py` shows the Keras implementation of the MNIST digit classifier model using MLP:

```python
import numpy as np
from keras.models import Sequential
from keras.layers import Dense, Activation, Dropout
from keras.utils import to_categorical, plot_model
from keras.datasets import mnist

# load mnist dataset
(x_train, y_train), (x_test, y_test) = mnist.load_data()

# compute the number of labels
num_labels = len(np.unique(y_train))

# convert to one-hot vector
y_train = to_categorical(y_train)
y_test = to_categorical(y_test)

# image dimensions (assumed square)
image_size = x_train.shape[1]
input_size = image_size * image_size

# resize and normalize
x_train = np.reshape(x_train, [-1, input_size])
x_train = x_train.astype('float32') / 255
x_test = np.reshape(x_test, [-1, input_size])
x_test = x_test.astype('float32') / 255

# network parameters
batch_size = 128
hidden_units = 256
dropout = 0.45

# model is a 3-layer MLP with ReLU and dropout after each layer
model = Sequential()
model.add(Dense(hidden_units, input_dim=input_size))
model.add(Activation('relu'))
model.add(Dropout(dropout))
model.add(Dense(hidden_units))
model.add(Activation('relu'))
model.add(Dropout(dropout))
model.add(Dense(num_labels))
# this is the output for one-hot vector
```

```
model.add(Activation('softmax'))
model.summary()
plot_model(model, to_file='mlp-mnist.png', show_shapes=True)

# loss function for one-hot vector
# use of adam optimizer
# accuracy is a good metric for classification tasks
model.compile(loss='categorical_crossentropy',
              optimizer='adam',
              metrics=['accuracy'])
# train the network
model.fit(x_train, y_train, epochs=20, batch_size=batch_size)

# validate the model on test dataset to determine generalization
loss, acc = model.evaluate(x_test, y_test, batch_size=batch_size)
print("\nTest accuracy: %.1f%%" % (100.0 * acc))
```

Before discussing the model implementation, the data must be in the correct shape and format. After loading the MNIST dataset, the number of labels is computed as:

```
# compute the number of labels
num_labels = len(np.unique(y_train))
```

Hard coding num_labels = 10 is also an option. But, it's always a good practice to let the computer do its job. The code assumes that y_train has labels 0 to 9.

At this point, the labels are in digits format, 0 to 9. This sparse scalar representation of labels is not suitable for the neural network prediction layer that outputs probabilities per class. A more suitable format is called a **one-hot vector**, a 10-dim vector with all elements 0, except for the index of the digit class. For example, if the label is 2, the equivalent one-hot vector is [0,0,1,0,0,0,0,0,0,0]. The first label has index 0.

The following lines convert each label into a one-hot vector:

```
# convert to one-hot vector
y_train = to_categorical(y_train)
y_test = to_categorical(y_test)
```

In deep learning, data is stored in **tensors**. The term tensor applies to a scalar (0D tensor), vector (1D tensor), matrix (2D tensor), and a multi-dimensional tensor. From this point, the term tensor is used unless scalar, vector, or matrix makes the explanation clearer.

The rest computes the image dimensions, `input_size` of the first `Dense` layer and scales each pixel value from 0 to 255 to range from 0.0 to 1.0. Although raw pixel values can be used directly, it is better to normalize the input data as to avoid large gradient values that could make training difficult. The output of the network is also normalized. After training, there is an option to put everything back to the integer pixel values by multiplying the output tensor by 255.

The proposed model is based on MLP layers. Therefore, the input is expected to be a 1D tensor. As such, `x_train` and `x_test` are reshaped to [60000, 28 * 28] and [10000, 28 * 28], respectively.

```
# image dimensions (assumed square)
image_size = x_train.shape[1]
input_size = image_size * image_size

# resize and normalize
x_train = np.reshape(x_train, [-1, input_size])
x_train = x_train.astype('float32') / 255
x_test = np.reshape(x_test, [-1, input_size])
x_test = x_test.astype('float32') / 255
```

Building a model using MLPs and Keras

After data preparation, building the model is next. The proposed model is made of three MLP layers. In Keras, an MLP layer is referred to as **Dense**, which stands for the densely connected layer. Both the first and second MLP layers are identical in nature with 256 units each, followed by `relu` activation and `dropout`. 256 units are chosen since 128, 512 and 1,024 units have lower performance metrics. At 128 units, the network converges quickly, but has a lower test accuracy. The added number units for 512 or 1,024 does not increase the test accuracy significantly.

The number of units is a **hyperparameter**. It controls the *capacity* of the network. The capacity is a measure of the complexity of the function that the network can approximate. For example, for polynomials, the degree is the hyperparameter. As the degree increases, the capacity of the function also increases.

As shown in the following model, the classifier model is implemented using a sequential model API of Keras. This is sufficient if the model requires one input and one output processed by a sequence of layers. For simplicity, we'll use this in the meantime, however, in *Chapter 2, Deep Neural Networks*, the Functional API of Keras will be introduced to implement advanced deep learning models.

```
# model is a 3-layer MLP with ReLU and dropout after each layer
model = Sequential()
model.add(Dense(hidden_units, input_dim=input_size))
```

```
model.add(Activation('relu'))
model.add(Dropout(dropout))
model.add(Dense(hidden_units))
model.add(Activation('relu'))
model.add(Dropout(dropout))
model.add(Dense(num_labels))
# this is the output for one-hot vector
model.add(Activation('softmax'))
```

Since a Dense layer is a linear operation, a sequence of Dense layers can only approximate a linear function. The problem is that the MNIST digit classification is inherently a non-linear process. Inserting a relu activation between Dense layers will enable MLPs to model non-linear mappings. relu or **Rectified Linear Unit (ReLU)** is a simple non-linear function. It's very much like a filter that allows positive inputs to pass through unchanged while clamping everything else to zero. Mathematically, relu is expressed in the following equation and plotted in *Figure 1.3.5*:

$$relu(\mathbf{x}) = max(0,x)$$

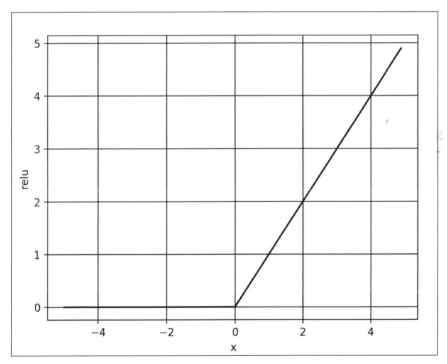

Figure 1.3.5: Plot of ReLU function. The ReLU function introduces non-linearity in neural networks.

There are other non-linear functions that can be used such as `elu`, `selu`, `softplus`, `sigmoid`, and `tanh`. However, `relu` is the most commonly used in the industry and is computationally efficient due to its simplicity. The `sigmoid` and `tanh` are used as activation functions in the output layer and described later. *Table 1.3.1* shows the equation for each of these activation functions:

relu	$relu(x) = max(0,x)$	1.3.1
softplus	$softplus(x) = \log(1 + e^x)$	1.3.2
elu	$$elu\left(x, a\right) = \begin{cases} x & if\ x \geq 0 \\ a\left(e^x - 1\right) & otherwise \end{cases}$$ where $a \geq 0$ and is a tunable hyperparameter	1.3.3
selu	$selu(x) = k \times elu(x, a)$ where k = 1.0507009873554804934193349852946 and a = 1.6732632423543772848170429916717	1.3.4

Table 1.3.1: Definition of common non-linear activation functions

Regularization

A neural network has the tendency to memorize its training data especially if it contains more than enough capacity. In such a case, the network fails catastrophically when subjected to the test data. This is the classic case of the network failing to generalize. To avoid this tendency, the model uses a regularizing layer or function. A common regularizing layer is referred to as a **dropout**.

The idea of dropout is simple. Given a dropout rate (here, it is set to `dropout=0.45`), the `Dropout` layer randomly removes that fraction of units from participating in the next layer. For example, if the first layer has 256 units, after `dropout=0.45` is applied, only *(1 - 0.45) * 256 units = 140* units from layer 1 participate in layer 2. The `Dropout` layer makes neural networks robust to unforeseen input data because the network is trained to predict correctly, even if some units are missing. It's worth noting that dropout is not used in the output layer and it is only active during training. Moreover, dropout is not present during prediction.

There are regularizers that can be used other than dropouts like `l1` or `l2`. In Keras, the bias, weight and activation output can be regularized per layer. `l1` and `l2` favor smaller parameter values by adding a penalty function. Both `l1` and `l2` enforce the penalty using a fraction of the sum of absolute (`l1`) or square (`l2`) of parameter values. In other words, the penalty function forces the optimizer to find parameter values that are small. Neural networks with small parameter values are more insensitive to the presence of noise from within the input data.

As an example, `l2` weight regularizer with `fraction=0.001` can be implemented as:

```
from keras.regularizers import l2
model.add(Dense(hidden_units,
         kernel_regularizer=l2(0.001),
         input_dim=input_size))
```

No additional layer is added if `l1` or `l2` regularization is used. The regularization is imposed in the `Dense` layer internally. For the proposed model, dropout still has a better performance than `l2`.

Output activation and loss function

The output layer has 10 units followed by `softmax` activation. The 10 units correspond to the 10 possible labels, classes or categories. The `softmax` activation can be expressed mathematically as shown in the following equation:

$$softmax\left(x_i\right) = \frac{e^{x_i}}{\sum_{j=0}^{N-1} e^{x_j}} \qquad \text{(Equation 1.3.5)}$$

The equation is applied to all $N = 10$ outputs, x_i for $i = 0, 1 \ldots 9$ for the final prediction. The idea of `softmax` is surprisingly simple. It squashes the outputs into probabilities by normalizing the prediction. Here, each predicted output is a probability that the index is the correct label of the given input image. The sum of all the probabilities for all outputs is 1.0. For example, when the `softmax` layer generates a prediction, it will be a 10-dim 1D tensor that may look like the following output:

```
[  3.57351579e-11    7.08998016e-08    2.30154569e-07    6.35787558e-07

   5.57471187e-11    4.15353840e-09    3.55973775e-16    9.99995947e-01

   1.29531730e-09    3.06023480e-06]
```

The prediction output tensor suggests that the input image is going to be 7 given that its index has the highest probability. The `numpy.argmax()` method can be used to determine the index of the element with the highest value.

There are other choices of output activation layer, like `linear`, `sigmoid`, and `tanh`. The `linear` activation is an identity function. It copies its input to its output. The `sigmoid` function is more specifically known as a **logistic sigmoid**. This will be used if the elements of the prediction tensor should be mapped between 0.0 and 1.0 independently. The summation of all elements of the predicted tensor is not constrained to 1.0 unlike in `softmax`. For example, `sigmoid` is used as the last layer in sentiment prediction (0.0 is bad to 1.0, which is good) or in image generation (0.0 is 0 to 1.0 is 255-pixel values).

The tanh function maps its input in the range -1.0 to 1.0. This is important if the output can swing in both positive and negative values. The tanh function is more popularly used in the internal layer of recurrent neural networks but has also been used as output layer activation. If tanh is used to replace sigmoid in the output activation, the data used must be scaled appropriately. For example, instead of scaling each grayscale pixel in the range [0.0 1.0] using $x = \dfrac{x}{255}$, it is assigned in the range [-1.0 1.0] by $x = \dfrac{x - 127.5}{127.5}$.

The following graph shows the sigmoid and tanh functions. Mathematically, sigmoid can be expressed in equation as follows:

$$sigmoid(x) = \sigma(x) = \frac{1}{1 + e^{-x}} \qquad \text{(Equation 1.3.6)}$$

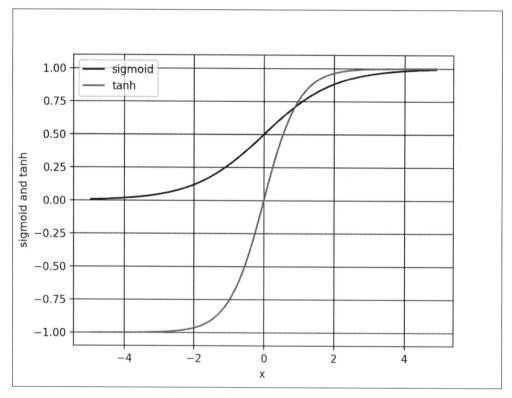

Figure 1.3.6: Plots of sigmoid and tanh

How far the predicted tensor is from the one-hot ground truth vector is called loss. One type of loss function is `mean_squared_error` (**mse**), or the average of the squares of the differences between target and prediction. In the current example, we are using `categorical_crossentropy`. It's the negative of the sum of the product of the target and the logarithm of the prediction. There are other loss functions that are available in Keras, such as `mean_absolute_error`, and `binary_crossentropy`. The choice of the loss function is not arbitrary but should be a criterion that the model is learning. For classification by category, `categorical_crossentropy` or `mean_squared_error` is a good choice after the `softmax` activation layer. The `binary_crossentropy` loss function is normally used after the `sigmoid` activation layer while `mean_squared_error` is an option for `tanh` output.

Optimization

With optimization, the objective is to minimize the loss function. The idea is that if the loss is reduced to an acceptable level, the model has indirectly learned the function mapping input to output. Performance metrics are used to determine if a model has learned the underlying data distribution. The default metric in Keras is **loss**. During training, validation, and testing, other metrics such as **accuracy** can also be included. Accuracy is the percent, or fraction, of correct predictions based on ground truth. In deep learning, there are many other performance metrics. However, it depends on the target application of the model. In literature, performance metrics of the trained model on the test dataset is reported for comparison to other deep learning models.

In Keras, there are several choices for optimizers. The most commonly used optimizers are; **Stochastic Gradient Descent (SGD)**, **Adaptive Moments (Adam)**, and **Root Mean Squared Propagation (RMSprop)**. Each optimizer features tunable parameters like learning rate, momentum, and decay. Adam and RMSprop are variations of SGD with adaptive learning rates. In the proposed classifier network, Adam is used since it has the highest test accuracy.

SGD is considered the most fundamental optimizer. It's a simpler version of the gradient descent in calculus. In **gradient descent (GD)**, tracing the curve of a function downhill finds the minimum value, much like walking downhill in a valley or opposite the gradient until the bottom is reached.

The GD algorithm is illustrated in *Figure 1.3.7*. Let's suppose x is the parameter (for example, weight) being tuned to find the minimum value of y (for example, loss function). Starting at an arbitrary point of $x = -0.5$ with the gradient being $\frac{dy}{dx} = -2.0$. The GD algorithm imposes that x is then updated to $x = -0.5 - \epsilon(-2.0)$. The new value of x is equal to the old value, plus the opposite of the gradient scaled by ϵ. The small number ϵ refers to the learning rate. If $\epsilon = 0.01$, then the new value of $x = -0.48$.

GD is performed iteratively. At each step, y will get closer to its minimum value. At $x = 0.5$ $\frac{dy}{dx} = 0.0$, the GD has found the absolute minimum value of $y = -1.25$. The gradient recommends no further change in x.

The choice of learning rate is crucial. A large value of $\in$ may not find the minimum value since the search will just swing back and forth around the minimum value. On the other hand, too small value of $\in$ may take a significant number of iterations before the minimum is found. In the case of multiple minima, the search might get stuck in a local minimum.

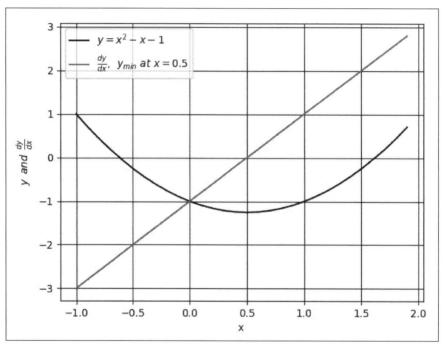

Figure 1.3.7: Gradient descent is similar to walking downhill on the function curve until the lowest point is reached. In this plot, the global minimum is at x = 0.5.

An example of multiple minima can be seen in *Figure 1.3.8*. If for some reason the search started at the left side of the plot and the learning rate is very small, there is a high probability that GD will find $x = -1.51$ as the minimum value of y. GD will not find the global minimum at $x = 1.66$. A sufficiently valued learning rate will enable the gradient descent to overcome the hill at $x = 0.0$. In deep learning practice, it is normally recommended to start at a bigger learning rate (for example. 0.1 to 0.001) and gradually decrease as the loss gets closer to the minimum.

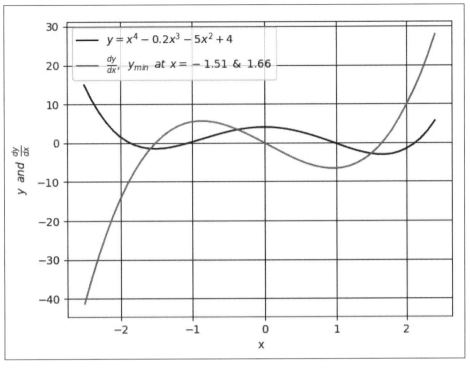

Figure 1.3.8: Plot of a function with 2 minima, x = -1.51 and x = 1.66.
Also shown is the derivative of the function.

Gradient descent is not typically used in deep neural networks since you'll often come upon millions of parameters that need to be trained. It is computationally inefficient to perform a full gradient descent. Instead, SGD is used. In SGD, a mini batch of samples is chosen to compute an approximate value of the descent. The parameters (for example, weights and biases) are adjusted by the following equation:

$$\theta \leftarrow \theta - \epsilon\, \mathbf{g} \qquad \text{(Equation 1.3.7)}$$

In this equation, θ and $\mathbf{g} = \frac{1}{m}\nabla_\theta \sum L$ are the parameters and gradients tensor of the loss function respectively. The $\mathbf{g}$ is computed from partial derivatives of the loss function. The mini-batch size is recommended to be a power of 2 for GPU optimization purposes. In the proposed network, `batch_size=128`.

Equation 1.3.7 computes the last layer parameter updates. So, how do we adjust the parameters of the preceding layers? For this case, the chain rule of differentiation is applied to propagate the derivatives to the lower layers and compute the gradients accordingly. This algorithm is known as **backpropagation** in deep learning. The details of backpropagation are beyond the scope of this book. However, a good online reference can be found at `http://neuralnetworksanddeeplearning.com`.

Since optimization is based on differentiation, it follows that an important criterion of the loss function is that it must be smooth or differentiable. This is an important constraint to keep in mind when introducing a new loss function.

Given the training dataset, the choice of the loss function, the optimizer, and the regularizer, the model can now be trained by calling the `fit()` function:

```
# loss function for one-hot vector
# use of adam optimizer
# accuracy is a good metric for classification tasks
model.compile(loss='categorical_crossentropy',
              optimizer='adam',
              metrics=['accuracy'])
# train the network
model.fit(x_train, y_train, epochs=20, batch_size=batch_size)
```

This is another helpful feature of Keras. By just supplying both the *x* and *y* data, the number of epochs to train, and the batch size, `fit()` does the rest. In other deep learning frameworks, this translates to multiple tasks such as preparing the input and output data in the proper format, loading, monitoring, and so on. While all of these must be done inside a `for` loop! In Keras, everything is done in just one line.

In the `fit()` function, an epoch is the complete sampling of the entire training data. The `batch_size` parameter is the sample size of the number of inputs to process at each training step. To complete one epoch, `fit()` requires the size of train dataset divided by batch size, plus 1 to compensate for any fractional part.

Performance evaluation

At this point, the model for the **MNIST** digit classifier is now complete. Performance evaluation will be the next crucial step to determine if the proposed model has come up with a satisfactory solution. Training the model for 20 epochs will be sufficient to obtain comparable performance metrics.

The following table, *Table 1.3.2*, shows the different network configurations and corresponding performance measures. Under *Layers*, the number of units is shown for layers 1 to 3. For each optimizer, the default parameters in Keras are used. The effects of varying the regularizer, optimizer and number of units per layer can be observed. Another important observation in *Table 1.3.2* is that bigger networks do not necessarily translate to better performance.

Increasing the depth of this network shows no added benefits in terms of accuracy for both training and testing datasets. On the other hand, a smaller number of units, like 128, could also lower both the test and train accuracy. The best train accuracy at 99.93% is obtained when the regularizer is removed, and 256 units per layer are used. The test accuracy, however, is much lower at 98.0%, as a result of the network overfitting.

The highest test accuracy is with the Adam optimizer and Dropout(0.45) at 98.5%. Technically, there is still some degree of overfitting given that its training accuracy is 99.39%. Both the train and test accuracy are the same at 98.2% for 256-512-256, Dropout(0.45) and SGD. Removing both the *Regularizer* and *ReLU* layers results in it having the worst performance. Generally, we'll find that the Dropout layer has better performance than l2.

Following table demonstrates a typical deep neural network performance during tuning. The example indicates that there is a need to improve the network architecture. In the following section, another model using CNNs shows a significant improvement in test accuracy:

Layers	Regularizer	Optimizer	ReLU	Train Accuracy, %	Test Accuracy, %
256-256-256	None	SGD	None	93.65	92.5
256-256-256	L2(0.001)	SGD	Yes	99.35	98.0
256-256-256	L2(0.01)	SGD	Yes	96.90	96.7
256-256-256	None	SGD	Yes	99.93	98.0
256-256-256	Dropout(0.4)	SGD	Yes	98.23	98.1
256-256-256	Dropout(0.45)	SGD	Yes	98.07	98.1
256-256-256	Dropout(0.5)	SGD	Yes	97.68	98.1
256-256-256	Dropout(0.6)	SGD	Yes	97.11	97.9
256-512-256	Dropout(0.45)	SGD	Yes	98.21	98.2
512-512-512	Dropout(0.2)	SGD	Yes	99.45	98.3
512-512-512	Dropout(0.4)	SGD	Yes	98.95	98.3
512-1024-512	Dropout(0.45)	SGD	Yes	98.90	98.2
1024-1024-1024	Dropout(0.4)	SGD	Yes	99.37	98.3
256-256-256	Dropout(0.6)	Adam	Yes	98.64	98.2
256-256-256	Dropout(0.55)	Adam	Yes	99.02	98.3
256-256-256	Dropout(0.45)	Adam	Yes	99.39	98.5
256-256-256	Dropout(0.45)	RMSprop	Yes	98.75	98.1
128-128-128	Dropout(0.45)	Adam	Yes	98.70	97.7

Table 1.3.2: Different MLP network configurations and performance measures

Model summary

Using the Keras library provides us with a quick mechanism to double check the model description by calling:

```
model.summary()
```

Listing 1.3.2 shows the model summary of the proposed network. It requires a total of 269,322 parameters. This is substantial considering that we have a simple task of classifying MNIST digits. MLPs are not parameter efficient. The number of parameters can be computed from *Figure 1.3.4* by focusing on how the output of the perceptron is computed. From input to Dense layer: 784 × 256 + 256 = 200,960. From first Dense to second Dense: 256 × 256 + 256 = 65,792. From second Dense to the output layer: 10 × 256 + 10 = 2,570. The total is 269,322.

Listing 1.3.2 shows a summary of an MLP MNIST digit classifier model:

Layer (type)	Output Shape	Param #
dense_1 (Dense)	(None, 256)	200960
activation_1 (Activation)	(None, 256)	0
dropout_1 (Dropout)	(None, 256)	0
dense_2 (Dense)	(None, 256)	65792
activation_2 (Activation)	(None, 256)	0
dropout_2 (Dropout)	(None, 256)	0
dense_3 (Dense)	(None, 10)	2570
activation_3 (Activation)	(None, 10)	0

Total params: 269,322
Trainable params: 269,322
Non-trainable params: 0

Another way of verifying the network is by calling:

```
plot_model(model, to_file='mlp-mnist.png', show_shapes=True)
```

Figure 1.3.9 shows the plot. You'll find that this is similar to the results of summary() but graphically shows the interconnection and I/O of each layer.

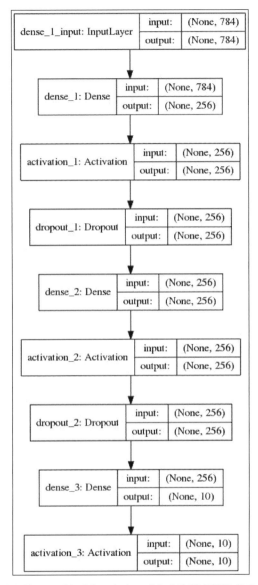

Figure 1.3.9: The graphical description of the MLP MNIST digit classifier

Convolutional neural networks (CNNs)

We're now going to move onto the second artificial neural network, **Convolutional Neural Networks (CNNs)**. In this section, we're going solve the same MNIST digit classification problem, instead this time using CNNs.

Figure 1.4.1 shows the CNN model that we'll use for the MNIST digit classification, while its implementation is illustrated in *Listing 1.4.1*. Some changes in the previous model will be needed to implement the CNN model. Instead of having input vector, the input tensor now has new dimensions (height, width, channels) or (image_size, image_size, 1) = (28, 28, 1) for the grayscale MNIST images. Resizing the train and test images will be needed to conform to this input shape requirement.

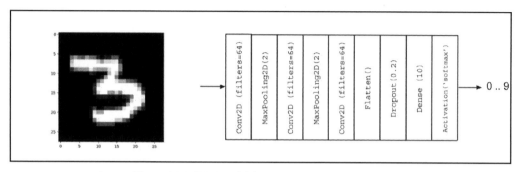

Figure 1.4.1: CNN model for MNIST digit classification

Listing 1.4.1, `cnn-mnist-1.4.1.py` shows the Keras code for the MNIST digit classification using CNN:

```python
import numpy as np
from keras.models import Sequential
from keras.layers import Activation, Dense, Dropout
from keras.layers import Conv2D, MaxPooling2D, Flatten
from keras.utils import to_categorical, plot_model
from keras.datasets import mnist

# load mnist dataset
(x_train, y_train), (x_test, y_test) = mnist.load_data()

# compute the number of labels
num_labels = len(np.unique(y_train))

# convert to one-hot vector
y_train = to_categorical(y_train)
y_test = to_categorical(y_test)

# input image dimensions
image_size = x_train.shape[1]
# resize and normalize
x_train = np.reshape(x_train,[-1, image_size, image_size, 1])
x_test = np.reshape(x_test,[-1, image_size, image_size, 1])
x_train = x_train.astype('float32') / 255
x_test = x_test.astype('float32') / 255

# network parameters
```

```
# image is processed as is (square grayscale)
input_shape = (image_size, image_size, 1)
batch_size = 128
kernel_size = 3
pool_size = 2
filters = 64
dropout = 0.2

# model is a stack of CNN-ReLU-MaxPooling
model = Sequential()
model.add(Conv2D(filters=filters,
                 kernel_size=kernel_size,
                 activation='relu',
                 input_shape=input_shape))
model.add(MaxPooling2D(pool_size))
model.add(Conv2D(filters=filters,
                 kernel_size=kernel_size,
                 activation='relu'))
model.add(MaxPooling2D(pool_size))
model.add(Conv2D(filters=filters,
                 kernel_size=kernel_size,
                 activation='relu'))
model.add(Flatten())
# dropout added as regularizer
model.add(Dropout(dropout))
# output layer is 10-dim one-hot vector
model.add(Dense(num_labels))
model.add(Activation('softmax'))
model.summary()
plot_model(model, to_file='cnn-mnist.png', show_shapes=True)

# loss function for one-hot vector
# use of adam optimizer
# accuracy is good metric for classification tasks
model.compile(loss='categorical_crossentropy',
              optimizer='adam',
              metrics=['accuracy'])
# train the network
model.fit(x_train, y_train, epochs=10, batch_size=batch_size)

loss, acc = model.evaluate(x_test, y_test, batch_size=batch_size)
print("\nTest accuracy: %.1f%%" % (100.0 * acc))
```

The major change here is the use of `Conv2D` layers. The `relu` activation function is already an argument of `Conv2D`. The `relu` function can be brought out as an `Activation` layer when the **batch normalization** layer is included in the model. Batch normalization is used in deep CNNs so that large learning rates can be used without causing instability during training.

Convolution

If in the MLP model the number of units characterizes the `Dense` layers, the kernel characterizes the CNN operations. As shown in *Figure 1.4.2*, the kernel can be visualized as a rectangular patch or window that slides through the whole image from left to right, and top to bottom. This operation is called **convolution**. It transforms the input image into a **feature maps**, which is a representation of what the kernel has *learned* from the input image. The feature maps are then transformed into another feature maps in the succeeding layer and so on. The number of feature maps generated per `Conv2D` is controlled by the `filters` argument.

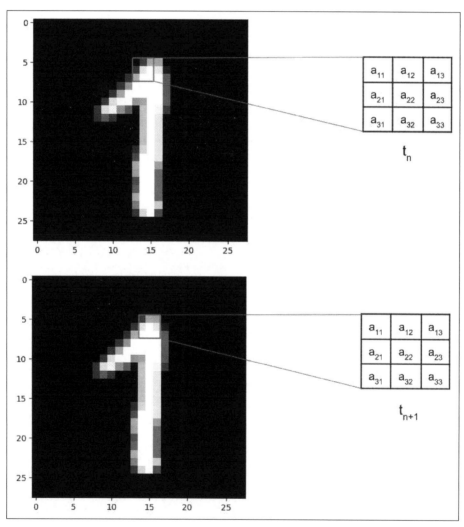

Figure 1.4.2: A 3 × 3 kernel is convolved with an MNIST digit image.
The convolution is shown in steps t_n and t_{n+1} where the kernel moved by a stride of 1 pixel to the right.

The computation involved in the convolution is shown in *Figure 1.4.3*. For simplicity, a 5 × 5 input image (or input feature map) where a 3 × 3 kernel is applied is illustrated. The resulting feature map is shown after the convolution. The value of one element of the feature map is shaded. You'll notice that the resulting feature map is smaller than the original input image, this is because the convolution is only performed on valid elements. The kernel cannot go beyond the borders of the image. If the dimensions of the input should be the same as the output feature maps, Conv2D will accept the option padding='same'. The input is padded with zeroes around its borders to keep the dimensions unchanged after the convolution:

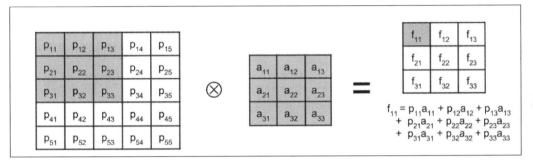

Figure 1.4.3: The convolution operation shows how one element of the feature map is computed

Pooling operations

The last change is the addition of a MaxPooling2D layer with the argument pool_size=2. MaxPooling2D compresses each feature map. Every patch of size pool_size × pool_size is reduced to one pixel. The value is equal to the maximum pixel value within the patch. MaxPooling2D is shown in the following figure for two patches:

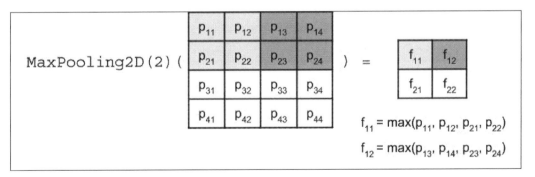

Figure 1.4.4: MaxPooling2D operation. For simplicity,
the input feature map is 4 × 4 resulting in a 2 × 2 feature map.

The significance of `MaxPooling2D` is the reduction in feature maps size which translates to increased kernel coverage. For example, after `MaxPooling2D(2)`, the 2 × 2 kernel is now approximately convolving with a 4 × 4 patch. The CNN has learned a new set of feature maps for a different coverage.

There are other means of pooling and compression. For example, to achieve a 50% size reduction as `MaxPooling2D(2)`, `AveragePooling2D(2)` takes the average of a patch instead of finding the maximum. Strided convolution, `Conv2D(strides=2,...)` will skip every two pixels during convolution and will still have the same 50% size reduction effect. There are subtle differences in the effectiveness of each reduction technique.

In `Conv2D` and `MaxPooling2D`, both `pool_size` and `kernel` can be non-square. In these cases, both the row and column sizes must be indicated. For example, `pool_size=(1, 2)` and `kernel=(3, 5)`.

The output of the last `MaxPooling2D` is a stack of feature maps. The role of `Flatten` is to convert the stack of feature maps into a vector format that is suitable for either `Dropout` or `Dense` layers, similar to the MLP model output layer.

Performance evaluation and model summary

As shown in *Listing 1.4.2*, the CNN model in *Listing 1.4.1* requires a smaller number of parameters at 80,226 compared to 269,322 when MLP layers are used. The `conv2d_1` layer has 640 parameters because each kernel has 3 × 3 = 9 parameters, and each of the 64 feature maps has one kernel and one bias parameter. The number of parameters for other convolution layers can be computed in a similar way. *Figure 1.4.5* shows the graphical representation of the CNN MNIST digit classifier.

Table 1.4.1 shows that the maximum test accuracy of 99.4% which can be achieved for a 3–layer network with 64 feature maps per layer using the Adam optimizer with `dropout=0.2`. CNNs are more parameter efficient and have a higher accuracy than MLPs. Likewise, CNNs are also suitable for learning representations from sequential data, images, and videos.

Listing 1.4.2 shows a summary of a CNN MNIST digit classifier:

Layer (type)	Output Shape	Param #
conv2d_1 (Conv2D)	(None, 26, 26, 64)	640
max_pooling2d_1 (MaxPooling2	(None, 13, 13, 64)	0
conv2d_2 (Conv2D)	(None, 11, 11, 64)	36928
max_pooling2d_2 (MaxPooling2	(None, 5, 5, 64)	0
conv2d_3 (Conv2D)	(None, 3, 3, 64)	36928
flatten_1 (Flatten)	(None, 576)	0
dropout_1 (Dropout)	(None, 576)	0
dense_1 (Dense)	(None, 10)	5770
activation_1 (Activation)	(None, 10)	0

Total params: 80,266
Trainable params: 80,266
Non-trainable params: 0

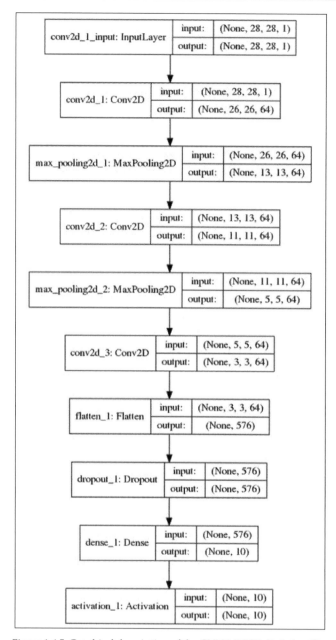

Figure 1.4.5: Graphical description of the CNN MNIST digit classifier

Layers	Optimizer	Regularizer	Train Accuracy, %	Test Accuracy, %
64-64-64	SGD	Dropout(0.2)	97.76	98.50

64-64-64	RMSprop	Dropout(0.2)	99.11	99.00
64-64-64	Adam	Dropout(0.2)	99.75	99.40
64-64-64	Adam	Dropout(0.4)	99.64	99.30

Table 1.4.1: Different CNN network configurations and performance
measures for the MNIST digit classification

Recurrent neural networks (RNNs)

We're now going to look at the last of our three artificial neural networks,
Recurrent neural networks, or RNNs.

RNNs are a family of networks that are suitable for learning representations of
sequential data like text in **Natural Language Processing** (**NLP**) or stream of sensor
data in instrumentation. While each MNIST data sample is not sequential in nature,
it is not hard to imagine that every image can be interpreted as a sequence of rows
or columns of pixels. Thus, a model based on RNNs can process each MNIST image
as a sequence of 28-element input vectors with **timesteps** equal to 28. The following
listing shows the code for the RNN model in *Figure 1.5.1*:

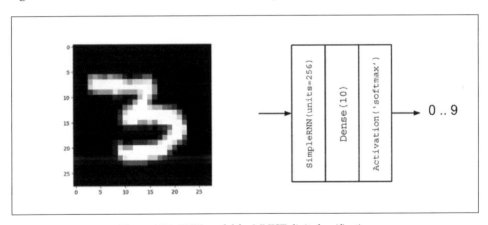

Figure 1.5.1: RNN model for MNIST digit classification

In the following listing, *Listing 1.5.1*, the `rnn-mnist-1.5.1.py` shows the Keras code
for MNIST digit classification using RNNs:

```
import numpy as np
from keras.models import Sequential
from keras.layers import Dense, Activation, SimpleRNN
from keras.utils import to_categorical, plot_model
from keras.datasets import mnist
```

```
# load mnist dataset
(x_train, y_train), (x_test, y_test) = mnist.load_data()

# compute the number of labels
num_labels = len(np.unique(y_train))

# convert to one-hot vector
y_train = to_categorical(y_train)
y_test = to_categorical(y_test)

# resize and normalize
image_size = x_train.shape[1]
x_train = np.reshape(x_train,[-1, image_size, image_size])
x_test = np.reshape(x_test,[-1, image_size, image_size])
x_train = x_train.astype('float32') / 255
x_test = x_test.astype('float32') / 255

# network parameters
input_shape = (image_size, image_size)
batch_size = 128
units = 256
dropout = 0.2

# model is RNN with 256 units, input is 28-dim vector 28 timesteps
model = Sequential()
model.add(SimpleRNN(units=units,
                    dropout=dropout,
                    input_shape=input_shape))
model.add(Dense(num_labels))
model.add(Activation('softmax'))
model.summary()
plot_model(model, to_file='rnn-mnist.png', show_shapes=True)

# loss function for one-hot vector
# use of sgd optimizer
# accuracy is good metric for classification tasks
model.compile(loss='categorical_crossentropy',
              optimizer='sgd',
              metrics=['accuracy'])
# train the network
model.fit(x_train, y_train, epochs=20, batch_size=batch_size)

loss, acc = model.evaluate(x_test, y_test, batch_size=batch_size)
print("\nTest accuracy: %.1f%%" % (100.0 * acc))
```

There are the two main differences between RNNs and the two previous models. First is the `input_shape = (image_size, image_size)` which is actually `input_shape = (timesteps, input_dim)` or a sequence of `input_dim`−dimension vectors of `timesteps` length. Second is the use of a `SimpleRNN` layer to represent an RNN cell with `units=256`. The `units` variable represents the number of output units. If the CNN is characterized by the convolution of kernel across the input feature map, the RNN output is a function not only of the present input but also of the previous output or hidden state. Since the previous output is also a function of the previous input, the current output is also a function of the previous output and input and so on. The `SimpleRNN` layer in Keras is a simplified version of the true RNN. The following, equation describes the output of SimpleRNN:

$$\mathbf{h}t = \tanh(\mathbf{b} + \mathbf{W}\mathbf{h}t\text{-}1 + \mathbf{U}\mathbf{x}t) \qquad (1.5.1)$$

In this equation, $\mathbf{b}$ is the bias, while $\mathbf{W}$ and $\mathbf{U}$ are called recurrent kernel (weights for previous output) and kernel (weights for the current input) respectively. Subscript t is used to indicate the position in the sequence. For `SimpleRNN` layer with `units=256`, the total number of parameters is $256 + 256 \times 256 + 256 \times 28 = 72{,}960$ corresponding to $\mathbf{b}$, $\mathbf{W}$, and $\mathbf{U}$ contributions.

Following figure shows the diagrams of both SimpleRNN and RNN that were used in the MNIST digit classification. What makes `SimpleRNN` simpler than RNN is the absence of the output values $\mathbf{O}t = \mathbf{V}\mathbf{h}t + \mathbf{c}$ before the softmax is computed:

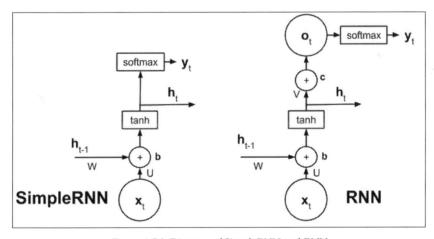

Figure 1.5.2: Diagram of SimpleRNN and RNN

RNNs might be initially harder to understand when compared to MLPs or CNNs. In MLPs, the perceptron is the fundamental unit. Once the concept of the perceptron is understood, MLPs are just a network of perceptrons. In CNNs, the kernel is a patch or window that slides through the feature map to generate another feature map. In RNNs, the most important is the concept of self-loop. There is in fact just one cell.

The illusion of multiple cells appears because a cell exists per timestep but in fact, it is just the same cell reused repeatedly unless the network is unrolled. The underlying neural networks of RNNs are shared across cells.

The summary in *Listing 1.5.2* indicates that using a `SimpleRNN` requires a fewer number of parameters. *Figure 1.5.3* shows the graphical description of the RNN MNIST digit classifier. The model is very concise. *Table 1.5.1* shows that the `SimpleRNN` has the lowest accuracy among the networks presented.

Listing 1.5.2, RNN MNIST digit classifier summary:

```
Layer (type)                Output Shape            Param #
=================================================================
simple_rnn_1 (SimpleRNN)    (None, 256)             72960


dense_1 (Dense)             (None, 10)              2570


activation_1 (Activation)   (None, 10)              0
=================================================================
Total params: 75,530

Trainable params: 75,530

Non-trainable params: 0
```

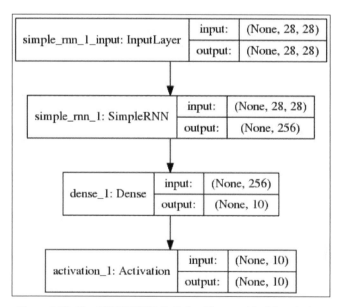

Figure 1.5.3: The RNN MNIST digit classifier graphical description

Layers	Optimizer	Regularizer	Train Accuracy, %	Test Accuracy, %
256	SGD	Dropout(0.2)	97.26	98.00
256	RMSprop	Dropout(0.2)	96.72	97.60
256	Adam	Dropout(0.2)	96.79	97.40
512	SGD	Dropout(0.2)	97.88	98.30

Table 1.5.1: The different SimpleRNN network configurations and performance measures

In many deep neural networks, other members of the RNN family are more commonly used. For example, **Long Short-Term Memory (LSTM)** networks have been used in both machine translation and question answering problems. LSTM networks address the problem of long-term dependency or remembering relevant past information to the present output.

Unlike RNNs or SimpleRNN, the internal structure of the LSTM cell is more complex. *Figure 1.5.4* shows a diagram of LSTM in the context of MNIST digit classification. LSTM uses not only the present input and past outputs or hidden states; it introduces a cell state, s_t, that carries information from one cell to the other. Information flow between cell states is controlled by three gates, f_t, i_t and q_t. The three gates have the effect of determining which information should be retained or replaced and the amount of information in the past and current input that should contribute to the current cell state or output. We will not discuss the details of the internal structure of the LSTM cell in this book. However, an intuitive guide to LSTM can be found at: `http://colah.github.io/posts/2015-08-Understanding-LSTMs`.

The `LSTM()` layer can be used as a drop-in replacement to `SimpleRNN()`. If LSTM is overkill for the task at hand, a simpler version called **Gated Recurrent Unit (GRU)** can be used. GRU simplifies LSTM by combining the cell state and hidden state together. GRU also reduces the number of gates by one. The `GRU()` function can also be used as a drop-in replacement for `SimpleRNN()`.

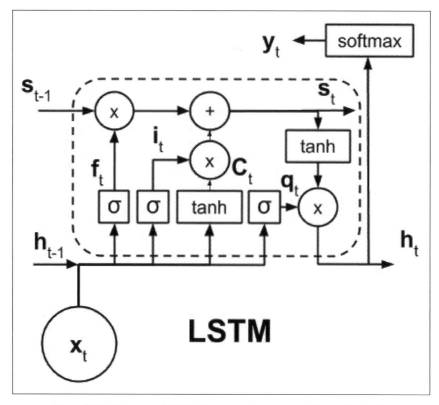

Figure 1.5.4: Diagram of LSTM. The parameters are not shown for clarity

There are many other ways to configure RNNs. One way is making an RNN model that is bidirectional. By default, RNNs are unidirectional in the sense that the current output is only influenced by the past states and the current input. In bidirectional RNNs, future states can also influence the present state and the past states by allowing information to flow backward. Past outputs are updated as needed depending on the new information received. RNNs can be made bidirectional by calling a wrapper function. For example, the implementation of bidirectional LSTM is `Bidirectional(LSTM())`.

For all types of RNNs, increasing the units will also increase the capacity. However, another way of increasing the capacity is by stacking the RNN layers. You should note though that as a general rule of thumb, the capacity of the model should only be increased if needed. Excess capacity may contribute to overfitting, and as a result, both longer training time and slower performance during prediction.

Conclusion

This chapter provided an overview of the three deep learning models – MLPs, RNNs, CNNs – and also introduced Keras, a library for the rapid development, training and testing those deep learning models. The sequential API of Keras was also discussed. In the next chapter, the Functional API will be presented, which will enable us to build more complex models specifically for advanced deep neural networks.

This chapter also reviewed the important concepts of deep learning such as optimization, regularization, and loss function. For ease of understanding, these concepts were presented in the context of the MNIST digit classification. Different solutions to the MNIST digit classification using artificial neural networks, specifically MLPs, CNNs, and RNNs, which are important building blocks of deep neural networks, were also discussed together with their performance measures.

With the understanding of deep learning concepts, and how Keras can be used as a tool with them, we are now equipped to analyze advanced deep learning models. After discussing Functional API in the next chapter, we'll move onto the implementation of popular deep learning models. Subsequent chapters will discuss advanced topics such as autoencoders, GANs, VAEs, and reinforcement learning. The accompanying Keras code implementations will play an important role in understanding these topics.

References

1. LeCun, Yann, Corinna Cortes, and C. J. Burges. *MNIST handwritten digit database*. AT&T Labs [Online]. Available: *http://yann. lecun. com/exdb/mnist 2* (2010).

2
Deep Neural Networks

In this chapter, we'll be examining deep neural networks. These networks have shown excellent performance in terms of the accuracy of their classification on more challenging and advanced datasets like ImageNet, CIFAR10 (https://www.cs.toronto.edu/~kriz/learning-features-2009-TR.pdf), and CIFAR100. For conciseness, we'll only be focusing on two networks, **ResNet** [2][4] and **DenseNet** [5]. While we will go into much more detail, it's important to take a minute to introduce these networks.

ResNet introduced the concept of residual learning which enabled it to build very deep networks by addressing the vanishing gradient problem in deep convolutional networks.

DenseNet improved the ResNet technique further by allowing every convolution to have direct access to inputs, and lower layer feature maps. It's also managed to keep the number of parameters low in deep networks by utilizing both the **Bottleneck** and **Transition** layers.

But why these two models, and not others? Well, since their introduction, there have been countless models such as **ResNeXt** [6] and **FractalNet** [7] which have been inspired by the technique used by these two networks. Likewise, with an understanding of both ResNet and DenseNet, we'll be able to use their design guidelines to build our own models. By using transfer learning, this will also allow us to take advantage of pretrained ResNet and DenseNet models for our own purposes. These reasons alone, along with their compatibility with Keras, make the two models ideal for exploring and complimenting the advanced deep learning scope of this book.

While this chapter's focus is on deep neural networks; we'll begin this chapter by discussing an important feature of Keras called the **Functional API**. This API acts as an alternative method for building networks in Keras and enables us to build more complex networks that cannot be accomplished by the sequential model. The reason why we're focusing so much on this API is that it will become a very useful tool for building deep networks such as the two we're focusing on in this chapter. It's recommended that you've completed, *Chapter 1, Introducing Advanced Deep Learning with Keras,* before moving onto this chapter as we'll refer to introductory level code and concepts explored in that chapter as we take them to an advanced level in this chapter.

The goals of this chapter is to introduce:

- The Functional API in Keras, as well as exploring examples of networks running it
- Deep Residual Networks (ResNet versions 1 and 2) implementation in Keras
- The implementation of Densely Connected Convolutional Networks (DenseNet) into Keras
- Explore two popular deep learning models, **ResNet,** and **DenseNet**

Functional API

In the sequential model that we first introduced in *Chapter 1, Introducing Advanced Deep Learning with Keras,* a layer is stacked on top of another layer. Generally, the model will be accessed through its input and output layers. We also learned that there is no simple mechanism if we find ourselves wanting to add an auxiliary input at the middle of the network, or even to extract an auxiliary output before the last layer.

That model also had its downside, for example, it doesn't support graph-like models or models that behave like Python functions. In addition, it's also difficult to share layers between the two models. Such limitations are addressed by the functional API and are the reason why it's a vital tool for anyone wanting to work with deep learning models.

The Functional API is guided by the following two concepts:

- A layer is an instance that accepts a tensor as an argument. The output of a layer is another tensor. To build a model, the layer instances are objects that are chained to one another through both input and output tensors. This will have similar end-result as would stacking multiple layers in the sequential model have. However, using layer instances makes it easier for models to have either auxiliary or multiple inputs and outputs since the input/output of each layer will be readily accessible.

- A model is a function between one or more input tensors and output tensors. In between the model input and output, tensors are the layer instances that are chained to one another by layer input and output tensors. A model is, therefore, a function of one or more input layers and one or more output layers. The model instance formalizes the computational graph on how the data flows from input(s) to output(s).

After you've completed building the functional API model, the training and evaluation are then performed by the same functions used in the sequential model. To illustrate, in a functional API, a 2D convolutional layer, Conv2D, with 32 filters and with x as the layer input tensor and y as the layer output tensor can be written as:

```
y = Conv2D(32)(x)
```

We're also able to stack multiple layers to build our models. For example, we can rewrite the CNN on MNIST code, the same code we created in the last chapter, as shown in following listing:

You'll find Listing 2.1.1, cnn-functional-2.1.1.py, as follows. This shows us how we can convert the cnn-mnist-1.4.1.py code using the functional API:

```
import numpy as np
from keras.layers import Dense, Dropout, Input
from keras.layers import Conv2D, MaxPooling2D, Flatten
from keras.models import Model
from keras.datasets import mnist
from keras.utils import to_categorical


# compute the number of labels
num_labels = len(np.unique(y_train))

# convert to one-hot vector
y_train = to_categorical(y_train)
y_test = to_categorical(y_test)
```

```
# reshape and normalize input images
image_size = x_train.shape[1]
x_train = np.reshape(x_train,[-1, image_size, image_size, 1])
x_test = np.reshape(x_test,[-1, image_size, image_size, 1])
x_train = x_train.astype('float32') / 255
x_test = x_test.astype('float32') / 255

# network parameters
# image is processed as is (square grayscale)
input_shape = (image_size, image_size, 1)
batch_size = 128
kernel_size = 3
filters = 64
dropout = 0.3

# use functional API to build cnn layers
inputs = Input(shape=input_shape)
y = Conv2D(filters=filters,
           kernel_size=kernel_size,
           activation='relu')(inputs)
y = MaxPooling2D()(y)
y = Conv2D(filters=filters,
           kernel_size=kernel_size,
           activation='relu')(y)
y = MaxPooling2D()(y)
y = Conv2D(filters=filters,
           kernel_size=kernel_size,
           activation='relu')(y)
# image to vector before connecting to dense layer
y = Flatten()(y)
# dropout regularization
y = Dropout(dropout)(y)
outputs = Dense(num_labels, activation='softmax')(y)

# build the model by supplying inputs/outputs
model = Model(inputs=inputs, outputs=outputs)
# network model in text
model.summary()

# classifier loss, Adam optimizer, classifier accuracy
model.compile(loss='categorical_crossentropy',
```

```
            optimizer='adam',
            metrics=['accuracy'])

# train the model with input images and labels
model.fit(x_train,
          y_train,
          validation_data=(x_test, y_test),
          epochs=20,
          batch_size=batch_size)

# model accuracy on test dataset
score = model.evaluate(x_test, y_test, batch_size=batch_size)
print("\nTest accuracy: %.1f%%" % (100.0 * score[1]))
```

By default, `MaxPooling2D` uses `pool_size=2`, so the argument has been removed.

In the preceding listing every layer is a function of a tensor. They each generate a tensor as an output which becomes the input to the next layer. To create this model, we can call `Model()` and supply both the `inputs` and `outputs` tensors, or alternatively the lists of tensors. Everything else remains the same.

The same listing can also be trained and evaluated using the `fit()` and `evaluate()` functions, similar to the sequential model. The `sequential` class is, in fact, a subclass of the `Model` class. We need to remember that we inserted the `validation_data` argument in the `fit()` function to see the progress of validation accuracy during training. The accuracy ranges from 99.3% to 99.4% in 20 epochs.

Creating a two-input and one-output model

We're now going to do something really exciting, creating an advanced model with two inputs and one output. Before we start, it's important to know that this is something that is not straightforward in the sequential model.

Let's suppose a new model for the MNIST digit classification is invented, and it's called the **Y-Network,** as shown in *Figure 2.1.1*. The Y-Network uses the same input twice, both on the left and right CNN branches. The network combines the results using `concatenate` layer. The merge operation `concatenate` is similar to stacking two tensors of the same shape along the concatenation axis to form one tensor. For example, concatenating two tensors of shape (3, 3, 16) along the last axis will result in a tensor of shape (3, 3, 32).

Everything else after the `concatenate` layer will remain the same as the previous CNN model. That is `Flatten-Dropout-Dense`:

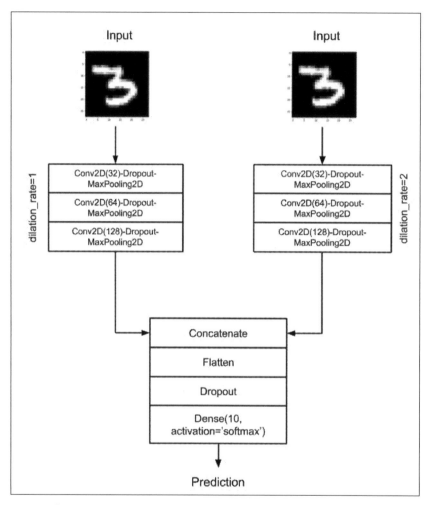

Figure 2.1.1: The Y-Network accepts the same input twice but processes the input in two branches of convolutional networks. The outputs of the branches are combined using the concatenate layer. The last layer prediction is going to be similar to the previous CNN example.

To improve the performance of the model in *Listing 2.1.1*, we can propose several changes. Firstly, the branches of the Y-Network are doubling the number of filters to compensate for the halving of the feature maps size after `MaxPooling2D()`. For example, if the output of the first convolution is (28, 28, 32), after max pooling the new shape is (14, 14, 32). The next convolution will have a filter size of 64 and output dimensions of (14, 14, 64).

Second, although both branches have the same kernel size of 3, the right branch use a dilation rate of 2. *Figure 2.1.2* shows the effect of different dilation rates on a kernel with size 3. The idea is that by increasing the coverage of the kernel using dilation rate, the CNN will enable the right branch to learn different feature maps. We'll use the option `padding='same'` to ensure that we will not have negative tensor dimensions when the dilated CNN is used. By using `padding='same'`, we'll keep the dimensions of the input the same as the output feature maps. This is accomplished by padding the input with zeros to make sure that the output has the *same* size:

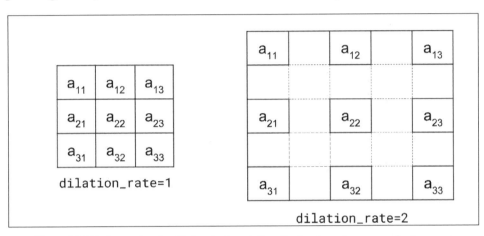

Figure 2.1.2: By increasing the dilate rate from 1, the effective kernel coverage also increases

Following listing shows the implementation of Y-Network. The two branches are created by the two for loops. Both branches expect the same input shape. The two `for` loops will create two 3-layer stacks of `Conv2D-Dropout-MaxPooling2D`. While we used the `concatenate` layer to combine the outputs of the left and right branches, we could also utilize the other merge functions of Keras, such as `add`, `dot`, `multiply`. The choice of the merge function is not purely arbitrary but must be based on a sound model design decision.

In the Y-Network, `concatenate` will not discard any portion of the feature maps. Instead, we'll let the `Dense` layer figure out what to do with the concatenated feature maps. Listing 2.1.2, `cnn-y-network-2.1.2.py` shows the Y-Network implementation using the Functional API:

```
import numpy as np

from keras.layers import Dense, Dropout, Input
from keras.layers import Conv2D, MaxPooling2D, Flatten
from keras.models import Model
from keras.layers.merge import concatenate
from keras.datasets import mnist
from keras.utils import to_categorical
```

```
from keras.utils import plot_model

# load MNIST dataset
(x_train, y_train), (x_test, y_test) = mnist.load_data()

    # compute the number of labels
    num_labels = len(np.unique(y_train))

    # convert to one-hot vector
    y_train = to_categorical(y_train)
y_test = to_categorical(y_test)

# reshape and normalize input images
image_size = x_train.shape[1]
x_train = np.reshape(x_train,[-1, image_size, image_size, 1])
x_test = np.reshape(x_test,[-1, image_size, image_size, 1])
x_train = x_train.astype('float32') / 255
x_test = x_test.astype('float32') / 255

# network parameters
input_shape = (image_size, image_size, 1)
batch_size = 32
kernel_size = 3
dropout = 0.4
n_filters = 32

# left branch of Y network
left_inputs = Input(shape=input_shape)
x = left_inputs
filters = n_filters
# 3 layers of Conv2D-Dropout-MaxPooling2D
# number of filters doubles after each layer (32-64-128)
for i in range(3):
    x = Conv2D(filters=filters,
               kernel_size=kernel_size,
               padding='same',
               activation='relu')(x)
    x = Dropout(dropout)(x)
    x = MaxPooling2D()(x)
    filters *= 2

# right branch of Y network
right_inputs = Input(shape=input_shape)
y = right_inputs
filters = n_filters
# 3 layers of Conv2D-Dropout-MaxPooling2D
# number of filters doubles after each layer (32-64-128)
for i in range(3):
    y = Conv2D(filters=filters,
               kernel_size=kernel_size,
```

```
                     padding='same',
                     activation='relu',
                     dilation_rate=2)(y)
       y = Dropout(dropout)(y)
       y = MaxPooling2D()(y)
       filters *= 2

   # merge left and right branches outputs
   y = concatenate([x, y])
   # feature maps to vector before connecting to Dense layer
   y = Flatten()(y)
   y = Dropout(dropout)(y)
   outputs = Dense(num_labels, activation='softmax')(y)

   # build the model in functional API
   model = Model([left_inputs, right_inputs], outputs)
   # verify the model using graph
   plot_model(model, to_file='cnn-y-network.png', show_shapes=True)
   # verify the model using layer text description
   model.summary()

   # classifier loss, Adam optimizer, classifier accuracy
   model.compile(loss='categorical_crossentropy',
                 optimizer='adam',
                 metrics=['accuracy'])

   # train the model with input images and labels
   model.fit([x_train, x_train],
             y_train,
             validation_data=([x_test, x_test], y_test),
             epochs=20,
             batch_size=batch_size)

   # model accuracy on test dataset
   score = model.evaluate([x_test, x_test], y_test, batch_size=batch_
   size)
   print("\nTest accuracy: %.1f%%" % (100.0 * score[1]))
```

Taking a step back, we can note that the Y-Network is expecting two inputs for training and validation. The inputs are identical, so [x_train, x_train] is supplied.

Over the course of the 20 epochs, the accuracy of the Y-Network ranges from 99.4% to 99.5%. This is a slight improvement over the 3-stack CNN which achieved a range between 99.3% and 99.4% accuracy range. However, this was at the cost of both higher complexity and more than double the number of parameters. The following figure, *Figure 2.1.3*, shows the architecture of the Y-Network as understood by Keras and generated by the plot_model() function:

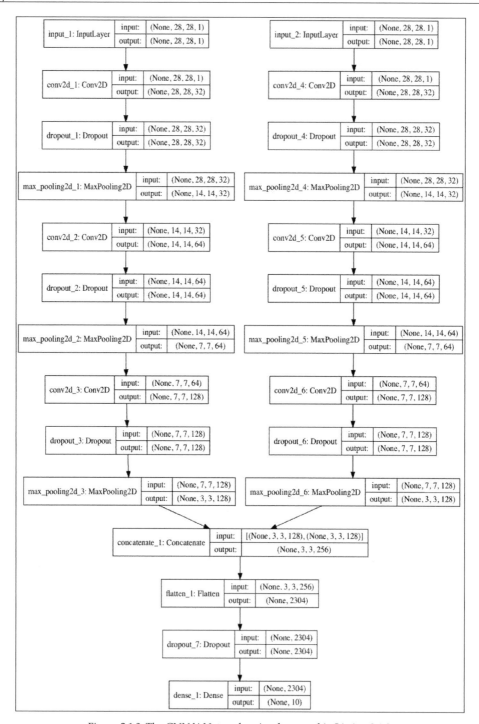

Figure 2.1.3: The CNN Y-Network as implemented in Listing 2.1.2

This concludes our look at the Functional API. We should take this time to remember that the focus of this chapter is building deep neural networks, specifically ResNet and DenseNet. Therefore, we're only covering the Functional API materials needed to build them, as to cover the entire API would be beyond the scope of this book.

 The reader is referred to visit `https://keras.io/` for additional information on functional API.

Deep residual networks (ResNet)

One key advantage of deep networks is that they have a great ability to learn different levels of representations from both inputs and feature maps. In both classification, segmentation, detection and a number of other computer vision problems, learning different levels of features generally leads to better performance.

However, you'll find that it's not easy to train deep networks as a result of the gradient vanishes (or explodes) with depth in the shallow layers during backpropagation. *Figure 2.2.1* illustrates the problem of vanishing gradient. The network parameters are updated by backpropagation from the output layer to all previous layers. Since backpropagation is based on the chain rule, there is a tendency for gradients to diminish as they reach the shallow layers. This is due to the multiplication of small numbers, especially for the small absolute value of errors and parameters.

The number of multiplication operations will be proportional to the depth of the network. It's also worth noting that if the gradient degrades, the parameters will not be updated appropriately.

Hence, the network will fail to improve its performance:

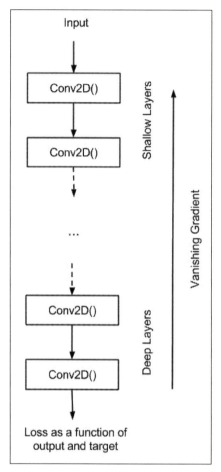

Figure 2.2.1: A common problem in deep networks is that the gradient
vanishes as it reaches the shallow layers during backpropagation.

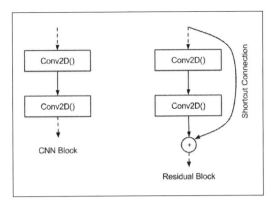

Figure 2.2.2: A comparison between a block in a typical CNN and a block in ResNet.
To prevent degradation in gradients during backpropagation, a shortcut connection is introduced.

To alleviate the degradation of the gradient in deep networks, ResNet introduced the concept of a deep residual learning framework. Let's analyze a block, a small segment of our deep network.

The preceding figure shows a comparison between a typical CNN block and a ResNet residual block. The idea of ResNet is that in order to prevent the gradient from degrading, we'll let the information flow through the shortcut connections to reach the shallow layers.

Next, we're going to look at more details within the discussion of the differences between the two blocks. *Figure 2.2.3* shows more details of the CNN block of another commonly used deep network, VGG[3], and ResNet. We'll represent the layer feature maps as **x**. The feature maps at layer l are $\mathbf{x}_l$. The operations in the CNN layer are **Conv2D-Batch Normalization (BN)-ReLU**.

Let's suppose we represent this set of operations in the form of $H()$ = Conv2D-Batch Normalization(BN)-ReLU, that will then mean that:

$$\mathbf{x}_{l-1} = H\left(\mathbf{x}_{l-2}\right) \qquad \text{(Equation 2.2.1)}$$

$$\mathbf{x}_l = H\left(\mathbf{x}_{l-1}\right) \qquad \text{(Equation 2.2.2)}$$

In other words, the feature maps at layer l - 2 are transformed to $\mathbf{x}_{l-1}$ by $H()$ = Conv2D-Batch Normalization(BN)-ReLU. The same set of operations is applied to transform $\mathbf{x}_{l-1}$ to $\mathbf{x}_l$. To put this another way, if we have an 18-layer VGG, then there are 18 $H()$ operations before the input image is transformed to the 18th layer feature maps.

Generally speaking, we can observe that the layer *l* output feature maps are directly affected by the previous feature maps only. Meanwhile, for ResNet:

$$\mathbf{x}_{l-1} = H\left(\mathbf{x}_{l-2}\right)$$ (Equation 2.2.3)

$$\mathbf{x}_{l} = ReLU\left(F\left(\mathbf{x}_{l-1}\right) + \mathbf{x}_{l-2}\right)$$ (Equation 2.2.4)

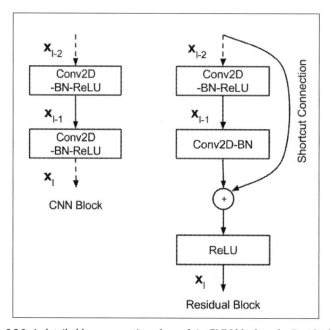

Figure 2.2.3: A detailed layer operations for a plain CNN block and a Residual block

$F\left(\mathbf{x}_{l-1}\right)$ is made of `Conv2D-BN`, which is also known as the residual mapping. The **+** sign is tensor element-wise addition between the shortcut connection and the output of $F\left(\mathbf{x}_{l-1}\right)$. The shortcut connection doesn't add extra parameters nor extra computational complexity.

The add operation can be implemented in Keras by the `add()` merge function. However, both the $F(\mathbf{x}_{l-1})$ equation and $\mathbf{x}$ should have the same dimensions. If the dimensions are different, for example, when changing the feature maps size, we should perform a linear projection on $\mathbf{x}$ as to match the size of $F(\mathbf{x}_{l-1})$. In the original paper, the linear projection for the case, when the feature maps size is halved, is done by a `Conv2D` with a 1 × 1 kernel and `strides=2`.

Back in *Chapter 1, Introducing Advanced Deep Learning with Keras*, we discussed that `stride > 1` is equivalent to skipping pixels during convolution. For example, if `strides=2`, we could skip every other pixel when we slide the kernel during the convolution process.

The preceding *Equations 2.2.3* and *2.2.4*, both model ResNet residual block operations. They imply that if the deeper layers can be trained to have fewer errors, then there is no reason why the shallower layers should have higher errors.

Knowing the basic building blocks of ResNet, we're able to design a deep residual network for image classification. This time, however, we're going to tackle a more challenging and advanced dataset.

In our examples, we're going to consider CIFAR10, which was one of the datasets the original paper was validated. In this example, Keras provides an API to conveniently access the CIFAR10 dataset, as shown:

```
from keras.datasets import cifar10
(x_train, y_train), (x_test, y_test) = cifar10.load_data()
```

Like MNIST, the CIFAR10 dataset has 10 categories. The dataset is a collection of small (32 × 32) RGB real-world images of an airplane, automobile, bird, cat, deer, dog, frog, horse, ship, and a truck corresponding to each of the 10 categories. *Figure 2.2.4* shows sample images from CIFAR10.

In the dataset, there are 50,000 labeled train images and 10,000 labeled test images for validation:

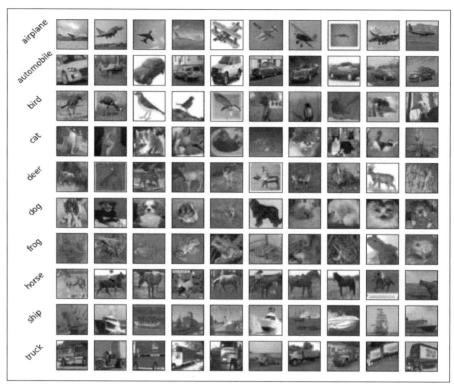

Figure 2.2.4: Sample images from the CIFAR10 dataset.
The full dataset has 50,000 labeled train images and 10,000 labeled test images for validation.

For the CIFAR10 data, ResNet can be built using different network architectures as shown in *Table 2.2.1*. The values of both *n* and the corresponding architectures of ResNet were validated in *Table 2.2.2*. *Table 2.2.1* means we have three sets of residual blocks. Each set has *2n* layers corresponding to *n* residual blocks. The extra layer in 32 × 32 is the first layer for the input image.

The kernel size is 3, except for the transition between two feature maps with different sizes that implements a linear mapping. For example, a `Conv2D` with a kernel size of 1 and `strides=2`. For the sake of consistency with DenseNet, we'll use the term Transition layer when we join two residual blocks of different sizes.

ResNet uses `kernel_initializer='he_normal'` in order to aid the convergence when backpropagation is taking place [1]. The last layer is made of `AveragePooling2D-Flatten-Dense`. It's worth noting at this point that ResNet does not use dropout. It also appears that the add merge operation and the 1 × 1 convolution have a self-regularizing effect. *Figure 2.2.4* shows the ResNet model architecture for the CIFAR10 dataset as described in *Table 2.2.1*.

The following listing shows the partial ResNet implementation within Keras. The code has been contributed to the Keras GitHub repository. From *Table 2.2.2* we can also see that by modifying the value of n, we're able to increase the depth of the networks. For example, for n = 18, we already have ResNet110, a deep network with 110 layers. To build ResNet20, we use n = 3:

```
n = 3

# model version
# orig paper: version = 1 (ResNet v1),
# Improved ResNet: version = 2 (ResNet v2)
version = 1

# computed depth from supplied model parameter n
if version == 1:
    depth = n * 6 + 2
elif version == 2:
    depth = n * 9 + 2
...
if version == 2:
    model = resnet_v2(input_shape=input_shape, depth=depth)
else:
    model = resnet_v1(input_shape=input_shape, depth=depth)
```

The resnet_v1() method is a model builder for ResNet. It uses a utility function, resnet_layer() to help build the stack of Conv2D-BN-ReLU.

It's referred to as version 1, as we will see in the next section, an improved ResNet was proposed, and that has been called ResNet version 2, or v2. Over ResNet, ResNet v2 has an improved residual block design resulting in better performance.

Layers	Output Size	Filter Size	Operations
Convolution	32×32	16	3×3 *Conv2D*
Residual Block (1)	32×32		$\begin{Bmatrix} 3 \times 3 & Conv2D \\ 3 \times 3 & Conv2D \end{Bmatrix} \times n$
Transition Layer (1)	32×32 16×16		$\{1 \times 1 \quad Conv2D, strides = 2\}$
Residual Block (2)	16×16	32	$\begin{Bmatrix} 3 \times 3 & Conv2D, strides = 2 \, if \, 1st \, Conv2D \\ 3 \times 3 & Conv2D \end{Bmatrix} \times n$

Transition Layer (2)	16×16		$\left\{1\times1 \quad Conv2\,D, strides = 2\right\}$
	8×8		
Residual Block (3)	8×8	64	$\left\{\begin{array}{l}3\times3 \quad Conv2D, strides = 2\,if\,1st\,Conv2D \\ 3\times3 \qquad\qquad Conv2D\end{array}\right\}\times n$
Average Pooling	1×1		$8\times8 \quad AveragePooling\,2D$

Table 2.2.1: ResNet network architecture configuration

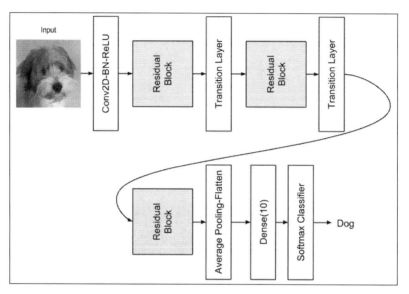

Figure 2.2.4: The model architecture of ResNet for the CIFAR10 dataset classification

# Layers	n	% Accuracy on CIFAR10 (Original paper)	% Accuracy on CIFAR10 (This book)
ResNet20	3	91.25	92.16
ResNet32	5	92.49	92.46
ResNet44	7	92.83	92.50
ResNet56	9	93.03	92.71
ResNet110	18	93.57	92.65

Table 2.2.2: ResNet architectures validated with CIFAR10

The following listing shows the partial code of `resnet-cifar10-2.2.1.py`, which is the Keras model implementation of ResNet v1:

```
def resnet_v1(input_shape, depth, num_classes=10):
```

```
    if (depth - 2) % 6 != 0:
        raise ValueError('depth should be 6n+2 (eg 20, 32,
44 in [a])')
    # Start model definition.
    num_filters = 16
    num_res_blocks = int((depth - 2) / 6)

    inputs = Input(shape=input_shape)
    x = resnet_layer(inputs=inputs)
    # Instantiate the stack of residual units
    for stack in range(3):
        for res_block in range(num_res_blocks):
            strides = 1
            if stack > 0 and res_block == 0:
                strides = 2   # downsample
            y = resnet_layer(inputs=x,
                             num_filters=num_filters,
                             strides=strides)
            y = resnet_layer(inputs=y,
                             num_filters=num_filters,
                             activation=None)
            if stack > 0 and res_block == 0
                # linear projection residual shortcut connection
                # to match changed dims
                x = resnet_layer(inputs=x,
                                 num_filters=num_filters,
                                 kernel_size=1,
                                 strides=strides,
                                 activation=None,
                                 batch_normalization=False)
            x = add([x, y])
            x = Activation('relu')(x)
        num_filters *= 2

    # Add classifier on top.
    # v1 does not use BN after last shortcut connection-ReLU
    x = AveragePooling2D(pool_size=8)(x)
    y = Flatten()(x)
    outputs = Dense(num_classes,
                    activation='softmax',
                    kernel_initializer='he_normal')(y)

    # Instantiate model.
    model = Model(inputs=inputs, outputs=outputs)
    return model
```

There are some minor differences from the original implementation of ResNet. In particular, we don't use SGD, and instead, we'll use Adam. This is because ResNet is easier to converge with Adam. We'll also use a learning rate (`lr`) scheduler, `lr_schedule()`, in order to schedule the decrease in `lr` at 80, 120, 160, and 180 epochs from the default 1e-3. The `lr_schedule()` function will be called after every epoch during training as part of the `callbacks` variable.

The other callback saves the checkpoint every time there is progress made in the validation accuracy. When training deep networks, it is a good practice to save the model or weight checkpoint. This is because it takes a substantial amount of time to train deep networks. When you want to use your network, all you need to do is simply reload the checkpoint, and the trained model is restored. This can be accomplished by calling Keras `load_model()`. The `lr_reducer()` function is included. In case the metric has plateaued before the schedule reduction, this callback will reduce the learning rate by the factor if the validation loss has not improved after `patience=5` epochs.

The `callbacks` variable is supplied when the `model.fit()` method is called. Similar to the original paper, the Keras implementation uses data augmentation, `ImageDataGenerator()`, in order to provide additional training data as part of the regularization schemes. As the number of training data increases, generalization will improve.

For example, a simple data augmentation is flipping the photo of the dog, as shown in following figure (`horizontal_flip=True`). If it is an image of a dog, then the flipped image is still an image of a dog. You can also perform other transformation, such as scaling, rotation, whitening, and so on, and the label will still remain the same:

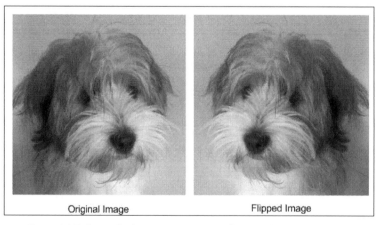

Figure 2.2.5: A simple data augmentation is flipping the original image

The complete code is available on GitHub: (`https://github.com/PacktPublishing/Advanced-Deep-Learning-with-Keras`).

It's often difficult to exactly duplicate the implementation of the original paper, especially in the optimizer used and data augmentation, as there are slight differences in the performance of the Keras ResNet implementation in this book and the model in the original paper.

ResNet v2

After the release of the second paper on ResNet [4], the original model presented in the previous section has been known as ResNet v1. The improved ResNet is commonly called ResNet v2. The improvement is mainly found in the arrangement of layers in the residual block as shown in following figure.

The prominent changes in ResNet v2 are:

- The use of a stack of $1 \times 1 - 3 \times 3 - 1 \times 1$ `BN-ReLU-Conv2D`
- Batch normalization and ReLU activation come before 2D convolution

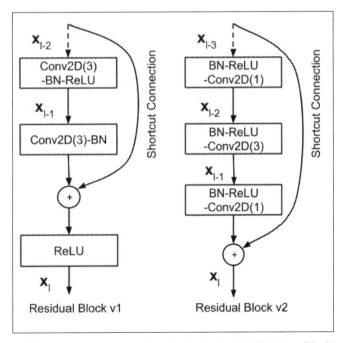

Figure 2.3.1: A comparison of residual blocks between ResNet v1 and ResNet v2

ResNet v2 is also implemented in the same code as `resnet-cifar10-2.2.1.py`:

```python
def resnet_v2(input_shape, depth, num_classes=10):
    if (depth - 2) % 9 != 0:
        raise ValueError('depth should be 9n+2 (eg 56 or 110 in [b])')
    # Start model definition.
    num_filters_in = 16
    num_res_blocks = int((depth - 2) / 9)

    inputs = Input(shape=input_shape)
    # v2 performs Conv2D with BN-ReLU on input
    # before splitting into 2 paths
    x = resnet_layer(inputs=inputs,
                     num_filters=num_filters_in,
                     conv_first=True)

    # Instantiate the stack of residual units
    for stage in range(3):
        for res_block in range(num_res_blocks):
            activation = 'relu'
            batch_normalization = True
            strides = 1
            if stage == 0:
                num_filters_out = num_filters_in * 4
                if res_block == 0:  # first layer and first stage
                    activation = None
                    batch_normalization = False
            else:
                num_filters_out = num_filters_in * 2
                if res_block == 0:  # 1st layer but not 1st stage
                    strides = 2    # downsample

            # bottleneck residual unit
            y = resnet_layer(inputs=x,
                             num_filters=num_filters_in,
                             kernel_size=1,
                             strides=strides,
                             activation=activation,
                             batch_normalization=batch_normalization,
                             conv_first=False)
            y = resnet_layer(inputs=y,
                             num_filters=num_filters_in,
                             conv_first=False)
            y = resnet_layer(inputs=y,
```

```
                            num_filters=num_filters_out,
                            kernel_size=1,
                            conv_first=False)
            if res_block == 0:
                # linear projection residual shortcut connection
                # to match changed dims
                x = resnet_layer(inputs=x,
                            num_filters=num_filters_out,
                            kernel_size=1,
                            strides=strides,
                            activation=None,
                            batch_normalization=False)
            x = add([x, y])

        num_filters_in = num_filters_out

    # add classifier on top.
    # v2 has BN-ReLU before Pooling
    x = BatchNormalization()(x)
    x = Activation('relu')(x)
    x = AveragePooling2D(pool_size=8)(x)
    y = Flatten()(x)
    outputs = Dense(num_classes,
                activation='softmax',
                kernel_initializer='he_normal')(y)

    # instantiate model.
    model = Model(inputs=inputs, outputs=outputs)
    return model
```

ResNet v2's model builder is shown in the following code. For example, to build ResNet110 v2, we'll use `n = 12`:

```
n = 12

# model version
# orig paper: version = 1 (ResNet v1), Improved ResNet: version = 2
(ResNet v2)
version = 2

# computed depth from supplied model parameter n
if version == 1:
    depth = n * 6 + 2
elif version == 2:
    depth = n * 9 + 2
```

```
...
if version == 2:
    model = resnet_v2(input_shape=input_shape, depth=depth)
else:
    model = resnet_v1(input_shape=input_shape, depth=depth)
```

The accuracy of ResNet v2 is shown in following table:

# Layers	n	% Accuracy on CIFAR10 (Original paper)	% Accuracy on CIFAR10 (This book)
ResNet56	9	NA	93.01
ResNet110	18	93.63	93.15

Table 2.3.1: The ResNet v2 architectures validated on the CIFAR10 dataset

In the Keras applications package, ResNet50 has been implemented as well with the corresponding checkpoint for reuse. This is an alternative implementation but tied to the 50-layer ResNet v1.

Densely connected convolutional networks (DenseNet)

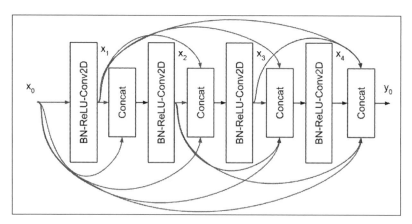

Figure 2.4.1: A 4-layer Dense block in DenseNet.
The input to each layer is made of all the previous feature maps.

DenseNet attacks the problem of vanishing gradient using a different approach. Instead of using shortcut connections, all the previous feature maps will become the input of the next layer. The preceding figure, shows an example of a dense interconnection in one Dense block.

For simplicity, in this figure, we'll only show four layers. Notice that the input to layer l is the concatenation of all previous feature maps. If we designate the `BN-ReLU-Conv2D` as the operation $H(x)$, then the output of layer l is:

$$\mathbf{x}_l = H\left(\mathbf{x}_0, \mathbf{x}_1, \mathbf{x}_2, \ldots, \mathbf{x}_{l-1}\right) \qquad \text{(Equation 2.4.1)}$$

`Conv2D` uses a kernel of size 3. The number of feature maps generated per layer is called the growth rate, k. Normally, $k = 12$, but $k = 24$ is also used in the paper, *Densely Connected Convolutional Networks*, Huang, and others, 2017 [5]. Therefore, if the number of feature maps x_0 is k_0, then the total number of feature maps at the end of the 4-layer Dense block in *Figure 2.4.1* will be $4 \times k + k_0$.

DenseNet also recommends that the Dense block is preceded by `BN-ReLU-Conv2D`, along with the number of feature maps twice the growth rate, $k_0 = 2 \times k$. Therefore, at the end of the Dense block, the total number of feature maps will be 72. We'll also use the same kernel size, which is 3. At the output layer, DenseNet suggests that we perform an average pooling before the `Dense()` and `softmax` classifier. If the data augmentation is not used, a dropout layer must follow the Dense block `Conv2D`:

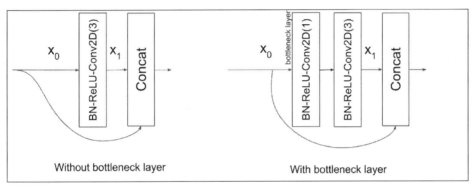

Figure 2.4.2: A layer in a Dense block of DenseNet, with and without the bottleneck layer BN-ReLU-Conv2D(1). We'll include the kernel size as an argument of Conv2D for clarity.

As the network gets deeper, two new problems will occur. Firstly, since every layer contributes k feature maps, the number of inputs at layer l is $(l-1) \times k + k_0$. Therefore, the feature maps can grow rapidly within deep layers, resulting in the computation becoming slow. For example, for a 101-layer network this will be 1200 + 24 = 1224 for $k = 12$.

Secondly, similar to ResNet, as the network gets deeper the feature maps size will be reduced to increase the coverage of the kernel. If DenseNet uses concatenation in the merge operation, it must reconcile the differences in size.

To prevent the number of feature maps from increasing to the point of being computationally inefficient, DenseNet introduced the Bottleneck layer as shown in *Figure 2.4.2*. The idea is that after every concatenation; a 1 × 1 convolution with a filter size equal to $4k$ is now applied. This dimensionality reduction technique prevents the number of feature maps to be processed by Conv2D(3) from rapidly increasing.

The Bottleneck layer then modifies the DenseNet layer as BN-ReLU-Conv2D(1)-BN-ReLU-Conv2D(3), instead of just BN-ReLU-Conv2D(3). We've included the kernel size as an argument of Conv2D for clarity. With the Bottleneck layer, every Conv2D(3) is processing just the $4k$ feature maps instead of $(l-1) \times k + k_0$ for layer l. For example, for the 101-layer network, the input to the last Conv2D(3) is still 48 feature maps for $k = 12$ instead of 1224 as computed previously:

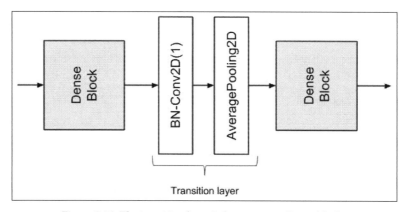

Figure 2.4.3: The transition layer in between two Dense blocks

To solve the problem in feature maps size mismatch, DenseNet divides a deep network into multiple dense blocks that are joined together by transition layers as shown in the preceding figure. Within each dense block, the feature map size (that is, width and height) will remain constant.

The role of the transition layer is to *transition* from one feature map size to a smaller feature map size between two dense blocks. The reduction in size is usually half. This is accomplished by the average pooling layer. For example, an AveragePooling2D with default pool_size=2 reduces the size from (64, 64, 256) to (32, 32, 256). The input to the transition layer is the output of the last concatenation layer in the previous dense block.

However, before the feature maps are passed to average pooling, their number will be reduced by a certain compression factor, $0 < \theta < 1$, using `Conv2D(1)`. DenseNet uses $\theta = 0.5$ in their experiment. For example, if the output of the last concatenation of the previous dense block is (64, 64, 512), then after `Conv2D(1)` the new dimensions of the feature maps will be (64, 64, 256). When compression and dimensionality reduction are put together, the transition layer is made of `BN-Conv2D(1)-AveragePooling2D` layers. In practice, batch normalization precedes the convolutional layer.

Building a 100-layer DenseNet-BC for CIFAR10

We're now going to build a **DenseNet-BC (Bottleneck-Compression)** with 100 layers for the CIFAR10 dataset, using the design principles that we discussed above.

Following table, shows the model configuration, while *Figure 2.4.3* shows the model architecture. *Listing 2.4.1* shows us the partial Keras implementation of DenseNet-BC with 100 layers. We need to take note that we use `RMSprop` since it converges better than SGD or Adam when using DenseNet.

Layers	Output Size	DenseNet-100 BC
Convolution	32 x 32	$3 \times 3 \quad Conv2D$
Dense Block (1)	32 x 32	$\begin{cases} 1 \times 1 & Conv2D \\ 3 \times 3 & Conv2D \end{cases} \times 16$
Transition Layer (1)	32 x 32 16 x 16	$\begin{cases} 1 \times 1 & Conv2D \\ 2 \times 2 & AveragePooling2D \end{cases}$
Dense Block (2)	16 x 16	$\begin{cases} 1 \times 1 & Conv2D \\ 3 \times 3 & Conv2D \end{cases} \times 16$
Transition Layer (2)	16 x 16 8 x 8	$\begin{cases} 1 \times 1 & Conv2D \\ 2 \times 2 & AveragePooling2D \end{cases}$
Dense Block (3)	8 x 8	$\begin{cases} 1 \times 1 & Conv2D \\ 3 \times 3 & Conv2D \end{cases} \times 16$

Average Pooling	1 x 1	8×8 *AveragePooling* 2*D*
Classification Layer		`Flatten-Dense(10)-softmax`

Table 2.4.1: DenseNet-BC with 100 layers for CIFAR10 classification

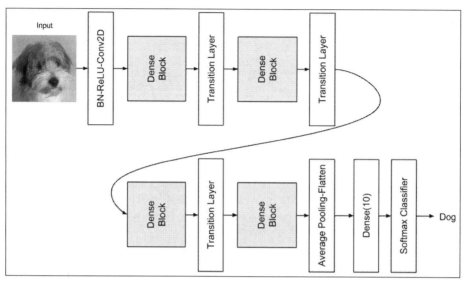

Figure 2.4.3: Model architecture of DenseNet-BC with 100 layers for CIFAR10 classification

Listing 2.4.1, `densenet-cifar10-2.4.1.py`: Partial Keras implementation of DenseNet-BC with 100 layers as shown in *Table 2.4.1*:

```
# start model definition
# densenet CNNs (composite function) are made of BN-ReLU-Conv2D
inputs = Input(shape=input_shape)
x = BatchNormalization()(inputs)
x = Activation('relu')(x)
x = Conv2D(num_filters_bef_dense_block,
           kernel_size=3,
           padding='same',
           kernel_initializer='he_normal')(x)
x = concatenate([inputs, x])

# stack of dense blocks bridged by transition layers
for i in range(num_dense_blocks):
    # a dense block is a stack of bottleneck layers
    for j in range(num_bottleneck_layers):
        y = BatchNormalization()(x)
        y = Activation('relu')(y)
```

```
        y = Conv2D(4 * growth_rate,
                   kernel_size=1,
                   padding='same',
                   kernel_initializer='he_normal')(y)
        if not data_augmentation:
            y = Dropout(0.2)(y)
        y = BatchNormalization()(y)
        y = Activation('relu')(y)
        y = Conv2D(growth_rate,
                   kernel_size=3,
                   padding='same',
                   kernel_initializer='he_normal')(y)
        if not data_augmentation:
            y = Dropout(0.2)(y)
        x = concatenate([x, y])

    # no transition layer after the last dense block
    if i == num_dense_blocks - 1:
        continue

    # transition layer compresses num of feature maps and
    # reduces the size by 2
    num_filters_bef_dense_block += num_bottleneck_layers * growth_rate
    num_filters_bef_dense_block = int(num_filters_bef_dense_block *
compression_factor)
    y = BatchNormalization()(x)
    y = Conv2D(num_filters_bef_dense_block,
               kernel_size=1,
               padding='same',
               kernel_initializer='he_normal')(y)
    if not data_augmentation:
        y = Dropout(0.2)(y)
    x = AveragePooling2D()(y)


# add classifier on top
# after average pooling, size of feature map is 1 x 1
x = AveragePooling2D(pool_size=8)(x)
y = Flatten()(x)
outputs = Dense(num_classes,
                kernel_initializer='he_normal',
                activation='softmax')(y)

# instantiate and compile model
```

```
# orig paper uses SGD but RMSprop works better for DenseNet
model = Model(inputs=inputs, outputs=outputs)
model.compile(loss='categorical_crossentropy',
              optimizer=RMSprop(1e-3),
              metrics=['accuracy'])
model.summary()
```

Training the Keras implementation in *Listing 2.4.1* for 200 epochs achieves a 93.74% accuracy vs. the 95.49% as reported in the paper. Data augmentation is used. We used the same callback functions in ResNet v1/v2 for DenseNet.

For the deeper layers, the `growth_rate` and `depth` variables must be changed using the table on the Python code. However, it will take a substantial amount of time to train the network at a depth of 250, or 190 as done in the paper. To give us an idea of training time, each epoch runs for about an hour on a 1060Ti GPU. Though there is also an implementation of DenseNet in the Keras applications module, it was trained on ImageNet.

Conclusion

In this chapter, we've presented Functional API as an advanced method for building complex deep neural network models using Keras. We also demonstrated how the Functional API could be used to build the multi-input-single-output Y-Network. This network, when compared to a single branch CNN network, archives better accuracy. For the rest of the book, we'll find the Functional API indispensable in building more complex and advanced models. For example, in the next chapter, the Functional API will enable us to build a modular encoder, decoder, and autoencoder.

We also spent a significant time exploring two important deep networks, ResNet and DenseNet. Both of these networks have been used not only in classification but also in other areas, such as segmentation, detection, tracking, generation, and visual/semantic understanding. We need to remember that it's more important that we understand the model design decisions in ResNet and DenseNet more closely than just following the original implementation. In that manner, we'll be able to use the key concepts of ResNet and DenseNet for our purposes.

References

1. Kaiming He and others. *Delving Deep into Rectifiers: Surpassing Human-Level Performance on ImageNet Classification*. Proceedings of the IEEE international conference on computer vision, 2015 (`https://www.cv-foundation.org/openaccess/content_iccv_2015/papers/He_Delving_Deep_into_ICCV_2015_paper.pdf?spm=5176.100239.blogcont55892.28.pm8zm1&file=He_Delving_Deep_into_ICCV_2015_paper.pdf`).

2. Kaiming He and others. *Deep Residual Learning for Image Recognition*. Proceedings of the IEEE conference on computer vision and pattern recognition, 2016a(`http://openaccess.thecvf.com/content_cvpr_2016/papers/He_Deep_Residual_Learning_CVPR_2016_paper.pdf`).

3. Karen Simonyan and Andrew Zisserman. *Very Deep Convolutional Networks for Large-Scale Image Recognition*. ICLR, 2015(`https://arxiv.org/pdf/1409.1556/`).

4. Kaiming He and others. *Identity Mappings in Deep Residual Networks*. European Conference on Computer Vision. Springer International Publishing, 2016b(`https://arxiv.org/pdf/1603.05027.pdf`).

5. Gao Huang and others. *Densely Connected Convolutional Networks*. Proceedings of the IEEE conference on computer vision and pattern recognition, 2017(`http://openaccess.thecvf.com/content_cvpr_2017/papers/Huang_Densely_Connected_Convolutional_CVPR_2017_paper.pdf`).

6. Saining Xie and others. *Aggregated Residual Transformations for Deep Neural Networks*. Computer Vision and Pattern Recognition (CVPR), 2017 IEEE Conference on. IEEE, 2017(`http://openaccess.thecvf.com/content_cvpr_2017/papers/Xie_Aggregated_Residual_Transformations_CVPR_2017_paper.pdf`).

7. Gustav Larsson, Michael Maire and Gregory Shakhnarovich. *Fractalnet: Ultra-Deep Neural Networks Without Residuals*. arXiv preprint arXiv:1605.07648, 2016 (`https://arxiv.org/pdf/1605.07648.pdf`).

3
Autoencoders

In the previous chapter, *Chapter 2, Deep Neural Networks*, you were introduced to the concepts of deep neural networks. We're now going to move on to look at autoencoders, which are a neural network architecture that attempts to find a compressed representation of the given input data.

Similar to the previous chapters, the input data may be in multiple forms including, speech, text, image, or video. An autoencoder will attempt to find a representation or code in order to perform useful transformations on the input data. As an example, in denoising autoencoders, a neural network will attempt to find a code that can be used to transform noisy data into clean ones. Noisy data could be in the form of an audio recording with static noise which is then converted into clear sound. Autoencoders will learn the code automatically from the data alone without human labeling. As such, autoencoders can be classified under **unsupervised** learning algorithms.

In later chapters of this book, we will look at **Generative Adversarial Networks (GANs)** and **Variational Autoencoders (VAEs)** which are also representative forms of unsupervised learning algorithms. This is in contrast to the supervised learning algorithms we discussed in the previous chapters where human annotations were required.

In its simplest form, an autoencoder will learn the representation or code by trying to copy the input to output. However, using an autoencoder is not as simple as copying the input to output. Otherwise, the neural network would not be able to uncover the hidden structure in the input distribution.

An autoencoder will encode the input distribution into a low-dimensional tensor, which usually takes the form of a vector. This will approximate the hidden structure that is commonly referred to as the latent representation, code, or vector. This process constitutes the encoding part. The latent vector will then be decoded by the decoder part to recover the original input.

As a result of the latent vector being a low-dimensional compressed representation of the input distribution, it should be expected that the output recovered by the decoder can only approximate the input. The dissimilarity between the input and the output can be measured by a loss function.

But why would we use autoencoders? Simply put, autoencoders have practical applications both in their original form or as part of more complex neural networks. They're a key tool in understanding the advanced topics of deep learning as they give you a low-dimensional latent vector. Furthermore, it can be efficiently processed to perform structural operations on the input data. Common operations include denoising, colorization, feature-level arithmetic, detection, tracking, and segmentation, to name just a few.

In summary, the goal of this chapter is to present:

- The principles of autoencoders
- How to implement autoencoders into the Keras neural network library
- The main features of denoising and colorization autoencoders

Principles of autoencoders

In this section, we're going to go over the principles of autoencoders. In this section, we're going to be looking at autoencoders with the MNIST dataset, which we were first introduced to in the previous chapters.

Firstly, we need to be made aware that an autoencoder has two operators, these are:

- **Encoder**: This transforms the input, x, into a low-dimensional latent vector, $z = f(x)$. Since the latent vector is of low dimension, the encoder is forced to learn only the most important features of the input data. For example, in the case of MNIST digits, the important features to learn may include writing style, tilt angle, roundness of stroke, thickness, and so on. Essentially, these are the most important information needed to represent digits zero to nine.

- **Decoder**: This tries to recover the input from the latent vector, $g(\mathbf{z}) = \tilde{x}$. Although the latent vector has a low dimension, it has a sufficient size to allow the decoder to recover the input data.

The goal of the decoder is to make $\tilde{x}$ as close as possible to x. Generally, both the encoder and decoder are non-linear functions. The dimension of z is a measure of the number of salient features it can represent. The dimension is usually much smaller than the input dimensions for efficiency and in order to constrain the latent code to learn only the most salient properties of the input distribution[1].

The autoencoder has the tendency to memorize the input when the dimension of the latent code is significantly bigger than x.

A suitable loss function, $\mathcal{L}(x,\tilde{x})$, is a measure of how dissimilar the input, x, from the output which is the recovered input, $\tilde{x}$. As shown in the following equation, the **Mean Squared Error (MSE)** is an example of such a loss function:

$$\mathcal{L}(x,\tilde{x}) = MSE = \frac{1}{m}\sum_{i=1}^{i=m}(x_i - \tilde{x}_i)^2 \qquad \text{(Equation 3.1.1)}$$

In this example, m is the output dimensions (For example, in MNIST $m = width \times height \times channels = 28 \times 28 \times 1 = 784$). x_i and $\tilde{x}_i$ are the elements of x and $\tilde{x}$ respectively. Since the loss function is a measure of dissimilarity between the input and output, we're able to use alternative reconstruction loss functions such as the binary cross entropy or **structural similarity index (SSIM)**.

Similar to the other neural networks, the autoencoder tries to make this error or loss function as small as possible during training. *Figure 3.1.1* shows the autoencoder. The encoder is a function that compresses the input, x, into a low-dimensional latent vector, z. This latent vector represents the important features of the input distribution. The decoder then tries to recover the original input from the latent vector in the form of $\tilde{x}$.

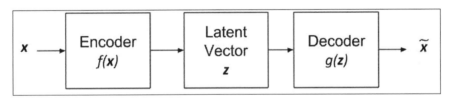

Figure 3.1.1: Block diagram of an autoencoder

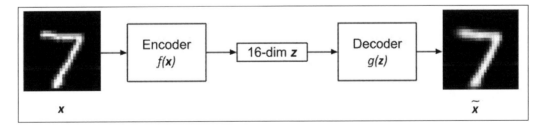

Figure 3.1.2: An autoencoder with MNIST digit input and output. The latent vector is 16-dim.

To put the autoencoder in context, x can be an MNIST digit which has a dimension of $28 \times 28 \times 1 = 784$. The encoder transforms the input into a low-dimensional z that can be a 16-dimension latent vector. The decoder will attempt to recover the input in the form of $\tilde{x}$ from z. Visually, every MNIST digit x will appear similar to $\tilde{x}$. *Figure 3.1.2* demonstrates this autoencoding process to us. We can observe that the decoded digit 7, while not exactly the same remains close enough.

Since both encoder and decoder are non-linear functions, we can use neural networks to implement both. For example, in the MNIST dataset, the autoencoder can be implemented by MLP or CNN. The autoencoder can be trained by minimizing the loss function through backpropagation. Similar to other neural networks, the only requirement is that the loss function must be differentiable.

If we treat the input as a distribution, we can interpret the encoder as an encoder of distribution, $p(z \mid x)$ and the decoder, as the decoder of distribution, $p(x \mid z)$. The loss function of the autoencoder is expressed as follows:

$$\mathcal{L} = -\log p\left(x \mid z\right) \qquad \text{(Equation 3.1.2)}$$

The loss function simply means that we would like to maximize the chances of recovering the input distribution given the latent vector distribution. If the decoder output distribution is assumed to be Gaussian, then the loss function boils down to MSE since:

$$\mathcal{L} = -\log p\left(x \mid z\right) = -\log \prod_{i=1}^{m} \mathcal{N}\left(x_i; \tilde{x}_i, \sigma^2\right) = -\sum_{i=1}^{m} \log \mathcal{N}\left(x_i; \tilde{x}_i, \sigma^2\right) \alpha \sum_{i=1}^{m} \left(x_i - \tilde{x}_i\right)^2 \qquad \text{(Equation 3.1.3)}$$

In this example, $\mathcal{N}\left(x_i; \tilde{x}_i, \sigma^2\right)$ represents a Gaussian distribution with a mean of $\tilde{x}_i$ and variance of σ^2. A constant variance is assumed. The decoder output $\tilde{x}_i$ is assumed to be independent. While m is the output dimension.

Building autoencoders using Keras

We're now going to move onto something really exciting, building an autoencoder using Keras library. For simplicity, we'll be using the MNIST dataset for the first set of examples. The autoencoder will then generate a latent vector from the input data and recover the input using the decoder. The latent vector in this first example is 16-dim.

Firstly, we're going to implement the autoencoder by building the encoder. *Listing 3.2.1* shows the encoder that compresses the MNIST digit into a 16-dim latent vector. The encoder is a stack of two `Conv2D`. The final stage is a `Dense` layer with 16 units to generate the latent vector. *Figure 3.2.1* shows the architecture model diagram generated by `plot_model()` which is the same as the text version produced by `encoder.summary()`. The shape of the output of the last `Conv2D` is saved to compute the dimensions of the decoder input layer for easy reconstruction of the MNIST image.

The following Listing 3.2.1, shows `autoencoder-mnist-3.2.1.py`. This is an autoencoder implementation using Keras. The latent vector is 16-dim:

```python
from keras.layers import Dense, Input
from keras.layers import Conv2D, Flatten
from keras.layers import Reshape, Conv2DTranspose
from keras.models import Model
from keras.datasets import mnist
from keras.utils import plot_model
from keras import backend as K

import numpy as np
import matplotlib.pyplot as plt

# load MNIST dataset
(x_train, _), (x_test, _) = mnist.load_data()

# reshape to (28, 28, 1) and normalize input images
image_size = x_train.shape[1]
x_train = np.reshape(x_train, [-1, image_size, image_size, 1])
x_test = np.reshape(x_test, [-1, image_size, image_size, 1])
x_train = x_train.astype('float32') / 255
x_test = x_test.astype('float32') / 255

# network parameters
input_shape = (image_size, image_size, 1)
batch_size = 32
kernel_size = 3
latent_dim = 16
# encoder/decoder number of filters per CNN layer
layer_filters = [32, 64]
```

```
# build the autoencoder model
# first build the encoder model
inputs = Input(shape=input_shape, name='encoder_input')
x = inputs
# stack of Conv2D(32)-Conv2D(64)
for filters in layer_filters:
    x = Conv2D(filters=filters,
               kernel_size=kernel_size,
               activation='relu',
               strides=2,
               padding='same')(x)

# shape info needed to build decoder model
# so we don't do hand computation
# the input to the decoder's first Conv2DTranspose
# will have this shape
# shape is (7, 7, 64) which is processed by
# the decoder back to (28, 28, 1)
shape = K.int_shape(x)

# generate latent vector
x = Flatten()(x)
latent = Dense(latent_dim, name='latent_vector')(x)

# instantiate encoder model
encoder = Model(inputs, latent, name='encoder')
encoder.summary()
plot_model(encoder, to_file='encoder.png', show_shapes=True)

# build the decoder model
latent_inputs = Input(shape=(latent_dim,), name='decoder_input')
# use the shape (7, 7, 64) that was earlier saved
x = Dense(shape[1] * shape[2] * shape[3])(latent_inputs)
# from vector to suitable shape for transposed conv
x = Reshape((shape[1], shape[2], shape[3]))(x)

# stack of Conv2DTranspose(64)-Conv2DTranspose(32)
for filters in layer_filters[::-1]:
    x = Conv2DTranspose(filters=filters,
                        kernel_size=kernel_size,
                        activation='relu',
                        strides=2,
                        padding='same')(x)
```

```python
# reconstruct the input
outputs = Conv2DTranspose(filters=1,
                          kernel_size=kernel_size,
                          activation='sigmoid',
                          padding='same',
                          name='decoder_output')(x)

# instantiate decoder model
decoder = Model(latent_inputs, outputs, name='decoder')
decoder.summary()
plot_model(decoder, to_file='decoder.png', show_shapes=True)

# autoencoder = encoder + decoder
# instantiate autoencoder model
   autoencoder = Model(inputs,
                       decoder(encoder(inputs)),
                       name='autoencoder')
   autoencoder.summary()
   plot_model(autoencoder,
              to_file='autoencoder.png',
           show_shapes=True)

# Mean Square Error (MSE) loss funtion, Adam optimizer
autoencoder.compile(loss='mse', optimizer='adam')

# train the autoencoder
autoencoder.fit(x_train,
                x_train,
                validation_data=(x_test, x_test),
                epochs=1,
                batch_size=batch_size)

# predict the autoencoder output from test data
x_decoded = autoencoder.predict(x_test)

# display the 1st 8 test input and decoded images
imgs = np.concatenate([x_test[:8], x_decoded[:8]])
imgs = imgs.reshape((4, 4, image_size, image_size))
imgs = np.vstack([np.hstack(i) for i in imgs])
plt.figure()
plt.axis('off')
```

```
plt.title('Input: 1st 2 rows, Decoded: last 2 rows')
plt.imshow(imgs, interpolation='none', cmap='gray')
plt.savefig('input_and_decoded.png')
plt.show()
```

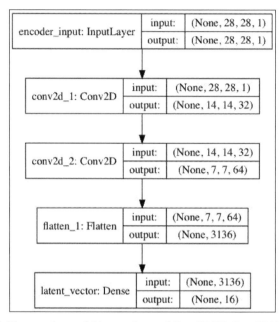

Figure 3.2.1: The encoder model is a made up of Conv2D(32)-Conv2D(64)-Dense(16)
in order to generate the low dimensional latent vector

The decoder in *Listing 3.2.1* decompresses the latent vector in order to recover the MNIST digit. The decoder input stage is a Dense layer that will accept the latent vector. The number of units is equal to the product of the saved Conv2D output dimensions from the encoder. This is done so we can easily resize the output of the Dense layer for Conv2DTranspose to finally recover the original MNIST image dimensions.

The decoder is made of a stack of three Conv2DTranspose. In our case, we're going to use a **Transposed CNN** (sometimes called deconvolution), which is more commonly used in decoders. We can imagine transposed CNN (Conv2DTranspose) as the reversed process of CNN. In a simple example, if the CNN converts an image to feature maps, the transposed CNN will produce an image given feature maps. *Figure 3.2.2* shows the decoder model.

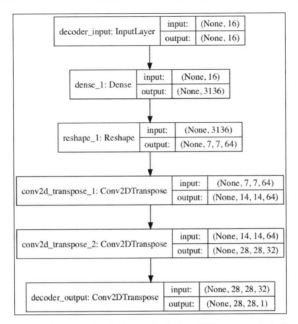

Figure 3.2.2: The decoder model is made of a Dense(16)-Conv2DTranspose(64) -Conv2DTranspose(32)-Conv2DTranspose(1). The input is the latent vector decoded to recover the original input.

By joining the encoder and decoder together, we're able to build the autoencoder. *Figure 3.2.3* illustrates the model diagram of the autoencoder. The tensor output of the encoder is also the input to a decoder which generates the output of the autoencoder. In this example, we'll be using the MSE loss function and Adam optimizer. During training, the input is the same as the output, x_train. We should note that in our example, there are only a few layers which are sufficient enough to drive the validation loss to 0.01 in one epoch. For more complex datasets, you may need a deeper encoder, decoder as well as more epochs of training.

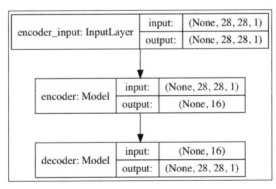

Figure 3.2.3: The autoencoder model is built by joining an encoder model and a decoder model together. There are 178k parameters for this autoencoder.

After training the autoencoder for one epoch with a validation loss of 0.01, we're able to verify if it can encode and decode the MNIST data that it has not seen before. *Figure 3.2.4* shows us eight samples from the test data and the corresponding decoded images. Except for minor blurring in the images, we're able to easily recognize that the autoencoder is able to recover the input with good quality. The results will improve as we train for a larger number of epochs.

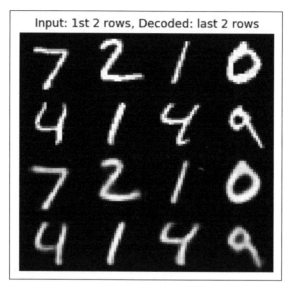

Figure 3.2.4: Prediction of the autoencoder from the test data.
The first 2 rows are the original input test data. The last 2 rows are the predicted data.

At this point, we may be wondering how we can visualize the latent vector in space. A simple method for visualization is to force the autoencoder to learn the MNIST digits features using a 2-dim latent vector. From there, we're able to project this latent vector on a 2D space in order to see how the MNIST codes are distributed. By setting the `latent_dim = 2` in `autoencoder-mnist-3.2.1.py` code and by using the `plot_results()` to plot the MNIST digit as a function of the 2-dim latent vector, *Figure 3.2.5* and *Figure 3.2.6* shows the distribution of MNIST digits as a function of latent codes. These figures were generated after 20 epochs of training. For convenience, the program is saved as `autoencoder-2dim-mnist-3.2.2.py` with the partial code shown in *Listing 3.2.2*.

Following is Listing 3.2.2, `autoencoder-2dim-mnist-3.2.2.py`, which shows the function for visualization of the MNIST digits distribution over 2-dim latent codes. The rest of the code is practically similar to *Listing 3.2.1* and no longer shown here.

```
def plot_results(models,
                 data,
```

```
                batch_size=32,
                model_name="autoencoder_2dim"):
"""Plots 2-dim latent values as color gradient
    then, plot MNIST digits as function of 2-dim latent vector

Arguments:
    models (list): encoder and decoder models
    data (list): test data and label
    batch_size (int): prediction batch size
    model_name (string): which model is using this function
"""

encoder, decoder = models
x_test, y_test = data
os.makedirs(model_name, exist_ok=True)

filename = os.path.join(model_name, "latent_2dim.png")
# display a 2D plot of the digit classes in the latent space
z = encoder.predict(x_test,
                    batch_size=batch_size)
plt.figure(figsize=(12, 10))
plt.scatter(z[:, 0], z[:, 1], c=y_test)
plt.colorbar()
plt.xlabel("z[0]")
plt.ylabel("z[1]")
plt.savefig(filename)
plt.show()

filename = os.path.join(model_name, "digits_over_latent.png")
# display a 30x30 2D manifold of the digits
n = 30
digit_size = 28
figure = np.zeros((digit_size * n, digit_size * n))
# linearly spaced coordinates corresponding to the 2D plot
# of digit classes in the latent space
grid_x = np.linspace(-4, 4, n)
grid_y = np.linspace(-4, 4, n)[::-1]

for i, yi in enumerate(grid_y):
    for j, xi in enumerate(grid_x):
        z = np.array([[xi, yi]])
        x_decoded = decoder.predict(z)
        digit = x_decoded[0].reshape(digit_size, digit_size)
        figure[i * digit_size: (i + 1) * digit_size,
```

```
                    j * digit_size: (j + 1) * digit_size] = digit

    plt.figure(figsize=(10, 10))
    start_range = digit_size // 2
    end_range = n * digit_size + start_range + 1
    pixel_range = np.arange(start_range, end_range, digit_size)
    sample_range_x = np.round(grid_x, 1)
    sample_range_y = np.round(grid_y, 1)
    plt.xticks(pixel_range, sample_range_x)
    plt.yticks(pixel_range, sample_range_y)
    plt.xlabel("z[0]")
    plt.ylabel("z[1]")
    plt.imshow(figure, cmap='Greys_r')
    plt.savefig(filename)
    plt.show()
```

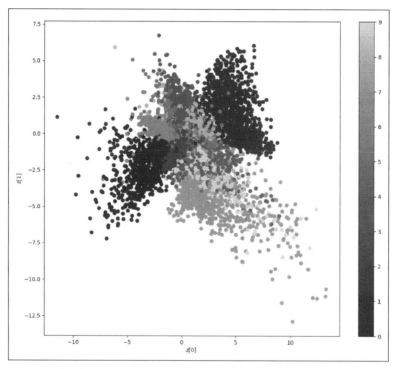

Figure 3.2.5: A MNIST digit distribution as a function of latent code dimensions, $z[0]$ and $z[1]$.
Original color photo can be found on the book GitHub repository, https://github.com/PacktPublishing/
Advanced-Deep-Learning-with-Keras/blob/master/chapter3-autoencoders/README.md.

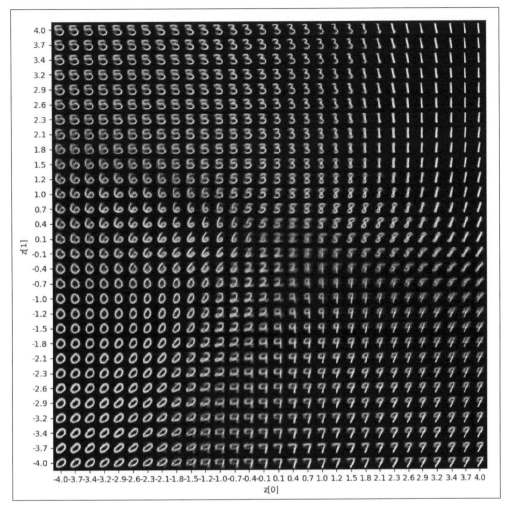

Figure 3.2.6: Digits generated as the 2-dim latent vector space is navigated

In *Figure 3.2.5*, we'll be able to see that the latent codes for a specific digit are clustering on a region in space. For example, digit 0 is on the lower left quadrant, while digit 1 is on the upper right quadrant. Such clustering is mirrored in *Figure 3.2.6*. In fact, the same figure shows the result of navigating or generating new digits from the latent space as shown in the *Figure 3.2.5*.

For example, starting from the center and varying the value of a 2-dim latent vector towards the lower left quadrant, shows us that the digit changes from 2 to 0. This is expected since from *Figure 3.2.5*, we're able to see that the codes for the digit 2 clusters are near the center, and as discussed digit 0 codes cluster in the lower left quadrant. For *Figure 3.2.6*, we've only explored the regions between -4.0 and +4.0 for each latent dimension.

As can be seen in *Figure 3.2.5*, the latent code distribution is not continuous and ranges beyond ±4.0. Ideally, it should look like a circle where there are valid values everywhere. Because of this discontinuity, there are regions where if we decode the latent vector, hardly recognizable digits will be produced.

Denoising autoencoder (DAE)

We're now going to build an autoencoder with a practical application. Firstly, let's paint a picture and imagine that the MNIST digits images were corrupted by noise, thus making it harder for humans to read. We're able to build a **Denoising Autoencoder** (**DAE**) to remove the noise from these images. *Figure 3.3.1* shows us three sets of MNIST digits. The top rows of each set (for example, MNIST digits 7, 2, 1, 9, 0, 6, 3, 4, 9) are the original images. The middle rows show the inputs to DAE, which are the original images corrupted by noise. The last rows show the outputs of DAE:

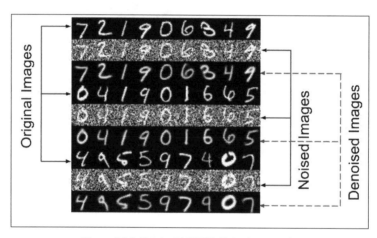

Figure 3.3.1: Original MNIST digits (top rows),
corrupted original images (middle rows) and denoised images (last rows)

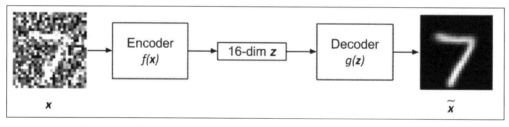

Figure 3.3.2: The input to the denoising autoencoder is the corrupted image.
The output is the clean or denoised image. The latent vector is assumed to be 16-dim.

As shown in *Figure 3.3.2*, the denoising autoencoder has practically the same structure as the autoencoder for MNIST that we presented in the previous section. The input is defined as:

$$x = x_{orig} + noise$$ (Equation 3.3.1)

In this formula, x_{orig} represents the original MNIST image corrupted by *noise*.

The objective of the encoder is to discover how to produce the latent vector, z, that will enable the decoder to recover x_{orig} by minimizing the dissimilarity loss function such as MSE, as shown here:

$$\mathcal{L}\left(x_{orig}, \tilde{x}\right) = MSE = \frac{1}{m} \sum_{i=1}^{i=m} \left(x_{orig_i} - \tilde{x}_i\right)^2$$ (Equation 3.3.2)

In this example, m is the output dimensions (for example, in MNIST $m = width \times height \times channels = 28 \times 28 \times 1 = 784$). x_{orig_i} and $\tilde{x}_i$ are the elements of x_{orig} and $\tilde{x}$, respectively.

To implement DAE, we're going to need to make a few changes on the autoencoder presented in the previous section. Firstly, the training input data should be corrupted MNIST digits. The training output data is the same original clean MNIST digits. This is like telling the autoencoder what the corrected images should be or asking it to figure out how to remove noise given a corrupted image. Lastly, we must validate the autoencoder on the corrupted MNIST test data.

The MNIST digit 7 shown on the left of *Figure 3.3.2* is an actual corrupted image input. The one on the right is the clean image output of a trained denoising autoencoder.

Listing 3.3.1 shows the denoising autoencoder which has been contributed to the Keras GitHub repository. Using the same MNIST dataset, we're able to simulate corrupted images by adding random noise. The noise added is a Gaussian distribution with a mean, $\mu = 0.5$ and standard deviation of $\sigma = 0.5$. Since adding random noise may push the pixel data into invalid values of less than 0 or greater than 1, the pixel values are clipped to [0.1, 1.0] range.

Everything else will remain practically the same as the autoencoder from the previous section. We'll use the same MSE loss function and Adam optimizer as the autoencoder. However, the number of epoch for training has increased to 10. This is to allow sufficient parameter optimization.

Figure 3.3.1 shows actual validation data with both the corrupted and denoised test MNIST digits. We're even able to see that humans will find it difficult to read the corrupted MNIST digits. *Figure 3.3.3* shows a certain level of robustness of DAE as the level of noise is increased from $\sigma = 0.5$ to $\sigma = 0.75$ and $\sigma = 1.0$. At $\sigma = 0.75$, DAE is still able to recover the original images. However, at $\sigma = 1.0$, a few digits such as 4 and 5 in the second and third sets can no longer be recovered correctly.

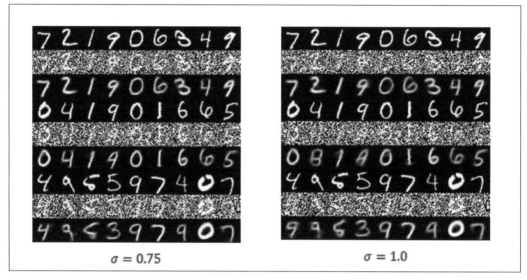

Figure 3.3.3: Performance of denoising autoencoder as the noise level is increased

As seen in Listing 3.3.1, `denoising-autoencoder-mnist-3.3.1.py` shows us a Denoising autoencoder:

```
from keras.layers import Dense, Input
from keras.layers import Conv2D, Flatten
from keras.layers import Reshape, Conv2DTranspose
from keras.models import Model
from keras import backend as K
from keras.datasets import mnist
import numpy as np
import matplotlib.pyplot as plt
from PIL import Image

np.random.seed(1337)

# load MNIST dataset
(x_train, _), (x_test, _) = mnist.load_data()

# reshape to (28, 28, 1) and normalize input images
```

```
image_size = x_train.shape[1]
x_train = np.reshape(x_train, [-1, image_size, image_size, 1])
x_test = np.reshape(x_test, [-1, image_size, image_size, 1])
x_train = x_train.astype('float32') / 255
x_test = x_test.astype('float32') / 255

# generate corrupted MNIST images by adding noise with normal dist
# centered at 0.5 and std=0.5
noise = np.random.normal(loc=0.5, scale=0.5, size=x_train.shape)
x_train_noisy = x_train + noise
noise = np.random.normal(loc=0.5, scale=0.5, size=x_test.shape)
x_test_noisy = x_test + noise

# adding noise may exceed normalized pixel values>1.0 or <0.0
# clip pixel values >1.0 to 1.0 and <0.0 to 0.0
x_train_noisy = np.clip(x_train_noisy, 0., 1.)
x_test_noisy = np.clip(x_test_noisy, 0., 1.)

# network parameters
input_shape = (image_size, image_size, 1)
batch_size = 32
kernel_size = 3
latent_dim = 16
# encoder/decoder number of CNN layers and filters per layer
layer_filters = [32, 64]

# build the autoencoder model
# first build the encoder model
inputs = Input(shape=input_shape, name='encoder_input')
x = inputs

# stack of Conv2D(32)-Conv2D(64)
for filters in layer_filters:
    x = Conv2D(filters=filters,
            kernel_size=kernel_size,
            strides=2,
            activation='relu',
            padding='same')(x)

# shape info needed to build decoder model
# so we don't do hand computation
# the input to the decoder's first Conv2DTranspose
# will have this shape
# shape is (7, 7, 64) which can be processed by
```

```
# the decoder back to (28, 28, 1)
shape = K.int_shape(x)

# generate the latent vector
x = Flatten()(x)
latent = Dense(latent_dim, name='latent_vector')(x)

# instantiate encoder model
encoder = Model(inputs, latent, name='encoder')
encoder.summary()


# build the decoder model
latent_inputs = Input(shape=(latent_dim,), name='decoder_input')
# use the shape (7, 7, 64) that was earlier saved
x = Dense(shape[1] * shape[2] * shape[3])(latent_inputs)
# from vector to suitable shape for transposed conv
x = Reshape((shape[1], shape[2], shape[3]))(x)

# stack of Conv2DTranspose(64)-Conv2DTranspose(32)
for filters in layer_filters[::-1]:
    x = Conv2DTranspose(filters=filters,
                        kernel_size=kernel_size,
                        strides=2,
                        activation='relu',
                        padding='same')(x)

# reconstruct the denoised input
outputs = Conv2DTranspose(filters=1,
                          kernel_size=kernel_size,
                          padding='same',
                          activation='sigmoid',
                          name='decoder_output')(x)

# instantiate decoder model
decoder = Model(latent_inputs, outputs, name='decoder')
decoder.summary()

# autoencoder = encoder + decoder
# instantiate autoencoder model
autoencoder = Model(inputs, decoder(encoder(inputs)),
name='autoencoder')
autoencoder.summary()
```

```
# Mean Square Error (MSE) loss function, Adam optimizer
autoencoder.compile(loss='mse', optimizer='adam')

# train the autoencoder
autoencoder.fit(x_train_noisy,
                x_train,
                validation_data=(x_test_noisy, x_test),
                epochs=10,
                batch_size=batch_size)

# predict the autoencoder output from corrupted test images
x_decoded = autoencoder.predict(x_test_noisy)

# 3 sets of images with 9 MNIST digits
# 1st rows - original images
# 2nd rows - images corrupted by noise
# 3rd rows - denoised images
rows, cols = 3, 9
num = rows * cols
imgs = np.concatenate([x_test[:num], x_test_noisy[:num], x_
decoded[:num]])
imgs = imgs.reshape((rows * 3, cols, image_size, image_size))
imgs = np.vstack(np.split(imgs, rows, axis=1))
imgs = imgs.reshape((rows * 3, -1, image_size, image_size))
imgs = np.vstack([np.hstack(i) for i in imgs])
imgs = (imgs * 255).astype(np.uint8)
plt.figure()
plt.axis('off')
plt.title('Original images: top rows, '
          'Corrupted Input: middle rows, '
          'Denoised Input:  third rows')
plt.imshow(imgs, interpolation='none', cmap='gray')
Image.fromarray(imgs).save('corrupted_and_denoised.png')
plt.show()
```

Automatic colorization autoencoder

We're now going to work on another practical application of autoencoders. In this case, we're going to imagine that we have a grayscale photo and that we want to build a tool that will automatically add color to them. We would like to replicate the human abilities in identifying that the sea and sky are blue, the grass field and trees are green, while clouds are white, and so on.

As shown in *Figure 3.4.1*, if we are given a grayscale photo of a rice field on the foreground, a volcano in the background and sky on top, we're able to add the appropriate colors.

Figure 3.4.1: Adding color to a grayscale photo of the Mayon Volcano. A colorization network should replicate human abilities by adding color to a grayscale photo. Left photo is grayscale. The right photo is color. Original color photo can be found on the book GitHub repository, https://github.com/PacktPublishing/Advanced-Deep-Learning-with-Keras/blob/master/chapter3-autoencoders/README.md.

A simple automatic colorization algorithm seems like a suitable problem for autoencoders. If we can train the autoencoder with a sufficient number of grayscale photos as input and the corresponding colored photos as output, it could possibly discover the hidden structure on properly applying colors. Roughly, it is the reverse process of denoising. The question is, can an autoencoder add color (good noise) to the original grayscale image?

Listing 3.4.1 shows the colorization autoencoder network. The colorization autoencoder network is a modified version of denoising autoencoder that we used for the MNIST dataset. Firstly, we need a dataset of grayscale to colored photos. The CIFAR10 database, which we have used before, has 50,000 training and 10,000 testing 32 × 32 RGB photos that can be converted to grayscale. As shown in the following listing, we're able to use the `rgb2gray()` function to apply weights on R, G, and B components to convert from color to grayscale.

Listing 3.4.1, `colorization-autoencoder-cifar10-3.4.1.py`, shows us a colorization autoencoder using the CIFAR10 dataset:

```
from keras.layers import Dense, Input
from keras.layers import Conv2D, Flatten
```

```
from keras.layers import Reshape, Conv2DTranspose
from keras.models import Model
from keras.callbacks import ReduceLROnPlateau, ModelCheckpoint
from keras.datasets import cifar10
from keras.utils import plot_model
from keras import backend as K

import numpy as np
import matplotlib.pyplot as plt
import os


# convert from color image (RGB) to grayscale
# source: opencv.org
# grayscale = 0.299*red + 0.587*green + 0.114*blue
def rgb2gray(rgb):
    return np.dot(rgb[...,:3], [0.299, 0.587, 0.114])


# load the CIFAR10 data
(x_train, _), (x_test, _) = cifar10.load_data()

# input image dimensions
# we assume data format "channels_last"
img_rows = x_train.shape[1]
img_cols = x_train.shape[2]
channels = x_train.shape[3]

# create saved_images folder
imgs_dir = 'saved_images'
save_dir = os.path.join(os.getcwd(), imgs_dir)
if not os.path.isdir(save_dir):
        os.makedirs(save_dir)

# display the 1st 100 input images (color and gray)
imgs = x_test[:100]
imgs = imgs.reshape((10, 10, img_rows, img_cols, channels))
imgs = np.vstack([np.hstack(i) for i in imgs])
plt.figure()
plt.axis('off')
plt.title('Test color images (Ground Truth)')
plt.imshow(imgs, interpolation='none')
plt.savefig('%s/test_color.png' % imgs_dir)
plt.show()
```

```
# convert color train and test images to gray
x_train_gray = rgb2gray(x_train)
x_test_gray = rgb2gray(x_test)

# display grayscale version of test images
imgs = x_test_gray[:100]
imgs = imgs.reshape((10, 10, img_rows, img_cols))
imgs = np.vstack([np.hstack(i) for i in imgs])
plt.figure()
plt.axis('off')
plt.title('Test gray images (Input)')
plt.imshow(imgs, interpolation='none', cmap='gray')
plt.savefig('%s/test_gray.png' % imgs_dir)
plt.show()


# normalize output train and test color images
x_train = x_train.astype('float32') / 255
x_test = x_test.astype('float32') / 255

# normalize input train and test grayscale images
x_train_gray = x_train_gray.astype('float32') / 255
x_test_gray = x_test_gray.astype('float32') / 255

# reshape images to row x col x channel for CNN output/validation
x_train = x_train.reshape(x_train.shape[0], img_rows, img_cols,
channels)
x_test = x_test.reshape(x_test.shape[0], img_rows, img_cols, channels)

# reshape images to row x col x channel for CNN input
x_train_gray = x_train_gray.reshape(x_train_gray.shape[0], img_rows,
img_cols, 1)
x_test_gray = x_test_gray.reshape(x_test_gray.shape[0], img_rows, img_
cols, 1)

# network parameters
input_shape = (img_rows, img_cols, 1)
batch_size = 32
kernel_size = 3
latent_dim = 256
# encoder/decoder number of CNN layers and filters per layer
layer_filters = [64, 128, 256]
```

```
# build the autoencoder model
# first build the encoder model
inputs = Input(shape=input_shape, name='encoder_input')
x = inputs
# stack of Conv2D(64)-Conv2D(128)-Conv2D(256)
for filters in layer_filters:
    x = Conv2D(filters=filters,
                kernel_size=kernel_size,
                strides=2,
                activation='relu',
                padding='same')(x)

# shape info needed to build decoder model
# so we don't do hand computation
# the input to the decoder's first Conv2DTranspose
# will have this shape
# shape is (4, 4, 256) which is processed
# by the decoder to (32, 32, 3)
shape = K.int_shape(x)

# generate a latent vector
x = Flatten()(x)
latent = Dense(latent_dim, name='latent_vector')(x)

# instantiate encoder model
encoder = Model(inputs, latent, name='encoder')
encoder.summary()

# build the decoder model
latent_inputs = Input(shape=(latent_dim,), name='decoder_input')
x = Dense(shape[1]*shape[2]*shape[3])(latent_inputs)
x = Reshape((shape[1], shape[2], shape[3]))(x)

# stack of Conv2DTranspose(256)-Conv2DTranspose(128)-
# Conv2DTranspose(64)
for filters in layer_filters[::-1]:
    x = Conv2DTranspose(filters=filters,
                        kernel_size=kernel_size,
                        strides=2,
                        activation='relu',
                        padding='same')(x)

outputs = Conv2DTranspose(filters=channels,
                          kernel_size=kernel_size,
```

```
                                        activation='sigmoid',
                                        padding='same',
                                        name='decoder_output')(x)

# instantiate decoder model
decoder = Model(latent_inputs, outputs, name='decoder')
decoder.summary()

# autoencoder = encoder + decoder
# instantiate autoencoder model
autoencoder = Model(inputs, decoder(encoder(inputs)),
name='autoencoder')
autoencoder.summary()

# prepare model saving directory.
save_dir = os.path.join(os.getcwd(), 'saved_models')
model_name = 'colorized_ae_model.{epoch:03d}.h5'
if not os.path.isdir(save_dir):
        os.makedirs(save_dir)
filepath = os.path.join(save_dir, model_name)

# reduce learning rate by sqrt(0.1) if the loss does not improve in 5
epochs
lr_reducer = ReduceLROnPlateau(factor=np.sqrt(0.1),
                               cooldown=0,
                               patience=5,
                               verbose=1,
                               min_lr=0.5e-6)

# save weights for future use
# (e.g. reload parameters w/o training)
checkpoint = ModelCheckpoint(filepath=filepath,
                             monitor='val_loss',
                             verbose=1,
                             save_best_only=True)

# Mean Square Error (MSE) loss function, Adam optimizer
autoencoder.compile(loss='mse', optimizer='adam')

# called every epoch
callbacks = clr_reducer, checkpoint]

# train the autoencoder
autoencoder.fit(x_train_gray,
```

```
                    x_train,
                    validation_data=(x_test_gray, x_test),
                    epochs=30,
                    batch_size=batch_size,
                    callbacks=callbacks)

# predict the autoencoder output from test data
x_decoded = autoencoder.predict(x_test_gray)

# display the 1st 100 colorized images
imgs = x_decoded[:100]
imgs = imgs.reshape((10, 10, img_rows, img_cols, channels))
imgs = np.vstack([np.hstack(i) for i in imgs])
plt.figure()
plt.axis('off')
plt.title('Colorized test images (Predicted)')
plt.imshow(imgs, interpolation='none')
plt.savefig('%s/colorized.png' % imgs_dir)
plt.show()
```

We've increased the capacity of the autoencoder by adding one more block of convolution and transposed convolution. We've also doubled the number of filters at each CNN block. The latent vector is now 256-dim in order to increase the number of salient properties it can represent as discussed in the autoencoder section. Finally, the output filter size has increased to three, or equal to the number of channels in RGB of the expected colored output.

The colorization autoencoder is now trained with the grayscale as inputs and original RGB images as outputs. The training will take more epochs and uses the learning rate reducer to scale down the learning rate when the validation loss is not improving. This can be easily done by telling the callbacks argument in the Keras fit() function to call the lr_reducer() function.

Figure 3.4.2 demonstrates colorization of grayscale images from the test dataset of CIFAR10. *Figure 3.4.3* compares the ground truth with the colorization autoencoder prediction. The autoencoder performs an acceptable colorization job. The sea or sky is predicted to be blue, animals have varying brown shades, the cloud is white, and so on.

There are some noticeable wrong predictions like red vehicles have become blue or blue vehicles become red, and the occasional green field has been mistaken as blue skies, and dark or golden skies are converted to blue skies.

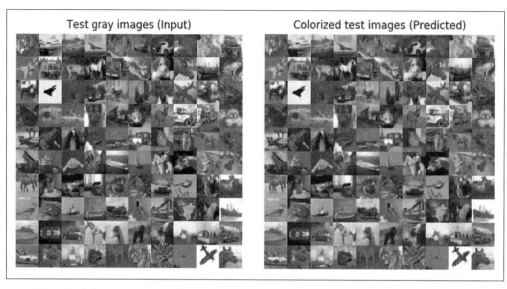

Figure 3.4.2: Automatic grayscale to color image conversion using the autoencoder. CIFAR10 test grayscale input images (left) and predicted color images (right). Original color photo can be found on the book GitHub repository, https://github.com/PacktPublishing/Advanced-Deep-Learning-with-Keras/blob/master/chapter3-autoencoders/README.md.

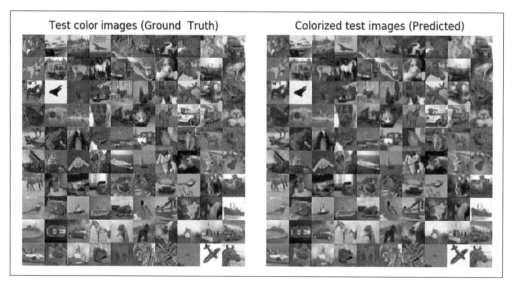

Figure 3.4.3: Side by side comparison of ground truth color images and predicted colorized images. Original color photos can be found on the book GitHub repository, https://github.com/PacktPublishing/Advanced-Deep-Learning-with-Keras/blob/master/chapter3-autoencoders/README.md.

Conclusion

In this chapter, we've been introduced to autoencoders, which are neural networks that compress input data into low-dimensional codes in order to efficiently perform structural transformations such as denoising and colorization. We've laid the foundations to the more advanced topics of GANs and VAEs, that we will introduce in later chapters, while still exploring how autoencoders can utilize Keras. We've demonstrated how to implement an autoencoder from two building block models, both encoder and decoder. We've also learned how the extraction of a hidden structure of input distribution is one of the common tasks in AI.

Once the latent code has been uncovered, there are many structural operations that can be performed on the original input distribution. In order to gain a better understanding of the input distribution, the hidden structure in the form of the latent vector can be visualized using low-level embedding similar to what we did in this chapter or through more sophisticated dimensionality reduction techniques such t-SNE or PCA.

Apart from denoising and colorization, autoencoders are used in converting input distribution to low-dimensional latent codes that can be further processed for other tasks such as segmentation, detection, tracking, reconstruction, visual understanding, and so on. In *Chapter 8, Variational Autoencoders (VAEs)*, we will discuss VAEs which are structurally the same as autoencoder but differ by having an interpretable latent code that can produce a continuous latent codes projection. In the next chapter, we will embark on one of the most important recent breakthroughs in AI, the introduction of GANs where we will learn of the core strengths of GANs and their ability to synthesize data or signals that look real.

References

1. Ian Goodfellow and others. *Deep learning*. Vol. 1. Cambridge: MIT press, 2016 (`http://www.deeplearningbook.org/`).

4
Generative Adversarial Networks (GANs)

In this chapter, we'll be investigating **Generative Adversarial Networks (GANs)** [1], the first of three artificial intelligence algorithms that we'll be looking at. GANs belong to the family of generative models. However, unlike autoencoders, generative models are able to create new and meaningful outputs given arbitrary encodings.

In this chapter, the working principles of GANs will be discussed. We'll also review the implementations of several early GANs within Keras. While later on the chapter, we'll be demonstrating the techniques needed to achieve stable training. The scope of this chapter covers two popular examples of GAN implementations, **Deep Convolutional GAN (DCGAN)** [2] and **Conditional GAN (CGAN)** [3].

In summary, the goal of this chapter is to:

- Introduce the principles of GANs
- How to implement GANs such as DCGAN and CGAN in Keras

An overview of GANs

Before we move into the more advanced concepts of GANs, let's start by going over GANs, and introducing the underlying concepts of them. GANs are very powerful; this simple statement is proven by the fact that they can generate new celebrity faces that are not of real people by performing latent space interpolations.

A great example of the advanced features of GANs [4] can be seen with this YouTube video (https://youtu.be/G06dEcZ-QTg). The video, which shows how GANs can be utilized to produce realistic faces just shows how powerful they can be. This topic is much more advanced than anything we've looked at before in this book. For example, the above video is something that can't be accomplished easily by autoencoders, which we covered in *Chapter 3, Autoencoders*.

GANs are able to learn how to model the input distribution by training two competing (and cooperating) networks referred to as **generator** and **discriminator** (sometimes known as **critic**). The role of the generator is to keep on figuring out how to generate fake data or signals (this includes, audio and images) that can fool the discriminator. Meanwhile, the discriminator is trained to distinguish between fake and real signals. As the training progresses, the discriminator will no longer be able to see the difference between the synthetically generated data and the real ones. From there, the discriminator can be discarded, and the generator can now be used to create new realistic signals that have never been observed before.

The underlying concept of GANs is straightforward. However, one thing we'll find is that the most challenging aspect is how do we achieve stable training of the generator-discriminator network? There must be a healthy competition between the generator and discriminator in order for both networks to be able to learn simultaneously. Since the loss function is computed from the output of the discriminator, its parameters update is fast. When the discriminator converges faster, the generator no longer receives sufficient gradient updates for its parameters and fails to converge. Other than being hard to train, GANs can also suffer from either a partial or total modal collapse, a situation wherein the generator is producing almost similar outputs for different latent encodings.

Principles of GANs

As shown in *Figure 4.1.1* a GAN is analogous to a counterfeiter (generator) - police (discriminator) scenario. At the academy, the police are taught how to determine if a dollar bill is either genuine or fake. Samples of real dollar bills from the bank and fake money from the counterfeiter are used to train the police. However, from time to time, the counterfeiter will attempt to pretend that he printed real dollar bills. Initially, the police will not be fooled and will tell the counterfeiter why the money is fake. Taking into consideration this feedback, the counterfeiter hones his skills again and attempts to produce new fake dollar bills. As expected the police will be able to both spot the money as fake and justify why the dollar bills are fake.

Figure 4.1.1: The generator and discriminator of GANs are analogous to the counterfeiter and the police.
The goal of the counterfeiter is to fool the police into believing that the dollar bill is real.

This scenario continues indefinitely but eventually, a time will come when the counterfeiter has mastered his skills in making fake dollar bills that are indistinguishable from real ones. The counterfeiter can then infinitely print dollar bills without getting caught by the police as they are no longer indefinable as counterfeit.

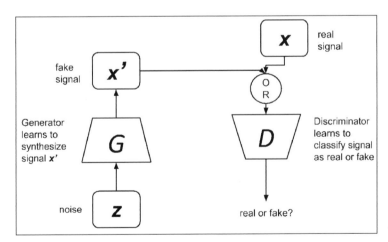

Figure 4.1.2: A GAN is made up of two networks, a generator, and a discriminator.
The discriminator is trained to distinguish between real and fake signals or data.
The generator's job is to generate fake signals or data that can eventually fool the discriminator.

As shown in *Figure 4.1.2*, a GAN is made up of two networks, a generator, and a discriminator. The input to the generator is noise, and the output is a synthesized signal. Meanwhile, the discriminator's input will be either a real or a synthesized signal. Genuine signals come from the true sampled data, while the fake signals come from the generator. All of the valid signals are labeled 1.0 (that is, 100% probability of being real) while all the synthesized signals are labeled 0.0 (that is, 0% probability of being real). Since the labeling process is automated, GANs are still considered part of the unsupervised learning approach in deep learning.

The objective of the discriminator is to learn from this supplied dataset on how to distinguish real signals from fake signals. During this part of GAN training, only the discriminator parameters will be updated. Like a typical binary classifier, the discriminator is trained to predict on a range of 0.0 to 1.0 in confidence values on how close a given input signal is to the true one. However, this is only half of the story.

At regular intervals, the generator will pretend that its output is a genuine signal and will ask the GAN to label it as 1.0. When the fake signal is then presented to the discriminator, naturally it will be classified as fake with a label close to 0.0. The optimizer computes the generator parameter updates based on the presented label (that is, 1.0). It also takes its own prediction into account when training on this new data. In other words, the discriminator has some doubt about its prediction, and so, GANs takes that into consideration. This time, GANs will let the gradients backpropagate from the last layer of the discriminator down to the first layer of the generator. However, in most practices, during this phase of training, the discriminator parameters are temporarily frozen. The generator will use the gradients to update its parameters and improve its ability to synthesize fake signals.

Overall, the whole process is akin to two networks competing with one another while still cooperating at the same time. When the GAN training converges, the end result is a generator that can synthesize signals. The discriminator thinks these synthesized signals are real or with a label near 1.0, which means the discriminator can then be discarded. The generator part will be useful in producing meaningful outputs from arbitrary noise inputs.

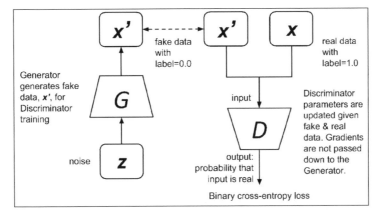

Figure 4.1.3: Training the discriminator is similar to training a binary classifier network using binary cross-entropy loss. The fake data is supplied by the generator while real data is from true samples.

As shown in the preceding figure, the discriminator can be trained by minimizing the loss function in the following equation:

$$\mathcal{L}^{(D)}\left(\theta^{(G)}, \theta^{(D)}\right) = -\mathbb{E}_{x \sim p_{data}} \log \mathcal{D}(x) - \mathbb{E}_z \log\left(1 - \mathcal{D}(\mathcal{G}(z))\right) \qquad \text{(Equation 4.1.1)}$$

The equation is just the standard binary cross-entropy cost function. The loss is the negative sum of the expectation of correctly identifying real data, $\mathcal{D}(x)$, and the expectation of 1.0 minus correctly identifying synthetic data, $1 - \mathcal{D}(\mathcal{G}(z))$. The log does not change the location of the local minima. Two mini-batches of data are supplied to the discriminator during training:

1. x, real from sampled data (that is, $x \sim p_{data}$) with label 1.0
2. $x' = \mathcal{G}(z)$, fake data from the generator with label 0.0

In order to minimize the loss function, the discriminator parameters, $\theta^{(D)}$, will be updated through backpropagation by correctly identifying the genuine data, $\mathcal{D}(x)$, and synthetic data, $1 - \mathcal{D}(\mathcal{G}(z))$. Correctly identifying real data is equivalent to $\mathcal{D}(x) \to 1.0$ while correctly classifying fake data is the same as $\mathcal{D}(\mathcal{G}(z)) \to 0.0$ or $\left(1 - \mathcal{D}(\mathcal{G}(z))\right) \to 1.0$. In this equation, z is the arbitrary encoding or noise vector that is used by the generator to synthesize new signals. Both contribute to minimizing the loss function.

To train the generator, GAN considers the total of the discriminator and generator losses as a zero-sum game. The generator loss function is simply the negative of the discriminator loss function:

$$\mathcal{L}^{(G)}\left(\theta^{(G)}, \theta^{(D)}\right) = -\mathcal{L}^{(D)}\left(\theta^{(G)}, \theta^{(D)}\right) \qquad \text{(Equation 4.1.2)}$$

This can then be rewritten more aptly as a value function:

$$\mathcal{V}^{(G)}\left(\theta^{(G)},\theta^{(D)}\right)=-\mathcal{L}^{(D)}\left(\theta^{(G)},\theta^{(D)}\right) \qquad \text{(Equation 4.1.3)}$$

From the perspective of the generator, *Equation 4.1.3* should be minimized. From the point of view of the discriminator, the value function should be maximized. Therefore, the generator training criterion can be written as a minimax problem:

$$\theta^{(G)*}=arg \min_{\theta^{(G)}} \min_{\theta^{(D)}} \mathcal{V}^{(D)}\left(\theta^{(G)},\theta^{(D)}\right) \qquad \text{(Equation 4.1.4)}$$

Occasionally, we'll try to fool the discriminator by pretending that the synthetic data is real with label 1.0. By maximizing with respect to $\theta^{(D)}$, the optimizer sends gradient updates to the discriminator parameters to consider this synthetic data as real. At the same time, by minimizing with respect to $\theta^{(G)}$, the optimizer will train the generator's parameters on how to trick the discriminator. However, in practice, the discriminator is confident in its prediction in classifying the synthetic data as fake and will not update its parameters. Furthermore, the gradient updates are small and have diminished significantly as they propagate to the generator layers. As a result, the generator fails to converge:

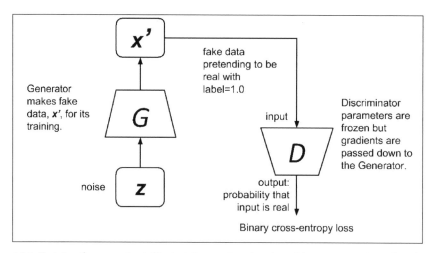

Figure 4.1.4: Training the generator is like training a network using a binary cross-entropy loss function. The fake data from the generator is presented as genuine.

The solution is to reformulate the loss function of the generator in the form:

$$\mathcal{L}^{(G)}\left(\theta^{(G)},\theta^{(D)}\right)=-\mathbb{E}_{z} \log \mathcal{D}\left(\mathcal{G}(z)\right) \qquad \text{(Equation 4.1.5)}$$

The loss function simply maximizes the chance of the discriminator into believing that the synthetic data is real by training the generator. The new formulation is no longer zero-sum and is purely heuristics-driven. *Figure 4.1.4* shows the generator during training. In this figure, the generator parameters are only updated when the whole adversarial network is trained. This is because the gradients are passed down from the discriminator to the generator. However, in practice, the discriminator weights are only temporarily frozen during adversarial training.

In deep learning, both the generator and discriminator can be implemented using a suitable neural network architecture. If the data or signal is an image, both the generator and discriminator networks will use a CNN. For single-dimensional sequences like in NLP, both networks are usually recurrent (RNN, LSTM or GRU).

GAN implementation in Keras

In the previous section, we learned that the principles behind GANs are straightforward. We also learned how GANs could be implemented by familiar network layers such as CNNs and RNNs. What differentiates GANs from other networks is they are notoriously difficult to train. Something as simple as a minor change in the layers can drive the network to training instability.

In this section, we'll examine one of the early successful implementations of GANs using deep CNNs. It is called DCGAN [3].

Figure 4.2.1 shows DCGAN that is used to generate fake MNIST images. DCGAN recommends the following design principles:

- Use of *strides* > 1 convolution instead of `MaxPooling2D` or `UpSampling2D`. With *strides* > 1, the CNN learns how to resize the feature maps.

- Avoid using `Dense` layers. Use CNN in all layers. The `Dense` layer is utilized only as the first layer of the generator to accept the *z*-vector. The output of the `Dense` layer is resized and becomes the input of the succeeding CNN layers.

- Use of **Batch Normalization (BN)** to stabilize learning by normalizing the input to each layer to have zero mean and unit variance. No BN in the generator output layer and discriminator input layer. In the implementation example to be presented here, no batch normalization is used in the discriminator.

- **Rectified Linear Unit (ReLU)** is used in all layers of the generator except in the output layer where the *tanh* activation is utilized. In the implementation example to be presented here, *sigmoid* is used instead of *tanh* in the output of the generator since it generally results in a more stable training for MNIST digits.

- Use of **Leaky ReLU** in all layers of the discriminator. Unlike ReLU, instead of zeroing out all outputs when the input is less than zero, Leaky ReLU generates a small gradient equal to *alpha* × *input*. In the following example, *alpha* = 0.2.

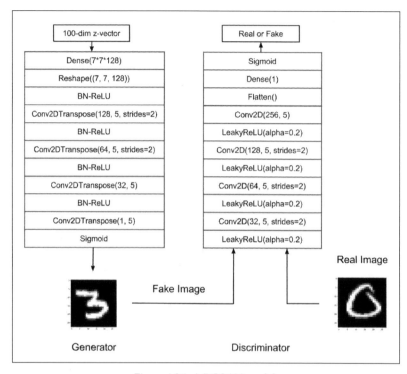

Figure 4.2.1: A DCGAN model

The generator learns to generate fake images from 100-dim input vectors ([-1.0, 1.0] range 100-dim random noise with uniform distribution). The discriminator classifies real from fake images but inadvertently coaches the generator how to generate real images when the adversarial network is trained. The kernel size used in our DCGAN implementation is 5, this is to allow it to increase the coverage and expressive power of the convolution.

The generator accepts the 100-dim *z*-vector generated by a uniform distribution with a range of -1.0 to 1.0. The first layer of the generator is a 7 × 7 ×128 = 6,272 - *unit* Dense layer. The number of units is computed based on the intended ultimate dimensions of the output image (28 × 28 × 1, 28 is a multiple of 7) and the number of filters of the first Conv2DTranspose, which is equal to 128. We can imagine transposed CNNs (Conv2DTranspose) as the reversed process of CNN. In a simple example, if a CNN converts an image to feature maps, a transposed CNN will produce an image given feature maps. Hence, transposed CNNs were used in the decoder in the previous chapter and here on generators.

After undergoing two `Conv2DTranspose` with `strides = 2`, the feature maps will have a size of 28 × 28 × *number of filters*. Each `Conv2DTranspose` is preceded by batch normalization and ReLU. The final layer has *sigmoid* activation that generates the 28 × 28 × 1 fake MNIST images. Each pixel is normalized to [0.0, 1.0] corresponding to [0, 255] grayscale levels. Following listing shows the implementation of the generator network in Keras. A function is defined to build the generator model. Due to the length of the entire code, we will limit the listing to the particular lines being discussed.

The complete code is available on GitHub: `https://github.com/PacktPublishing/Advanced-Deep-Learning-with-Keras`.

Listing 4.2.1, `dcgan-mnist-4.2.1.py` shows us the generator network builder function for DCGAN:

```python
def build_generator(inputs, image_size):
    """Build a Generator Model

    Stack of BN-ReLU-Conv2DTranpose to generate fake images.
    Output activation is sigmoid instead of tanh in [1].
    Sigmoid converges easily.

    # Arguments
        inputs (Layer): Input layer of the generator (the z-vector)
        image_size: Target size of one side (assuming square image)

    # Returns
        Model: Generator Model
    """

    image_resize = image_size // 4
    # network parameters
    kernel_size = 5
    layer_filters = [128, 64, 32, 1]

    x = Dense(image_resize * image_resize * layer_filters[0])(inputs)
    x = Reshape((image_resize, image_resize, layer_filters[0]))(x)

    for filters in layer_filters:
        # first two convolution layers use strides = 2
        # the last two use strides = 1
        if filters > layer_filters[-2]:
            strides = 2
```

```
    else:
        strides = 1
    x = BatchNormalization()(x)
    x = Activation('relu')(x)
    x = Conv2DTranspose(filters=filters,
                        kernel_size=kernel_size,
                        strides=strides,
                        padding='same')(x)

x = Activation('sigmoid')(x)
generator = Model(inputs, x, name='generator')
return generator
```

The discriminator is similar to many CNN-based classifiers. The input is a 28 × 28 × 1 MNIST image that is classified as either real (1.0) or fake (0.0). There are four CNN layers. Except for the last convolution, each `Conv2D` uses `strides = 2` to down sample the feature maps by two. Each `Conv2D` is then preceded by a Leaky ReLU layer. The final filter size is 256, while the initial filter size is 32 and doubles every convolution layer. The final filter size of 128 also works. However, we'll find that the generated images look better with 256. The final output layer is flattened, and a single unit `Dense` layer generates the prediction between 0.0 to 1.0 after scaling by the sigmoid activation layer. The output is modeled as a Bernoulli distribution. Hence, the binary cross-entropy loss function is used.

After building the generator and discriminator models, the adversarial model is made by concatenating the generator and discriminator networks. Both discriminator and adversarial networks use the RMSprop optimizer. The learning rate for the discriminator is 2e-4 while for the adversarial network, it is 1e-4. RMSprop decay rates of 6e-8 for discriminator and 3e-8 for the adversarial network are applied. Setting the learning rate of the adversarial equal to half of the discriminator will result in a more stable training. We'll recall from *Figure 4.1.3* and *4.1.4*, that the GAN training has two parts: discriminator training and generator training, which is adversarial training, with discriminator weights frozen.

Listing 4.2.2 shows the implementation of the discriminator in Keras. A function is defined to build the discriminator model. In *Listing 4.2.3*, we'll illustrate how to build GAN models. Firstly, the discriminator model is built and following on from that the generator model is instantiated. The adversarial model is just the generator and the discriminator put together. Across many GANs, the batch size of 64 appears to be the most common. The network parameters are shown in *Listing 4.2.3*.

As can be seen in *Listing 4.2.1* and *4.2.2*, the DCGAN models are straightforward. What makes it difficult to build is small changes in the network design can easily break the training convergence. For example, if batch normalization is used in the discriminator or if `strides = 2` in the generator is transferred to the latter CNN layers, DCGAN will fail to converge.

Listing 4.2.2, `dcgan-mnist-4.2.1.py` shows us the discriminator network builder function for DCGAN:

```
def build_discriminator(inputs):
    """Build a Discriminator Model

    Stack of LeakyReLU-Conv2D to discriminate real from fake.
    The network does not converge with BN so it is not used here
    unlike in [1] or original paper.

    # Arguments
        inputs (Layer): Input layer of the discriminator (the image)

    # Returns
        Model: Discriminator Model
    """
    kernel_size = 5
    layer_filters = [32, 64, 128, 256]

    x = inputs
    for filters in layer_filters:
        # first 3 convolution layers use strides = 2
        # last one uses strides = 1
        if filters == layer_filters[-1]:
            strides = 1
        else:
            strides = 2
        x = LeakyReLU(alpha=0.2)(x)
        x = Conv2D(filters=filters,
                   kernel_size=kernel_size,
                   strides=strides,
                   padding='same')(x)

    x = Flatten()(x)
    x = Dense(1)(x)
    x = Activation('sigmoid')(x)
    discriminator = Model(inputs, x, name='discriminator')
    return discriminator
```

Listing 4.2.3, `dcgan-mnist-4.2.1.py`: Function to build DCGAN models and call the training routine:

```
def build_and_train_models():
    # load MNIST dataset
    (x_train, _), (_, _) = mnist.load_data()

    # reshape data for CNN as (28, 28, 1) and normalize
    image_size = x_train.shape[1]
    x_train = np.reshape(x_train, [-1, image_size, image_size, 1])
    x_train = x_train.astype('float32') / 255

    model_name = "dcgan_mnist"
    # network parameters
    # the latent or z vector is 100-dim
    latent_size = 100
    batch_size = 64
    train_steps = 40000
    lr = 2e-4
    decay = 6e-8
    input_shape = (image_size, image_size, 1)

    # build discriminator model
    inputs = Input(shape=input_shape, name='discriminator_input')
    discriminator = build_discriminator(inputs)
    # [1] or original paper uses Adam,
    # but discriminator converges easily with RMSprop
    optimizer = RMSprop(lr=lr, decay=decay)
    discriminator.compile(loss='binary_crossentropy',
                          optimizer=optimizer,
                          metrics=['accuracy'])
    discriminator.summary()

    # build generator model
    input_shape = (latent_size, )
    inputs = Input(shape=input_shape, name='z_input')
    generator = build_generator(inputs, image_size)
    generator.summary()

    # build adversarial model
    optimizer = RMSprop(lr=lr * 0.5, decay=decay * 0.5)
    # freeze the weights of discriminator
    # during adversarial training
```

```
discriminator.trainable = False
# adversarial = generator + discriminator
adversarial = Model(inputs,
                    discriminator(generator(inputs)),
                    name=model_name)
adversarial.compile(loss='binary_crossentropy',
                    optimizer=optimizer,
                    metrics=['accuracy'])
adversarial.summary()

# train discriminator and adversarial networks
models = (generator, discriminator, adversarial)
params = (batch_size, latent_size, train_steps, model_name)
train(models, x_train, params)
```

Listing 4.2.4 shows the function dedicated to training the discriminator and adversarial networks. Due to custom training, the usual `fit()` function is not going to be used. Instead, `train_on_batch()` is called up to run a single gradient update for the given batch of data. The generator is then trained via an adversarial network. The training first randomly picks a batch of real images from the dataset. This is labeled as real (1.0). Then a batch of fake images will be generated by the generator. This is labeled as fake (0.0). The two batches are concatenated and are used to train the discriminator.

After this is completed, a new batch of fake images will be generated by the generator and labeled as real (1.0). This batch will be used to train the adversarial network. The two networks are trained alternately for about 40,000 steps. At regular intervals, the generated MNIST digits based on a certain noise vector are saved on the filesystem. At the last training step, the network has converged. The generator model is also saved on a file so we can easily reuse the trained model for future MNIST digits generation. However, only the generator model is saved since that is the useful part of GANs in the generation of new MNIST digits. For example, we can generate new and random MNIST digits by executing:

python3 dcgan-mnist-4.2.1.py --generator=dcgan_mnist.h5

Listing 4.2.4, `dcgan-mnist-4.2.1.py` shows us the function to train the discriminator and adversarial networks:

```
def train(models, x_train, params):
    """Train the Discriminator and Adversarial Networks

    Alternately train Discriminaor and Adversarial networks by batch.
    Discriminator is trained first with properly real and fake images.
    Adversarial is trained next with fake images pretending to be real
    Generate sample images per save_interval.
```

```
    # Arguments
        models (list): Generator, Discriminator, Adversarial models
        x_train (tensor): Train images
        params (list) : Networks parameters

    """
    # the GAN models
    generator, discriminator, adversarial = models
    # network parameters
    batch_size, latent_size, train_steps, model_name = params
    # the generator image is saved every 500 steps
    save_interval = 500
    # noise vector to see how the generator output evolves
    # during training
    noise_input = np.random.uniform(-1.0, 1.0, size=[16, latent_size])
    # number of elements in train dataset
    train_size = x_train.shape[0]
    for i in range(train_steps):
        # train the discriminator for 1 batch
        # 1 batch of real (label=1.0) and fake images (label=0.0)
        # randomly pick real images from dataset
        rand_indexes = np.random.randint(0, train_size, size=batch_
size)
        real_images = x_train[rand_indexes]
        # generate fake images from noise using generator
        # generate noise using uniform distribution
        noise = np.random.uniform(-1.0, 1.0, size=[batch_size, latent_
size])
        # generate fake images
        fake_images = generator.predict(noise)
        # real + fake images = 1 batch of train data
        x = np.concatenate((real_images, fake_images))
        # label real and fake images
        # real images label is 1.0
        y = np.ones([2 * batch_size, 1])
        # fake images label is 0.0
        y[batch_size:, :] = 0.0
        # train discriminator network, log the loss and accuracy
        loss, acc = discriminator.train_on_batch(x, y)
        log = "%d: [discriminator loss: %f, acc: %f]" % (i, loss, acc)

        # train the adversarial network for 1 batch
        # 1 batch of fake images with label=1.0
        # since the discriminator weights are frozen in adversarial
network
```

```
            # only the generator is trained
            # generate noise using uniform distribution
            noise = np.random.uniform(-1.0, 1.0, size=[batch_size, latent_
    size])
            # label fake images as real or 1.0
            y = np.ones([batch_size, 1])
            # train the adversarial network
            # note that unlike in discriminator training,
            # we do not save the fake images in a variable
            # the fake images go to the discriminator input of the
    adversarial
            # for classification
            # log the loss and accuracy
            loss, acc = adversarial.train_on_batch(noise, y)
            log = "%s [adversarial loss: %f, acc: %f]" % (log, loss, acc)
            print(log)
            if (i + 1) % save_interval == 0:
                if (i + 1) == train_steps:
                    show = True
                else:
                    show = False

                # plot generator images on a periodic basis
                plot_images(generator,
                            noise_input=noise_input,
                            show=show,
                            step=(i + 1),
                            model_name=model_name)

        # save the model after training the generator
        # the trained generator can be reloaded for future MNIST digit
    generation
        generator.save(model_name + ".h5")
```

Figure 4.2.1 shows the evolution of fake images from the generator as a function of training steps. At 5,000 steps, the generator is already producing recognizable images. It's very much like having an agent that knows how to draw digits. It's worth noting that some digits change from one recognizable form (for example, 8 on the 2nd column of the last row) to another (for example, 0). When the training converges, the discriminator loss reaches near 0.5 while the adversarial loss approaches near 1.0 as follows:

```
39997: [discriminator loss: 0.423329, acc: 0.796875] [adversarial loss:
0.819355, acc: 0.484375]
39998: [discriminator loss: 0.471747, acc: 0.773438] [adversarial loss:
1.570030, acc: 0.203125]
```

```
39999: [discriminator loss: 0.532917, acc: 0.742188] [adversarial loss:
0.824350, acc: 0.453125]
```

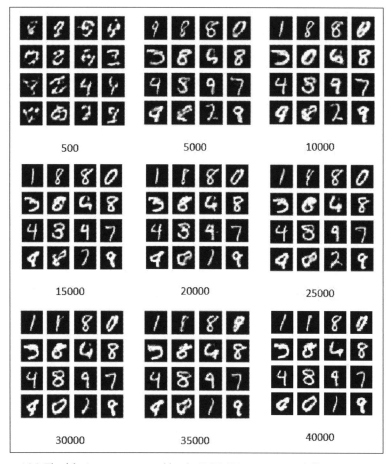

Figure 4.2.2: The fake images generated by the DCGAN generator at different training steps

Conditional GAN

In the previous section, the fake images generated by the DCGAN are random. There is no control over which specific digits will be produced by the generator. There is no mechanism for how to request a particular digit from the generator. This problem can be addressed by a variation of GAN called **Conditional GAN (CGAN)** [4].

Using the same GAN, a condition is imposed on both the generator and discriminator inputs. The condition is in the form of a one-hot vector version of the digit. This is associated with the image to produce (generator) or classified as real or fake (discriminator). The CGAN model is shown in *Figure 4.3.1*.

CGAN is similar to DCGAN except for the additional one-hot vector input. For the generator, the one-hot label is concatenated with the latent vector before the `Dense` layer. For the discriminator, a new `Dense` layer is added. The new layer is used to process the one-hot vector and reshape it so that it is suitable for concatenation to the other input of the succeeding CNN layer:

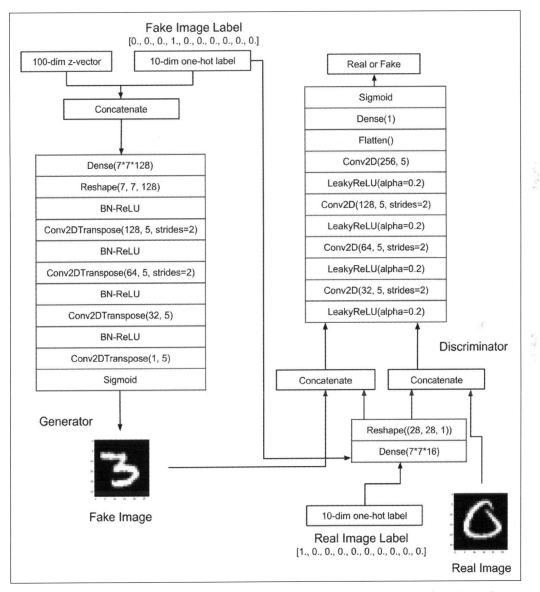

Figure 4.3.1: The CGAN model is similar to DCGAN except for the one-hot vector, which is used to condition the generator and discriminator outputs

The generator learns to generate fake images from a 100-dim input vector and a specified digit. The discriminator classifies real from fake images based on real and fake images and their corresponding labels.

The basis of CGAN is still the same as the original GAN principle except that the discriminator and generator inputs are conditioned on one-hot labels, *y*. By incorporating this condition in *Equations 4.1.1* and *4.1.5*, the loss functions for the discriminator and generator are shown in *Equations 4.3.1* and *4.3.2* respectively.

Given *Figure 4.3.2*, it may be more appropriate to write the loss functions as:

$$\mathcal{L}^{(D)}\left(\theta^{(G)},\theta^{(D)}\right) = -\mathbb{E}_{x \sim p_{data}} \log \mathcal{D}(x \mid y) - \mathbb{E}_z \log\left(1 - \mathcal{D}\left(\mathcal{G}(z \mid y') \mid y'\right)\right)$$

and

$$\mathcal{L}^{(G)}\left(\theta^{(G)},\theta^{(D)}\right) = -\mathbb{E}_z \log \mathcal{D}\left(\mathcal{G}(z \mid y') \mid y'\right)$$.

$$\mathcal{L}^{(D)}\left(\theta^{(G)},\theta^{(D)}\right) = -\mathbb{E}_{x \sim p_{data}} \log \mathcal{D}(x \mid y) - \mathbb{E}_z \log\left(1 - \mathcal{D}\left(\mathcal{G}(z \mid y')\right)\right) \qquad \text{(Equation 4.3.1)}$$

$$\mathcal{L}^{(G)}\left(\theta^{(G)},\theta^{(D)}\right) = -\mathbb{E}_z \log D\left(\mathcal{G}(z \mid y')\right) \qquad \text{(Equation 4.3.2)}$$

The new loss function of the discriminator aims to minimize the error of predicting real images coming from the dataset and fake images coming from the generator given their one-hot labels. *Figure 4.3.2* shows how to train the discriminator.

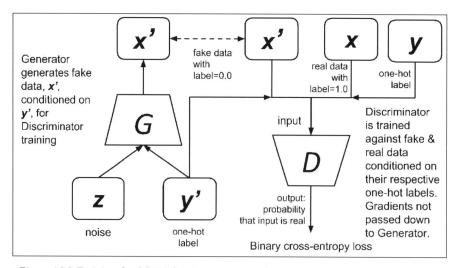

Figure 4.3.2: Training the CGAN discriminator is similar to training the GAN discriminator. The only difference is both the generated fake and the dataset's real images are conditioned with their corresponding one-hot labels.

The new loss function of the generator minimizes the correct prediction of the discriminator on fake images conditioned on the specified one-hot labels. The generator learns how to generate the specific MNIST digit given its one-hot vector that can fool the discriminator. The following figure shows how to train the generator:

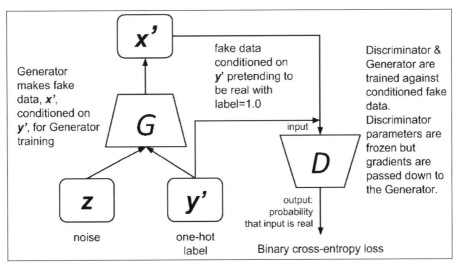

Figure 4.3.3: Training the CGAN generator through the adversarial network is similar to training GAN generator. The only difference is the generated fake images are conditioned with one-hot labels.

Following listing highlights the minor changes needed in the discriminator model. The code processes the one-hot vector using a Dense layer and concatenates it with the image input. The Model instance is modified for the image and one-hot vector inputs.

Listing 4.3.1, cgan-mnist-4.3.1.py shows us the CGAN discriminator. In highlight are the changes made in DCGAN.

```
def build_discriminator(inputs, y_labels, image_size):
    """Build a Discriminator Model

    Inputs are concatenated after Dense layer.
    Stack of LeakyReLU-Conv2D to discriminate real from fake.
    The network does not converge with BN so it is not used here
    unlike in DCGAN paper.

    # Arguments
        inputs (Layer): Input layer of the discriminator (the image)
        y_labels (Layer): Input layer for one-hot vector to condition
            the inputs
        image_size: Target size of one side (assuming square image)
```

```
    # Returns
        Model: Discriminator Model
    """
    kernel_size = 5
    layer_filters = [32, 64, 128, 256]

    x = inputs

    y = Dense(image_size * image_size)(y_labels)
    y = Reshape((image_size, image_size, 1))(y)
    x = concatenate([x, y])

    for filters in layer_filters:
        # first 3 convolution layers use strides = 2
        # last one uses strides = 1
        if filters == layer_filters[-1]:
            strides = 1
        else:
            strides = 2
        x = LeakyReLU(alpha=0.2)(x)
        x = Conv2D(filters=filters,
                   kernel_size=kernel_size,
                   strides=strides,
                   padding='same')(x)

    x = Flatten()(x)
    x = Dense(1)(x)
    x = Activation('sigmoid')(x)
    # input is conditioned by y_labels
    discriminator = Model([inputs, y_labels],
                          x,
                          name='discriminator')
    return discriminator
```

Following listing highlights the code changes to incorporate the conditioning one-hot labels in the generator builder function. The Model instance is modified for the *z*-vector and one-hot vector inputs.

Listing 4.3.2, cgan-mnist-4.3.1.py shows us the CGAN generator. In highlight are the changes made in DCGAN:

```
def build_generator(inputs, y_labels, image_size):
    """Build a Generator Model
```

```
    Inputs are concatenated before Dense layer.
    Stack of BN-ReLU-Conv2DTranpose to generate fake images.
    Output activation is sigmoid instead of tanh in orig DCGAN.
    Sigmoid converges easily.

    # Arguments
        inputs (Layer): Input layer of the generator (the z-vector)
        y_labels (Layer): Input layer for one-hot vector to condition
            the inputs
        image_size: Target size of one side (assuming square image)

    # Returns
        Model: Generator Model
    """
    image_resize = image_size // 4
    # network parameters
    kernel_size = 5
    layer_filters = [128, 64, 32, 1]

    x = concatenate([inputs, y_labels], axis=1)
    x = Dense(image_resize * image_resize * layer_filters[0])(x)
    x = Reshape((image_resize, image_resize, layer_filters[0]))(x)

    for filters in layer_filters:
        # first two convolution layers use strides = 2
        # the last two use strides = 1
        if filters > layer_filters[-2]:
            strides = 2
        else:
            strides = 1
        x = BatchNormalization()(x)
        x = Activation('relu')(x)
        x = Conv2DTranspose(filters=filters,
                            kernel_size=kernel_size,
                            strides=strides,
                            padding='same')(x)

    x = Activation('sigmoid')(x)
    # input is conditioned by y_labels
    generator = Model([inputs, y_labels], x, name='generator')
    return generator
```

Listing 4.3.3 highlights the changes made in the `train()` function to accommodate the conditioning one-hot vector for the discriminator and the generator. The CGAN discriminator is firstly trained with one batch of real and fake data conditioned on their respective one-hot labels. Then, the generator parameters are updated by training the adversarial network given one-hot label conditioned fake data pretending to be real. Similar to DCGAN, the discriminator weights are frozen during adversarial training.

Listing 4.3.3, `cgan-mnist-4.3.1.py` shows us the CGAN training. In highlight are the changes made in DCGAN:

```python
def train(models, data, params):
    """Train the Discriminator and Adversarial Networks

    Alternately train Discriminator and Adversarial networks by batch.
    Discriminator is trained first with properly labelled real and
fake images.
    Adversarial is trained next with fake images pretending to be
real.
    Discriminator inputs are conditioned by train labels for real
images,
    and random labels for fake images.
    Adversarial inputs are conditioned by random labels.
    Generate sample images per save_interval.

    # Arguments
        models (list): Generator, Discriminator, Adversarial models
        data (list): x_train, y_train data
        params (list): Network parameters

    """
    # the GAN models
    generator, discriminator, adversarial = models
    # images and labels
    x_train, y_train = data
    # network parameters
    batch_size, latent_size, train_steps, num_labels, model_name =
params
    # the generator image is saved every 500 steps
    save_interval = 500
    # noise vector to see how the generator output evolves during
training
    noise_input = np.random.uniform(-1.0, 1.0, size=[16, latent_size])
    # one-hot label the noise will be conditioned to
```

```
noise_class = np.eye(num_labels)[np.arange(0, 16) % num_labels]
# number of elements in train dataset
train_size = x_train.shape[0]

print(model_name,
      "Labels for generated images: ",
      np.argmax(noise_class, axis=1))

for i in range(train_steps):
    # train the discriminator for 1 batch
    # 1 batch of real (label=1.0) and fake images (label=0.0)
    # randomly pick real images from dataset
    rand_indexes = np.random.randint(0, train_size,
size=batch_size)
    real_images = x_train[rand_indexes]
    # corresponding one-hot labels of real images
    real_labels = y_train[rand_indexes]
    # generate fake images from noise using generator
    # generate noise using uniform distribution
    noise = np.random.uniform(-1.0, 1.0, size=[batch_size,
latent_size])
    # assign random one-hot labels
    fake_labels = np.eye(num_labels)[np.random.choice(num_labels,
                                                     batch_size)]

    # generate fake images conditioned on fake labels
    fake_images = generator.predict([noise, fake_labels])
    # real + fake images = 1 batch of train data
    x = np.concatenate((real_images, fake_images))
    # real + fake one-hot labels = 1 batch of train one-hot labels
    y_labels = np.concatenate((real_labels, fake_labels))

    # label real and fake images
    # real images label is 1.0
    y = np.ones([2 * batch_size, 1])
    # fake images label is 0.0
    y[batch_size:, :] = 0.0
    # train discriminator network, log the loss and accuracy
    loss, acc = discriminator.train_on_batch([x, y_labels], y)
    log = "%d: [discriminator loss: %f, acc: %f]" % (i, loss, acc)

    # train the adversarial network for 1 batch
    # 1 batch of fake images conditioned on fake 1-hot labels
w/ label=1.0
    # since the discriminator weights are frozen in adversarial
network
```

```
        # only the generator is trained
        # generate noise using uniform distribution
        noise = np.random.uniform(-1.0, 1.0, size=[batch_size,
latent_size])
        # assign random one-hot labels
        fake_labels = np.eye(num_labels)[np.random.choice
(num_labels,batch_size)]
        # label fake images as real or 1.0
        y = np.ones([batch_size, 1])
        # train the adversarial network
        # note that unlike in discriminator training,
        # we do not save the fake images in a variable
        # the fake images go to the discriminator input of the
adversarial
        # for classification
        # log the loss and accuracy
        loss, acc = adversarial.train_on_batch([noise, fake_labels],
y)
        log = "%s [adversarial loss: %f, acc: %f]" % (log, loss, acc)
        print(log)
        if (i + 1) % save_interval == 0:
            if (i + 1) == train_steps:
                show = True
            else:
                show = False

            # plot generator images on a periodic basis
            plot_images(generator,
                        noise_input=noise_input,
                        noise_class=noise_class,
                        show=show,
                        step=(i + 1),
                        model_name=model_name)

    # save the model after training the generator
    # the trained generator can be reloaded for
    # future MNIST digit generation
    generator.save(model_name + ".h5")
```

Figure 4.3.4 shows the evolution of MNIST digits generated when the generator is conditioned to produce digits with the following labels:

[0 1 2 3

4 5 6 7

8 9 0 1

2 3 4 5]

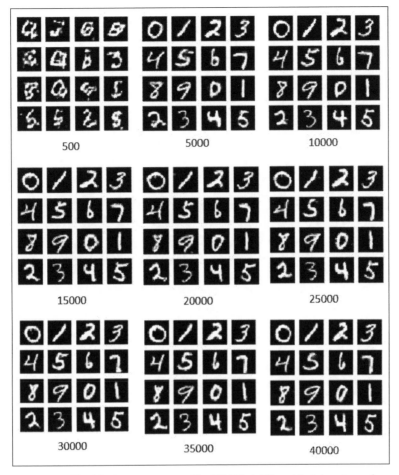

Figure 4.3.4: The fake images generated by CGAN at different training steps when conditioned with labels [0 1 2 3 4 5 6 7 8 9 0 1 2 3 4 5]

You're encouraged to run the trained generator model to see new synthesized MNIST digits images:

```
python3 cgan-mnist-4.3.1.py --generator=cgan_mnist.h5
```

Alternatively, a specific digit (for example, 8) to be generated can also be requested:

```
cgan-mnist-4.3.1.py --generator=cgan_mnist.h5 --digit=8
```

With CGAN it's like having an agent that we can ask to draw digits similar to how humans write digits. The key advantage of CGAN over DCGAN is that we can specify which digit we want the agent to draw.

Conclusion

This chapter discussed the general principles behind GANs, to give you a foundation to the more advanced topics we'll now move on to, including Improved GANs, Disentangled Representations GANs, and Cross-Doman GANs. We started this chapter by understanding how GANs are made up of two networks called generator and discriminator. The role of the discriminator is to discriminate between real and fake signals. The aim of the generator is to fool the discriminator. The generator is normally combined with the discriminator to form an adversarial network. It is through training the adversarial network that the generator learns how to produce fake signals that can trick the discriminator.

We also learned how GANs are easy to build but notoriously difficult to train. Two example implementations in Keras were presented. DCGAN demonstrated that it is possible to train GANs to generate fake images using deep CNNs. The fake images are MNIST digits. However, the DCGAN generator has no control over which specific digit it should draw. CGAN addressed this problem by conditioning the generator to draw a specific digit. The condition is in the form of a one-hot label. CGAN is useful if we want to build an agent that can generate data of a specific class.

In the next chapter, improvements on the DCGAN and CGAN will be introduced. In particular, the focus is on how to stabilize the training of DCGAN and how to improve the perceptive quality of CGAN. This will be done by introducing new loss functions and slightly different model architectures.

References

1. Ian Goodfellow. *NIPS 2016 Tutorial: Generative Adversarial Networks*. arXiv preprint arXiv:1701.00160, 2016 (`https://arxiv.org/pdf/1701.00160.pdf`).

2. Alec Radford, Luke Metz, and Soumith Chintala. *Unsupervised Representation Learning with Deep Convolutional Generative Adversarial Networks*. arXiv preprint arXiv:1511.06434, 2015 (`https://arxiv.org/pdf/1511.06434.pdf`).

3. Mehdi Mirza and Simon Osindero. *Conditional Generative Adversarial Nets*. arXiv preprint arXiv:1411.1784, 2014 (`https://arxiv.org/pdf/1411.1784.pdf`).

4. Tero Karras and others. *Progressive Growing of GANs for Improved Quality, Stability, and Variation*. ICLR, 2018 (`https://arxiv.org/pdf/1710.10196.pdf`).

5
Improved GANs

Since the introduction of the **Generative Adversarial Networks (GANs)** in 2014[1], its popularity has rapidly increased. GANs have proved to be a useful generative model that can synthesize new data that look real. Many of the research papers in deep learning that followed, proposed measures to address the difficulties and limitations of the original GAN.

As we discussed in previous chapters, GANs can be notoriously difficult to train and prone to mode collapse. Mode collapse is a situation where the generator is producing outputs that look the same even though the loss functions are already optimized. In the context of MNIST digits, with mode collapse, the generator may only be producing digits 4 and 9 since they look similar. **Wasserstein GAN (WGAN)**[2] addressed these problems by arguing that stable training and mode collapse can be avoided by simply replacing the GAN loss function based on Wasserstein 1 or **Earth-Mover distance (EMD)**.

However, the issue of stability is not the only problem of GANs. There is also the increasing need to improve the perceptive quality of the generated images. **Least Squares GAN (LSGAN)**[3] proposed to address both these problems simultaneously. The basic premise is that sigmoid cross entropy loss leads to a vanishing gradient during training. This results in poor image quality. Least squares loss does not induce vanishing gradients. The resulting generated images are of higher perceptive quality when compared to vanilla GAN generated images.

In the previous chapter, CGAN introduced a method for conditioning the output of the generator. For example, if we wanted to get digit 8, we would include the conditioning label in the input to the generator. Inspired by CGAN, the **Auxiliary Classifier GAN (ACGAN)**[4] proposed a modified conditional algorithm that results in better perceptive quality and diversity of the outputs.

In summary, the goal of this chapter is to introduce these improved GANs and to present:

- The theoretical formulation of the WGAN
- An understanding of the principles of LSGAN
- An understanding of the principles of ACGAN
- Knowledge of how to implement improved GANs - WGAN, LSGAN, and ACGAN using Keras

Wasserstein GAN

As we've mentioned before, GANs are notoriously hard to train. The opposing objectives of the two networks, the discriminator and the generator, can easily cause training instability. The discriminator attempts to correctly classify the fake data from the real data. Meanwhile, the generator tries its best to trick the discriminator. If the discriminator learns faster than the generator, the generator parameters will fail to optimize. On the other hand, if the discriminator learns more slowly, then the gradients may vanish before reaching the generator. In the worst case, if the discriminator is unable to converge, the generator is not going to be able to get any useful feedback.

Distance functions

The stability in training a GAN can be understood by examining its loss functions. To better understand the GAN loss functions, we're going to review the common distance or divergence functions between two probability distributions. Our concern is the distance between p_{data} for true data distribution and p_g for generator data distribution. The goal of GANs is to make $p_g \rightarrow p_{data}$. *Table 5.1.1* shows the divergence functions.

In most maximum likelihood tasks, we'll use **Kullback-Leibler (KL)** divergence or D_{KL} in the loss function as a measure of how far our neural network model prediction is from the true distribution function. As shown in *Equation 5.1.1*, D_{KL} is not symmetric since $D_{KL}\left(p_{data} \| p_g\right) \neq D_{KL}\left(p_g \| p_{data}\right)$.

Jensen-Shannon (JS) or D_{JS} is a divergence that is based on D_{KL}. However, unlike D_{KL}, D_{JS} is symmetrical and will be finite. In this section, we'll show that optimizing the GAN loss functions is equivalent to optimizing D_{JS}.

Divergence	Expression
Kullback-Leibler (KL) 5.1.1	$$D_{KL}\left(p_{data} \parallel p_g\right) = E_{x \sim pdata} \log \frac{p_{data}(x)}{p_g(x)}$$ $$\neq D_{KL}\left(p_g \parallel p_{data}\right) = \mathbb{E}_{x \sim p_g} \log \frac{p_{data}(x)}{p_g(x)}$$
Jensen-Shannon (JS) 5.1.2	$$D_{JS}\left(p_{data} \parallel p_g\right) = \frac{1}{2}\mathbb{E}_{x \sim pdata} \log \frac{p_{data}(x)}{\frac{p_{data}(x)+p_g(x)}{2}} + \frac{1}{2}\mathbb{E}_{x \sim p_g} \log \frac{p_g(x)}{\frac{p_{data}(x)+p_g(x)}{2}} = D_{JS}\left(p_g \parallel p_{data}\right)$$
Earth-Mover Distance (EMD) or Wasserstein 1 5.1.3	$$W\left(p_{data}, p_g\right) = \inf_{\gamma \in \Pi\left(p_{data}, p_g\right)} \mathbb{E}_{(x,y) \sim \gamma} \left[\|x - y\|\right]$$ where $\Pi\left(p_{data}, p_g\right)$ is the set of all joint distributions $y(x,y)$ whose marginal are p_{data} and p_g.

Table 5.1.1: The divergence functions between two probability distribution functions p_{data} and p_g

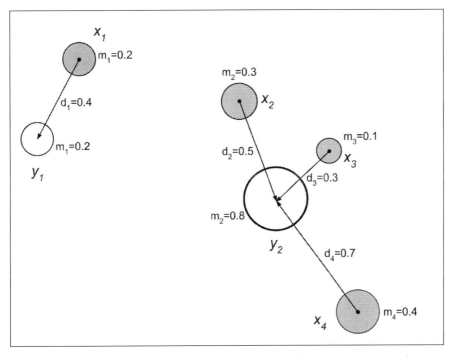

Figure 5.1.1: The EMD is the weighted amount of mass from *x* to be transported in order to match the target distribution, *y*

The intuition behind EMD is that it is a measure of how much mass $\gamma(x,y)$ should be transported by $d = ||x - y||$ for the probability distribution p_{data} in order to match the probability distribution p_g. $\gamma(x,y)$ is a joint distribution in the space of all possible joint distributions $\prod(p_{data}, p_g)$. $\gamma(x,y)$ is also known as a transport plan to reflect the strategy for transporting masses to match the two probability distributions. There are many possible transport plans given the two probability distributions. Roughly speaking, *inf* indicates a transport plan with the minimum cost.

For example, *Figure 5.1.1* shows us two simple discrete distributions x and y. x has masses m_i for i = 1, 2, 3 and 4 at locations x_i for i = 1, 2, 3 and 4. Meanwhile y has masses m_i for i =1 and 2 at locations y_i for i = 1 and 2. To match the distribution y, the arrows show the minimum transport plan to move each mass x_i by d_i. The EMD is computed as:

$$EMD = \sum_{i=1}^{4} x_i d_i = 0.2(0.4) + 0.3(0.5) + 0.1(0.3) + 0.4(0.7) = 0.54 \qquad \text{(Equation 5.1.4)}$$

In *Figure 5.1.1*, the EMD can be interpreted as the least amount of work needed to move the pile of dirt x to fill the hole y. While in this example, the *inf* can also be deduced from the figure, in most cases especially in continuous distributions, it is intractable to exhaust all possible transport plans. We will come back to this problem later on in this chapter. In the meantime, we'll show how the GAN loss functions are, in fact, minimizing the **Jensen-Shannon (JS)** divergence.

Distance function in GANs

We're now going to compute the optimal discriminator given any generator from the loss function in the previous chapter. We'll recall the following equation:

$$\mathcal{L}^{(D)} = -\mathbb{E}_{x \sim p_{data}} \log \mathcal{D}(x) - \mathbb{E}_z \log\left(1 - \mathcal{D}(\mathcal{G}(z))\right) \qquad \text{(Equation 4.1.1)}$$

Instead of sampling from the noise distribution, the preceding equation can also be expressed as sampling from the generator distribution:

$$\mathcal{L}^{(D)} = -\mathbb{E}_{x \sim p_{data}} \log \mathcal{D}(x) - \mathbb{E}_{x \sim p_g} \log\left(1 - \mathcal{D}(x)\right) \qquad \text{(Equation 5.1.5)}$$

To find the minimum $\mathcal{L}^{(D)}$:

$$\mathcal{L}^{(D)} = -\int_x p_{data}(x) \log \mathcal{D}(x)\, dx - \int_x p_g(x) \log(1 - \mathcal{D}(x))\, dx \qquad \text{(Equation 5.1.6)}$$

$$\mathcal{L}^{(D)} = -\int_x \left(p_{data}(x) \log \mathcal{D}(x) + p_g(x) \log(1 - D(x)) \right) dx \qquad \text{(Equation 5.1.7)}$$

The term inside the integral is in the form of $y \to a \log y + b \log(1 - y)$ which has a known maximum value at $\frac{a}{a+b}$ for $y \in [0,1]$, for any $a, b \in \mathbb{R}^2$ not including $\{0,0\}$. Since the integral does not change the location of the maximum value (or the minimum value of $\mathcal{L}^{(D)}$) for this expression, the optimal discriminator is:

$$\mathcal{D}^*(x) = \frac{p_{data}}{p_{data} + p_g} \qquad \text{(Equation 5.1.8)}$$

Consequently, the loss function is given the optimal discriminator:

$$\mathcal{L}^{(D^*)} = -\mathbb{E}_{x \sim pdata} \log \frac{p_{data}}{p_{data} + p_g} - E_{x \sim p_g} \log \left(1 - \frac{p_{data}}{p_{data} + p_g} \right) \qquad \text{(Equation 5.1.9)}$$

$$\mathcal{L}^{(D^*)} = -\mathbb{E}_{x \sim pdata} \log \frac{p_{data}}{p_{data} + p_g} - \mathbb{E}_{x \sim p_g} \log \left(\frac{p_g}{p_{data} + p_g} \right) \qquad \text{(Equation 5.1.10)}$$

$$\mathcal{L}^{(D^*)} = 2 \log 2 - D_{KL} \left(p_{data} \middle\| \frac{p_{data} + p_g}{2} \right) - D_{KL} \left(p_g \middle\| \frac{p_{data} + p_g}{2} \right) \qquad \text{(Equation 5.1.11)}$$

$$\mathcal{L}^{(D^*)} = 2 \log 2 - 2 D_{JS} \left(p_{data} \middle\| p_g \right) \qquad \text{(Equation 5.1.12)}$$

We can observe from *Equation 5.1.12* that the loss function of the optimal discriminator is a constant minus twice the Jensen-Shannon divergence between the true distribution, *pdata*, and any generator distribution, p_g. Minimizing $\mathcal{L}^{(D^*)}$ implies maximizing $D_{JS}\left(p_{data} \middle\| p_g \right)$ or the discriminator must correctly classify fake from real data.

Meanwhile, we can safely argue that the optimal generator is when the generator distribution is equal to the true data distribution:

$$\mathcal{G}^*(x) \to p_g = p_{data} \qquad \text{(Equation 5.1.13)}$$

This makes sense since the objective of the generator is to fool the discriminator by learning the true data distribution. Effectively, we can arrive at the optimal generator by minimizing D_{JS}, or by making $p_g \rightarrow p_{data}$. Given an optimal generator, the optimal discriminator is $D*(x) = \frac{1}{2}$ with $\mathcal{L}^{(D*)} = 2\log 2 = 0.60$.

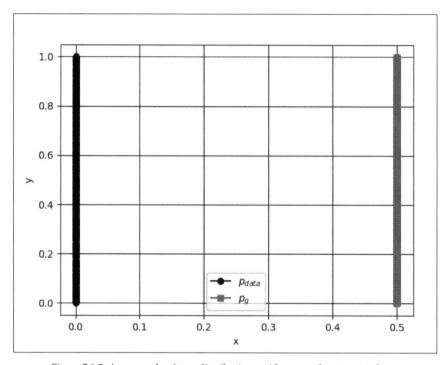

Figure 5.1.2: An example of two distributions with no overlap. $\theta = 0.5$ for p_g

The problem is that when the two distributions have no overlap, there's no smooth function that will help to close the gap between them. Training the GANs will not converge by gradient descent. For example, let's suppose:

$$p_{data} = (x, y) \text{ where } x = 0, y \sim U(0,1) \quad \text{(Equation 5.1.14)}$$

$$p_g = (x, y) \text{ where } x = \theta, y \sim U(0,1) \quad \text{(Equation 5.1.15)}$$

As shown in *Figure 5.1.2*. U(0,1) is the uniform distribution. The divergence for each distance function is as follows:

- $D_{KL}\left(p_g \| p_{data}\right) = \mathbb{E}_{x=\theta, y \sim U(0,1)} \log \frac{p_g(x,y)}{p_{data}(x,y)} = \sum 1\log\frac{1}{0} = +\infty$
- $D_{KL}\left(p_g \| p_{data}\right) = \mathbb{E}_{x=\theta, y \sim U(0,1)} \log \frac{p_g(x,y)}{p_{data}(x,y)} = \sum 1\log\frac{1}{0} = +\infty$

- $D_{JS}\left(p_{data}\|p_g\right) = \frac{1}{2}\mathbb{E}_{x=0,\,y\sim U(0,1)}\log\dfrac{p_{data}(x,y)}{\dfrac{p_{data}(x,y)+p_g(x,y)}{2}} + \frac{1}{2}\mathbb{E}_{x=\theta,\,y\sim uU(0,1)}\log\dfrac{p_g}{\dfrac{p_{data}(x,y)+p_g(x,y)}{2}} = \frac{1}{2}\sum 1\log\dfrac{1}{\frac{1}{2}} + \frac{1}{2}\sum 1\log\dfrac{1}{\frac{1}{2}} = \log 2$

- $W\left(p_{data}, p_g\right) = |\theta|$

Since D_{JS} is a constant, the GAN will not have a sufficient gradient to drive $p_g \to p_{data}$. We'll also find that D_{KL} or reverse D_{KL} is not helpful either. However, with $W(p_{data}, p_g)$ we can have a smooth function in order to attain $p_g \to p_{data}$ by gradient descent. EMD or Wasserstein 1 seems to be a more logical loss function in order to optimize GANs since D_{JS} fails in situations when two distributions have minimal to no overlap.

For further understanding, an excellent discussion on distance functions can be found at https://lilianweng.github.io/lil-log/2017/08/20/from-GAN-to-WGAN.html.

Use of Wasserstein loss

Before using EMD or Wasserstein 1, there is one more problem to overcome. It is intractable to exhaust the space of $\Pi\left(p_{data}, p_g\right)$ to find $\overset{\text{inf}}{\gamma \in \Pi\left(p_{data}, p_g\right)}$. The proposed solution is to use its Kantorovich-Rubinstein dual:

$$W\left(p_{data}, p_g\right) = \frac{1}{K}\sup_{\|f\|L \le K}\mathbb{E}_{x \sim p_{data}}\left[f(x)\right] - \mathbb{E}_{x \sim p_g}\left[f(x)\right] \qquad \text{(Equation 5.1.16)}$$

Equivalently, EMD, $\underset{\|f\|L\le 1}{\sup}$, is the supremum (roughly, maximum value) over all the K-Lipschitz functions: $f : x \to \mathbb{R}$. K-Lipschitz functions satisfy the constraint:

$$\left|f(x_1) - f(x_2)\right| \le K\left|x_1 - x_2\right| \qquad \text{(Equation 5.1.17)}$$

For all $x_1, x_2 \in \mathbb{R}$, the K-Lipschitz functions have bounded derivatives and almost always continuously differentiable (for example, $f(x)$, $= |x|$ has bounded derivatives and continuous but not differentiable at $x = 0$).

Equation 5.1.16 can be solved by finding a family of K-Lipschitz functions $\left\{f_w\right\}_{w \in \mathcal{W}}$:

$$W\left(p_{data}, p_g\right) = \max_{w \in \mathcal{W}}\mathbb{E}_{x \sim p_{data}}\left[f_w(x)\right] - \mathbb{E}_{x \sim p_g}\left[f_w(x)\right] \qquad \text{(Equation 5.1.18)}$$

In the context of GANs, *Equation 5.1.18* can be rewritten by sampling from z-noise distribution and replacing f_w by the discriminator function, D_w:

$$W\left(p_{data}, p_g\right) = \max_{w \in \mathcal{W}} \mathbb{E}_{x \sim p_{data}}\left[\mathcal{D}_w(x)\right] - \mathbb{E}_z\left[\mathcal{D}_w\left(\mathcal{G}(z)\right)\right] \quad \text{(Equation 5.1.19)}$$

We use the bold letter to highlight the generality to multi-dimensional samples. The final problem we face is how to find the family of functions $w \in \mathcal{W}$. The proposed solution we're going to go over is that at every gradient update, the weights of the discriminator, w, are clipped between lower and upper bounds, (for example, -0.0,1 and 0.01):

$$w \leftarrow clip\left(w, -0.01, 0.01\right) \quad \text{(Equation 5.1.20)}$$

The small values of w constrains the discriminator to a compact parameter space thus ensuring Lipschitz continuity.

We can use *Equation 5.1.19* as the basis of our new GAN loss functions. EMD or Wasserstein 1 is the loss function that the generator aims to minimize, and the cost function that the discriminator tries to maximize (or minimize $-W(p_{data}, p_g)$):

$$\mathcal{L}^{(D)} = -\mathbb{E}_{x \sim p_{data}} \mathcal{D}_w(x) + \mathbb{E}_z \mathcal{D}_w\left(\mathcal{G}(z)\right) \quad \text{(Equation 5.1.21)}$$

$$\mathcal{L}^{(G)} = -\mathbb{E}_z \mathcal{D}_w\left(\mathcal{G}(z)\right) \quad \text{(Equation 5.1.22)}$$

In the generator loss function, the first term disappears since it is not directly optimizing with respect to the real data.

Following table shows the difference between the loss functions of GAN and WGAN. For conciseness, we've simplified the notation for $\mathcal{L}^{(D)}$, and $\mathcal{L}^{(G)}$. These loss functions are used in training the WGAN as shown in *Algorithm 5.1.1*. *Figure 5.1.3* illustrates that the WGAN model is practically the same as the DCGAN model except for the fake/true data labels and loss functions:

Network	Loss Functions	Equation
GAN	$\mathcal{L}^{(D)} = -\mathbb{E}_{x \sim p_{data}} \log \mathcal{D}(x) - \mathbb{E}_z \log\left(1 - \mathcal{D}\left(\mathcal{G}(z)\right)\right)$	4.1.1
	$\mathcal{L}^{(G)} = -\mathbb{E}_z \log \mathcal{D}\left(\mathcal{G}(z)\right)$	4.1.5

WGAN	$\mathcal{L}^{(D)} = -\mathbb{E}_{x \sim p_{data}} \mathcal{D}_w(x) + \mathbb{E}_z \mathcal{D}_w(\mathcal{G}(z))$	5.1.21
	$\mathcal{L}^{(G)} = -\mathbb{E}_z \mathcal{D}_w(\mathcal{G}(z))$	5.1.22
	$w \leftarrow clip(w, -0.01, 0.01)$	5.1.20

Table 5.1.1: A comparison between the loss functions of GAN and WGAN

Algorithm 5.1.1 WGAN

The values of the parameters are $\alpha = 0.00005$, $c = 0.01$ $m = 64$, and $n_{critic} = 5$.

Require: a, the learning rate. c, the clipping parameter. m, the batch size. n_{critic}, the number of the critic (discriminator) iterations per generator iteration.

Require: w_0, initial critic (discriminator) parameters. θ_0, initial generator parameters

1. while θ has not converged do
2.   for $t = 1, ..., n_{critic}$ do
3.   Sample a batch $\{x^{(i)}\}_{i=1}^m \sim p_{data}$ from the real data
4.   Sample a batch $\{z^{(i)}\}_{i=1}^m \sim p(z)$ from the uniform noise distribution
5. $g_w \leftarrow \nabla_w \left[-\dfrac{1}{m} \sum_{i=1}^m \mathcal{D}_w(x^{(i)}) + \dfrac{1}{m} \sum_{i=1}^m \mathcal{D}_w(\mathcal{G}_\theta(z^{(i)})) \right]$, compute the discriminator gradients
6. $w \leftarrow w - \alpha \times RMSProp(w, g_w)$, update the discriminator parameters
7. $w \leftarrow clip(w, -c, c)$, clip discriminator weights
8.   end for
9.   Sample a batch $\{z^{(i)}\}_{i=1}^m \sim p(z)$ from the uniform noise distribution
10. $g_\theta \leftarrow -\nabla_\theta \dfrac{1}{m} \sum_{i=1}^m \mathcal{D}_w(\mathcal{G}_\theta(z^{(i)}))$, compute the generator gradients
11. $\theta \leftarrow \theta - \alpha \times RMSProp(\theta, \mathcal{G}_\theta)$, update generator parameters
12. end while

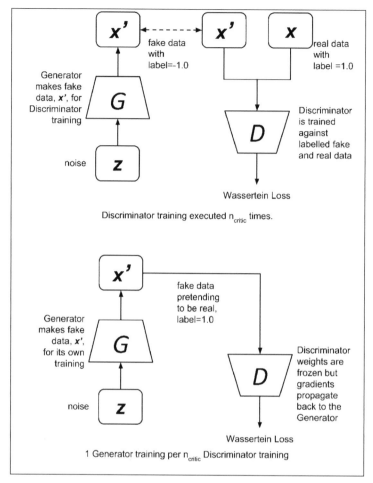

Figure 5.1.3: Top: Training the WGAN discriminator requires fake data from the generator and real data from the true distribution. Bottom: Training the WGAN generator requires fake data from the generator pretending to be real.

Similar to GANs, WGAN alternately trains the discriminator and generator (through adversarial). However, in WGAN, the discriminator (also called the critic) trains n_{critic} iterations (Lines 2 to 8) before training the generator for one iteration (Lines 9 to 11). This in contrast to GANs with an equal number of training iteration for both discriminator and generator. Training the discriminator means learning the parameters (weights and biases) of the discriminator. This requires sampling a batch from the real data (Line 3) and a batch from the fake data (Line 4) and computing the gradient of discriminator parameters (Line 5) after feeding the sampled data to the discriminator network. The discriminator parameters are optimized using RMSProp (Line 6). Both lines 5 and 6 are the optimization of *Equation 5.1.21*. Adam was found to be unstable in WGAN.

Lastly, the Lipschitz constraint in the EM distance optimization is imposed by clipping the discriminator parameters (Line 7). Line 7 is the implementation of *Equation 5.1.20*. After n_{critic} iterations of discriminator training, the discriminator parameters are frozen. The generator training starts by sampling a batch of fake data (Line 9). The sampled data is labeled as real (1.0) trying to fool the discriminator network. The generator gradients are computed in Line 10 and optimized using the RMSProp in Line 11. Lines 10 and 11 perform gradients update to optimize *Equation 5.1.22*.

After training the generator, the discriminator parameters are unfrozen, and another n_{critic} discriminator training iterations start. We should take note that there is no need to freeze the generator parameters during discriminator training as the generator is only involved in the fabrication of data. Similar to GANs, the discriminator can be trained as a separate network. However, training the generator always requires the participation of the discriminator through the adversarial network since the loss is computed from the output of the generator network.

Unlike GAN, in WGAN real data are labeled 1.0 while fake data are labeled -1.0 as a workaround in computing the gradient in Line 5. Lines 5-6 and 10-11 perform gradient update to optimize *Equations 5.1.21* and *5.1.22* respectively. Each term in Lines 5 and 10 is modelled as:

$$\mathcal{L} = -y_{label} \frac{1}{m} \sum_{i=1}^{m} y_{prediction} \qquad \text{(Equation 5.1.23)}$$

Where y_{label} = 1.0 for the real data and y_{label} = -1.0 for the fake data. We removed the superscript (i) for simplicity of the notation. For discriminator, WGAN increases $y_{prediction} = \mathcal{D}_w(x)$ to minimize the loss function when training using the real data. When training using fake data, WGAN decreases $y_{prediction} = \mathcal{D}_w(\mathcal{G}(z))$ to minimize the loss function. For the generator, WGAN increases $y_{prediction} = \mathcal{D}_w(\mathcal{G}(z))$ as to minimize the loss function when the fake data is labeled as real during training. Note that y_{label} has no direct contribution in the loss function other than its sign. In Keras, *Equation 5.1.23* is implemented as:

```
def wasserstein_loss(y_label, y_pred):
    return -K.mean(y_label * y_pred)
```

WGAN implementation using Keras

To implement WGAN within Keras, we can reuse the DCGAN implementation of GANs, something we introduced in the previous chapter. The DCGAN builder and utility functions are implemented in `gan.py` in `lib` folder as a module.

The functions include:

- `generator()`: A generator model builder
- `discriminator()`: Discriminator model builder
- `train()`: DCGAN trainer
- `plot_images()`: Generic generator outputs plotter
- `test_generator()`: Generic generator test utility

As shown in *Listing 5.1.1*, we can build a discriminator by simply calling:

```
discriminator = gan.discriminator(inputs, activation='linear')
```

WGAN uses linear output activation. For the generator, we execute:

```
generator = gan.generator(inputs, image_size)
```

The overall network model in Keras is similar to the one seen in *Figure 4.2.1* for DCGAN.

Listing 5.1.1 highlights the use of the RMSprop optimizer and Wasserstein loss function. The hyper-parameters in *Algorithm 5.1.1* are used during training. *Listing 5.1.2* is the training function that closely follows the *algorithm*. However, there is a minor tweak in the training of the discriminator. Instead of training the weights in a single combined batch of both real and fake data, we'll train with one batch of real data first and then a batch of fake data. This tweak will prevent the gradient from vanishing because of the opposite sign in the label of real and fake data and the small magnitude of weights due to clipping.

The complete code is available on GitHub:
https://github.com/PacktPublishing/Advanced-Deep-Learning-with-Keras

Figure 5.1.4 shows the evolution of the WGAN outputs on MNIST dataset.

Listing 5.1.1, `wgan-mnist-5.1.2.py`. The WGAN model instantiation and training. Both discriminator and generator use Wassertein 1 loss, `wasserstein_loss()`:

```
def build_and_train_models():
    # load MNIST dataset
    (x_train, _), (_, _) = mnist.load_data()

    # reshape data for CNN as (28, 28, 1) and normalize
    image_size = x_train.shape[1]
    x_train = np.reshape(x_train, [-1, image_size, image_size, 1])
```

```
x_train = x_train.astype('float32') / 255

model_name = "wgan_mnist"
# network parameters
# the latent or z vector is 100-dim
latent_size = 100
# hyper parameters from WGAN paper [2]
n_critic = 5
clip_value = 0.01
batch_size = 64
lr = 5e-5
train_steps = 40000
input_shape = (image_size, image_size, 1)

# build discriminator model
inputs = Input(shape=input_shape, name='discriminator_input')
# WGAN uses linear activation in paper [2]
discriminator = gan.discriminator(inputs, activation='linear')
optimizer = RMSprop(lr=lr)
# WGAN discriminator uses wassertein loss
discriminator.compile(loss=wasserstein_loss,
                      optimizer=optimizer,
                      metrics=['accuracy'])
discriminator.summary()

# build generator model
input_shape = (latent_size, )
inputs = Input(shape=input_shape, name='z_input')
generator = gan.generator(inputs, image_size)
generator.summary()

# build adversarial model = generator + discriminator
# freeze the weights of discriminator
# during adversarial training
discriminator.trainable = False
adversarial = Model(inputs,
                    discriminator(generator(inputs)),
                    name=model_name)
adversarial.compile(loss=wasserstein_loss,
                    optimizer=optimizer,
                    metrics=['accuracy'])
adversarial.summary()

# train discriminator and adversarial networks
```

```
models = (generator, discriminator, adversarial)
params = (batch_size,
          latent_size,
          n_critic,
          clip_value,
          train_steps,
          model_name)
train(models, x_train, params)
```

Listing 5.1.2, `wgan-mnist-5.1.2.py`. The training procedure for WGAN closely follows *Algorithm 5.1.1*. The discriminator is trained n_{critic} iterations per 1 generator training iteration:

```
def train(models, x_train, params):
    """Train the Discriminator and Adversarial Networks

    Alternately train Discriminator and Adversarial networks by batch.
    Discriminator is trained first with properly labeled real and fake
images
    for n_critic times.
    Discriminator weights are clipped as a requirement of Lipschitz
constraint.
    Generator is trained next (via Adversarial) with fake images
    pretending to be real.
    Generate sample images per save_interval

    # Arguments
        models (list): Generator, Discriminator, Adversarial models
        x_train (tensor): Train images
        params (list) : Networks parameters

    """
    # the GAN models
    generator, discriminator, adversarial = models
    # network parameters
    (batch_size, latent_size, n_critic,
        clip_value, train_steps, model_name) = params
    # the generator image is saved every 500 steps
    save_interval = 500
    # noise vector to see how the generator output
    # evolves during training
    noise_input = np.random.uniform(-1.0, 1.0, size=[16,
                                    latent_size])
    # number of elements in train dataset
    train_size = x_train.shape[0]
```

```
# labels for real data
real_labels = np.ones((batch_size, 1))
for i in range(train_steps):
    # train discriminator n_critic times
    loss = 0
    acc = 0
    for _ in range(n_critic):
        # train the discriminator for 1 batch
        # 1 batch of real (label=1.0) and
        # fake images (label=-1.0)
        # randomly pick real images from dataset
        rand_indexes = np.random.randint(0,
                                         train_size,
                                         size=batch_size)
        real_images = x_train[rand_indexes]
        # generate fake images from noise using generator
        # generate noise using uniform distribution
        noise = np.random.uniform(-1.0,
                                  1.0,
                                  size=[batch_size,
                                  latent_size])
        fake_images = generator.predict(noise)

        # train the discriminator network
        # real data label=1, fake data label=-1
        # instead of 1 combined batch of real and fake images,
        # train with 1 batch of real data first, then 1 batch
        # of fake images.
        # this tweak prevents the gradient from vanishing
        # due to opposite signs of real and
        # fake data labels (i.e. +1 and -1) and
        # small magnitude of weights due to clipping.
        real_loss, real_acc = \
                    discriminator.train_on_batch(real_images,
                                                 real_labels)
        fake_loss, fake_acc = \
                    discriminator.train_on_batch(fake_images,
                                                 real_labels)
        # accumulate average loss and accuracy
        loss += 0.5 * (real_loss + fake_loss)
        acc += 0.5 * (real_acc + fake_acc)

        # clip discriminator weights to satisfy
        # Lipschitz constraint
```

```
        for layer in discriminator.layers:
            weights = layer.get_weights()
            weights = [np.clip(weight,
                               -clip_value,
                               clip_value) for weight in weights]
            layer.set_weights(weights)

    # average loss and accuracy per n_critic
    # training iterations
    loss /= n_critic
    acc /= n_critic
    log = "%d: [discriminator loss: %f, acc: %f]" % (i, loss, acc)

    # train the adversarial network for 1 batch
    # 1 batch of fake images with label=1.0
    # since the discriminator weights are
    # frozen in adversarial network
    # only the generator is trained
    # generate noise using uniform distribution
    noise = np.random.uniform(-1.0, 1.0,
                              size=[batch_size, latent_size])
    # train the adversarial network
    # note that unlike in discriminator training,
    # we do not save the fake images in a variable
    # the fake images go to the discriminator input
    # of the adversarial for classification
    # fake images are labelled as real
    # log the loss and accuracy
    loss, acc = adversarial.train_on_batch(noise, real_labels)
    log = "%s [adversarial loss: %f, acc: %f]" % (log, loss, acc)
    print(log)
    if (i + 1) % save_interval == 0:
        if (i + 1) == train_steps:
            show = True
        else:
            show = False

        # plot generator images on a periodic basis
        gan.plot_images(generator,
                        noise_input=noise_input,
                        show=show,
                        step=(i + 1),
                        model_name=model_name)
```

```
# save the model after training the generator
# the trained generator can be reloaded for future
# MNIST digit generation
generator.save(model_name + ".h5")
```

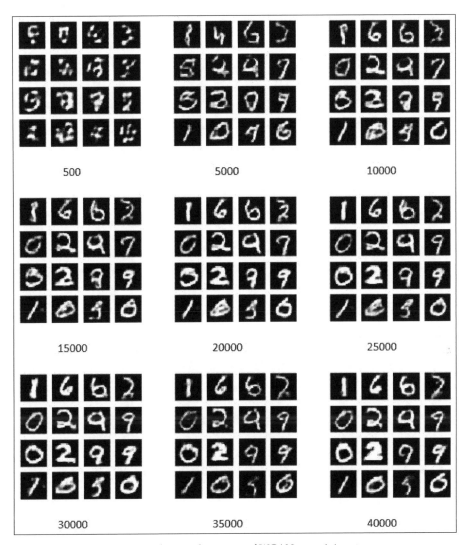

Figure 5.1.4: The sample outputs of WGAN vs. training steps.
WGAN does not suffer mode collapse in all the outputs during training and testing.

WGAN is stable even under network configuration changes. For example, DCGAN is known to be unstable when batch normalization is inserted before the ReLU in the discriminator network. The same configuration is stable in WGAN.

Following figure shows us the outputs of both DCGAN and WGAN with batch normalization on the discriminator network:

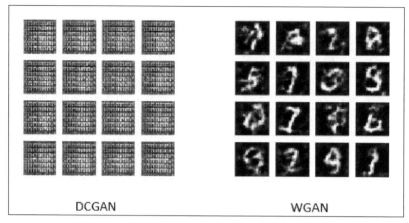

DCGAN   WGAN

Figure 5.1.5: A comparison of the output of the DCGAN (Left) and WGAN (Right)
when batch normalization is inserted before the ReLU activation in the discriminator network

Similar to the GAN training in the previous chapter, the trained model is saved on a file after 40,000 train steps. I would encourage you to run the trained generator model to see new synthesized MNIST digits images:

```
python3 wgan-mnist-5.1.2.py --generator=wgan_mnist.h5
```

Least-squares GAN (LSGAN)

As discussed in the previous section, the original GAN is difficult to train. The problem arises when the GAN optimizes its loss function; it's actually optimizing the *Jensen-Shannon* divergence, D_{JS}. It is difficult to optimize D_{JS} when there is little to no overlap between two distribution functions.

WGAN proposed to address the problem by using the EMD or Wasserstein 1 loss function which has a smooth differentiable function even when there is little or no overlap between the two distributions. However, WGAN is not concerned with the generated image quality. Apart from stability issues, there are still areas of improvement in terms of perceptive quality in the generated images of the original GAN. LSGAN theorizes that the twin problems can be solved simultaneously.

LSGAN proposes the least squares loss. *Figure 5.2.1* demonstrates why the use of a sigmoid cross entropy loss in the GAN results in poorly generated data quality. Ideally, the fake samples distribution should be as close as possible to the true samples' distribution. However, for GANs, once the fake samples are already on the correct side of the decision boundary, the gradients vanish.

This prevents the generator from having enough motivation to improve the quality of the generated fake data. Fake samples far from the decision boundary will no longer attempt to move closer to the true samples' distribution. Using the least squares loss function, the gradients do not vanish as long as the fake samples distribution is far from the real samples' distribution. The generator will strive to improve its estimate of real density distribution even if the fake samples are already on the correct side of the decision boundary:

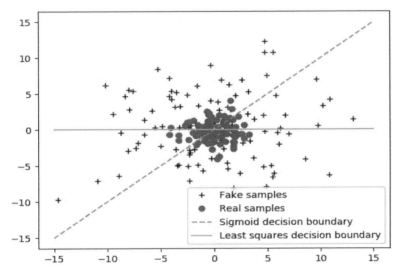

Figure 5.2.1: Both real and fake samples distributions divided by respective decision boundaries: Sigmoid and Least squares

Network	Loss Functions	Equation
GAN	$\mathcal{L}^{(D)} = -\mathbb{E}_{x \sim p_{data}} \log \mathcal{D}(x) - \mathbb{E}_z \log \left(1 - \mathcal{D}(\mathcal{G}(z))\right)$	4.1.1
	$\mathcal{L}^{(G)} = -\mathbb{E}_z \log \mathcal{D}(\mathcal{G}(z))$	4.1.5
LSGAN	$\mathcal{L}^{(D)} = \mathbb{E}_{x \sim p_{data}} \left(\mathcal{D}(x) - 1\right)^2 + \mathbb{E}_z \mathcal{D}(\mathcal{G}(z))^2$	5.2.1
	$\mathcal{L}^{(G)} = \mathbb{E}_z \left(\mathcal{D}(\mathcal{G}(z)) - 1\right)^2$	5.2.2

Table 5.2.1: A comparison between the loss functions of GAN and LSGAN

The preceding table shows the comparison of the loss functions between GAN and LSGAN. Minimizing *Equation 5.2.1* or the discriminator loss function implies that the MSE between real data classification and true label 1.0 should be close to zero. In addition, the MSE between the fake data classification and the true label 0.0 should be close to zero.

Similar to GANs, the LSGAN discriminator is trained to classify real from fake data samples. Minimizing *Equation 5.2.2* means fooling the discriminator to think that the generated fake sample data are real with label 1.0.

Implementing LSGAN using the DCGAN code in the previous chapter as the basis requires few changes only. As shown in *Listing 5.2.1*, the discriminator sigmoid activation is removed. The discriminator is built by calling:

```
discriminator = gan.discriminator(inputs, activation=None)
```

The generator is similar to the original DCGAN:

```
generator = gan.generator(inputs, image_size)
```

Both the discriminator and adversarial loss functions are replaced by mse. All the network parameters are the same as in DCGAN. The network model of LSGAN in Keras is similar to *Figure 4.2.1* except that there is no linear or output activation. The training process is similar to that seen in DCGAN and is provided by the utility function:

```
gan.train(models, x_train, params)
```

Listing 5.2.1, lsgan-mnist-5.2.1.py shows how the discriminator and generator are the same in DCGAN except for the discriminator output activation and the use of MSE loss function:

```
def build_and_train_models():
    # MNIST dataset
    (x_train, _), (_, _) = mnist.load_data()

    # reshape data for CNN as (28, 28, 1) and normalize
    image_size = x_train.shape[1]
    x_train = np.reshape(x_train, [-1, image_size, image_size, 1])
    x_train = x_train.astype('float32') / 255

    model_name = "lsgan_mnist"
    # network parameters
    # the latent or z vector is 100-dim
    latent_size = 100
```

```
input_shape = (image_size, image_size, 1)
batch_size = 64
lr = 2e-4
decay = 6e-8
train_steps = 40000

# build discriminator model
inputs = Input(shape=input_shape, name='discriminator_input')
discriminator = gan.discriminator(inputs, activation=None)
# [1] uses Adam, but discriminator converges
# easily with RMSprop
optimizer = RMSprop(lr=lr, decay=decay)
# LSGAN uses MSE loss [2]
discriminator.compile(loss='mse',
                      optimizer=optimizer,
                      metrics=['accuracy'])
discriminator.summary()

# build generator model
input_shape = (latent_size, )
inputs = Input(shape=input_shape, name='z_input')
generator = gan.generator(inputs, image_size)
generator.summary()

# build adversarial model = generator + discriminator
optimizer = RMSprop(lr=lr*0.5, decay=decay*0.5)
# freeze the weights of discriminator
# during adversarial training
discriminator.trainable = False
adversarial = Model(inputs,
                    discriminator(generator(inputs)),
                    name=model_name)
# LSGAN uses MSE loss [2]
adversarial.compile(loss='mse',
                    optimizer=optimizer,
                    metrics=['accuracy'])
adversarial.summary()

# train discriminator and adversarial networks
models = (generator, discriminator, adversarial)
params = (batch_size, latent_size, train_steps, model_name)
gan.train(models, x_train, params)
```

Following figure shows generated samples after training LSGAN using the MNIST dataset for 40,000 training steps. The output images have better perceptual quality compared to *Figure 4.2.1* in DCGAN:

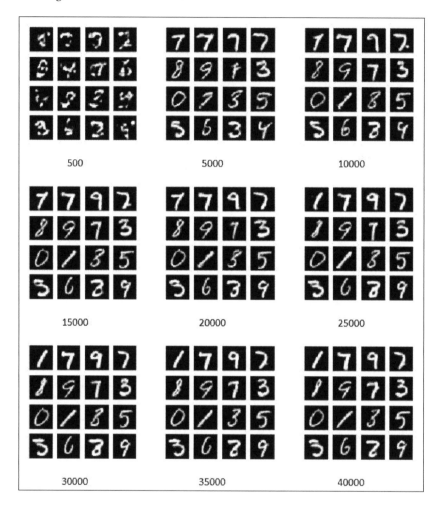

Figure 5.2.2: Sample outputs of LSGAN vs. training steps

I encourage you to run the trained generator model to see the new synthesized MNIST digits images:

```
python3 lsgan-mnist-5.2.1.py --generator=lsgan_mnist.h5
```

Auxiliary classifier GAN (ACGAN)

ACGAN is similar in principle to the **Conditional GAN (CGAN)** that we discussed in the previous chapter. We're going to compare both CGAN and ACGAN. For both CGAN and ACGAN, the generator inputs are noise and its label. The output is a fake image belonging to the input class label. For CGAN, the inputs to the discriminator are an image (fake or real) and its label. The output is the probability that the image is real. For ACGAN, the input to the discriminator is an image, whilst the output is the probability that the image is real and its class label. Following figure highlights the difference between CGAN and ACGAN during generator training:

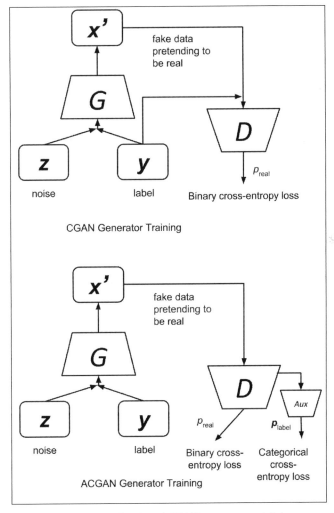

Figure 5.3.1: CGAN vs. ACGAN generator training.
The main difference is the input and output of the discriminator.

Essentially, in CGAN we feed the network with side information (label). In ACGAN, we try to reconstruct the side information using an auxiliary class decoder network. ACGAN argued that forcing the network to do additional tasks is known to improve the performance of the original task. In this case, the additional task is image classification. The original task is the generation of fake images.

Network	Loss Functions	Number
CGAN	$\mathcal{L}^{(D)} = -\mathbb{E}_{x \sim p_{data}} \log \mathcal{D}(x \mid y) - \mathbb{E}_z \log\left(1 - \mathcal{D}(\mathcal{D}(z \mid y))\right)$	4.3.1
	$\mathcal{L}^{(G)} = -\mathbb{E}_z \log \mathcal{D}(\mathcal{G}(z \mid y))$	4.3.2
ACGAN	$\mathcal{L}^{(D)} = -\mathbb{E}_{x \sim p_{data}} \log \mathcal{D}(x) - \mathbb{E}_z \log\left(1 - \mathcal{D}(\mathcal{G}(z \mid y))\right) - \mathbb{E}_{x \sim p_{data}} \log \mathcal{P}(c \mid x) - \mathbb{E}_z \log \mathcal{P}(c \mid \mathcal{G}(z \mid y))$	5.3.1
	$\mathcal{L}^{(G)} = -\mathbb{E}_z \log \mathcal{D}(\mathcal{G}(z \mid y)) - \mathbb{E}_z \log \mathcal{P}(c \mid \mathcal{G}(z \mid y))$	5.3.2

Table 5.3.1: A comparison between the loss functions of CGAN and ACGAN

Preceding table shows the ACGAN loss functions as compared to CGAN. The ACGAN loss functions are the same as CGAN except for the additional classifier loss functions. Apart from the original task of identifying real from fake images $\left(-\mathbb{E}_{x \sim p_{data}} \log \mathcal{D}(x \mid y) - \mathbb{E}_z \log\left(1 - \mathcal{D}(\mathcal{G}(z \mid y))\right)\right)$, *Equation 5.3.1* of the discriminator has the additional task of correctly classifying real and fake images $\left(-\mathbb{E}_{x \sim p_{data}} \log \mathcal{P}(c \mid x) - \mathbb{E}_z \log \mathcal{P}(c \mid \mathcal{G}(z \mid y))\right)$. *Equation 5.3.2* of the generator means that apart from trying to fool the discriminator with fake images $\left(-\mathbb{E}_z \log \mathcal{D}(\mathcal{G}(z \mid y))\right)$, it is asking the discriminator to correctly classify those fake images $\left(-\mathbb{E}_z \log \mathcal{P}(c \mid \mathcal{G}(z \mid y))\right)$.

Starting with the CGAN code, only the discriminator and the training function are modified to implement ACGAN. The discriminator and generator builder functions are also provided by gan.py. To see the changes made on the discriminator, following listing shows the builder function where the auxiliary decoder network that performs image classification and the dual outputs are highlighted.

Listing 5.3.1, gan.py shows how the discriminator model builder is the same as in DCGAN predicting if an image is real, the first output. An auxiliary decoder network is added to perform the image classification and produce the second output:

```
def discriminator(inputs,
                  activation='sigmoid',
                  num_labels=None,
                  num_codes=None):
    """Build a Discriminator Model
```

```
Stack of LeakyReLU-Conv2D to discriminate real from fake
The network does not converge with BN  so it is not used here
unlike in [1]

# Arguments
    inputs (Layer): Input layer of the discriminator (the image)
    activation (string): Name of output activation layer
    num_labels (int): Dimension of one-hot labels for ACGAN &
InfoGAN
    num_codes (int): num_codes-dim Q network as output
                if StackedGAN or 2 Q networks if InfoGAN


# Returns
    Model: Discriminator Model
"""
kernel_size = 5
layer_filters = [32, 64, 128, 256]

x = inputs
for filters in layer_filters:
    # first 3 convolution layers use strides = 2
    # last one uses strides = 1
    if filters == layer_filters[-1]:
        strides = 1
    else:
        strides = 2
    x = LeakyReLU(alpha=0.2)(x)
    x = Conv2D(filters=filters,
            kernel_size=kernel_size,
            strides=strides,
            padding='same')(x)

x = Flatten()(x)
# default output is probability that the image is real
outputs = Dense(1)(x)
if activation is not None:
    print(activation)
    outputs = Activation(activation)(outputs)

if num_labels:
    # ACGAN and InfoGAN have 2nd output
    # 2nd output is 10-dim one-hot vector of label
```

```
        layer = Dense(layer_filters[-2])(x)
        labels = Dense(num_labels)(layer)
        labels = Activation('softmax', name='label')(labels)
        if num_codes is None:
            outputs = [outputs, labels]
        else:
            # InfoGAN have 3rd and 4th outputs
            # 3rd output is 1-dim continous Q of 1st c given x
            code1 = Dense(1)(layer)
            code1 = Activation('sigmoid', name='code1')(code1)

            # 4th output is 1-dim continuous Q of 2nd c given x
            code2 = Dense(1)(layer)
            code2 = Activation('sigmoid', name='code2')(code2)

            outputs = [outputs, labels, code1, code2]
    elif num_codes is not None:
        # z0_recon is reconstruction of z0 normal distribution
        z0_recon =  Dense(num_codes)(x)
        z0_recon = Activation('tanh', name='z0')(z0_recon)
        outputs = [outputs, z0_recon]

    return Model(inputs, outputs, name='discriminator')
```

The discriminator is then built by calling:

```
discriminator = gan.discriminator(inputs, num_labels=num_labels)
```

The generator is the same as the one in ACGAN. To recall, the generator builder is shown in the following listing. We should note that both *Listings 5.3.1* and *5.3.2* are the same builder functions used by WGAN and LSGAN in the previous sections.

Listing 5.3.2, gan.py shows the generator model builder is the same as in CGAN:

```
def generator(inputs,
              image_size,
              activation='sigmoid',
              labels=None,
              codes=None):
    """Build a Generator Model

    Stack of BN-ReLU-Conv2DTranpose to generate fake images.
    Output activation is sigmoid instead of tanh in [1].
    Sigmoid converges easily.

    # Arguments
```

```
        inputs (Layer): Input layer of the generator (the z-vector)
        image_size (int): Target size of one side (assuming square
image)
        activation (string): Name of output activation layer
        labels (tensor): Input labels
        codes (list): 2-dim disentangled codes for InfoGAN

    # Returns
        Model: Generator Model
    """
    image_resize = image_size // 4
    # network parameters
    kernel_size = 5
    layer_filters = [128, 64, 32, 1]

    if labels is not None:
        if codes is None:
            # ACGAN labels
            # concatenate z noise vector and one-hot labels
            inputs = [inputs, labels]
        else:
            # infoGAN codes
            # concatenate z noise vector, one-hot labels
            # and codes 1 & 2
            inputs = [inputs, labels] + codes
        x = concatenate(inputs, axis=1)
    elif codes is not None:
        # generator 0 of StackedGAN
        inputs = [inputs, codes]
        x = concatenate(inputs, axis=1)
    else:
        # default input is just 100-dim noise (z-code)
        x = inputs

    x = Dense(image_resize * image_resize * layer_filters[0])(x)
    x = Reshape((image_resize, image_resize, layer_filters[0]))(x)

    for filters in layer_filters:
        # first two convolution layers use strides = 2
        # the last two use strides = 1
        if filters > layer_filters[-2]:
            strides = 2
        else:
            strides = 1
```

```
        x = BatchNormalization()(x)
        x = Activation('relu')(x)
        x = Conv2DTranspose(filters=filters,
                            kernel_size=kernel_size,
                            strides=strides,
                            padding='same')(x)

    if activation is not None:
        x = Activation(activation)(x)

    # generator output is the synthesized image x
    return Model(inputs, x, name='generator')
```

In ACGAN, the generator is instantiated as:

```
generator = gan.generator(inputs, image_size, labels=labels)
```

Following figure shows the network model of ACGAN in Keras:

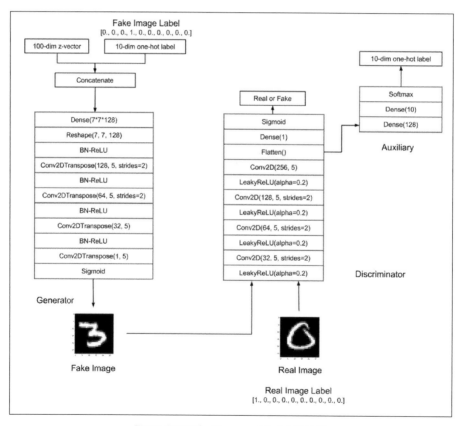

Figure 5.3.2: The Keras model of ACGAN

As shown in *Listing 5.3.3*, the discriminator and adversarial models are modified to accommodate the changes in the discriminator network. We now have two loss functions. The first is the original binary cross-entropy to train the discriminator in estimating the probability if the input image is real. The second is the image classifier predicting the class label. The output is a one-hot vector of 10 dimensions.

Referring to Listing 5.3.3, `acgan-mnist-5.3.1.py`, where highlighted are the changes implemented in the discriminator and adversarial models to accommodate the image classifier of the discriminator network. The two loss functions correspond to the two outputs of the discriminator:

```
def build_and_train_models():
    # load MNIST dataset
    (x_train, y_train), (_, _) = mnist.load_data()

    # reshape data for CNN as (28, 28, 1) and normalize
    image_size = x_train.shape[1]
    x_train = np.reshape(x_train, [-1, image_size, image_size, 1])
    x_train = x_train.astype('float32') / 255

    # train labels
    num_labels = len(np.unique(y_train))
    y_train = to_categorical(y_train)

    model_name = "acgan_mnist"
    # network parameters
    latent_size = 100
    batch_size = 64
    train_steps = 40000
    lr = 2e-4
    decay = 6e-8
    input_shape = (image_size, image_size, 1)
    label_shape = (num_labels, )

    # build discriminator Model
    inputs = Input(shape=input_shape, name='discriminator_input')
    # call discriminator builder with 2 outputs,
    # pred source and labels
    discriminator = gan.discriminator(inputs, num_labels=num_labels)
    # [1] uses Adam, but discriminator converges easily with RMSprop
    optimizer = RMSprop(lr=lr, decay=decay)
    # 2 loss fuctions: 1) probability image is real
    # 2) class label of the image
    loss = ['binary_crossentropy', 'categorical_crossentropy']
```

```
discriminator.compile(loss=loss,
                      optimizer=optimizer,
                      metrics=['accuracy'])
discriminator.summary()

# build generator model
input_shape = (latent_size, )
inputs = Input(shape=input_shape, name='z_input')
labels = Input(shape=label_shape, name='labels')
# call generator builder with input labels
generator = gan.generator(inputs, image_size, labels=labels)
generator.summary()

# build adversarial model = generator + discriminator
optimizer = RMSprop(lr=lr*0.5, decay=decay*0.5)
# freeze the weights of discriminator
# during adversarial training
discriminator.trainable = False
adversarial = Model([inputs, labels],
                    discriminator(generator([inputs, labels])),
                    name=model_name)
# same 2 loss fuctions: 1) probability image is real
# 2) class label of the image
adversarial.compile(loss=loss,
                    optimizer=optimizer,
                    metrics=['accuracy'])
adversarial.summary()

# train discriminator and adversarial networks
models = (generator, discriminator, adversarial)
data = (x_train, y_train)
params = (batch_size, latent_size, train_steps, num_labels, model_
name)
train(models, data, params)
```

In *Listing 5.3.4*, we highlight the changes implemented in the training routine. The main difference compared to CGAN code is that the output label must be supplied during discriminator and adversarial training.

As seen in Listing 5.3.4, `acgan-mnist-5.3.1.py`, the changes implemented in the train function are highlighted:

```
def train(models, data, params):
    """Train the discriminator and adversarial Networks
```

Alternately train discriminator and adversarial networks by batch.
Discriminator is trained first with real and fake images and
corresponding one-hot labels.
Adversarial is trained next with fake images pretending to be real
and
corresponding one-hot labels.
Generate sample images per save_interval.

```
# Arguments
    models (list): Generator, Discriminator, Adversarial models
    data (list): x_train, y_train data
    params (list): Network parameters


"""
# the GAN models
generator, discriminator, adversarial = models
# images and their one-hot labels
x_train, y_train = data
# network parameters
batch_size, latent_size, train_steps, num_labels, model_name =
params
# the generator image is saved every 500 steps
save_interval = 500
# noise vector to see how the generator output
# evolves during training
noise_input = np.random.uniform(-1.0,
                                 1.0,
                                 size=[16, latent_size])
# class labels are 0, 1, 2, 3, 4, 5, 6, 7, 8, 9, 0, 1, 2, 3, 4, 5
# the generator must produce these MNIST digits
noise_label = np.eye(num_labels)[np.arange(0, 16) % num_labels]
# number of elements in train dataset
train_size = x_train.shape[0]
print(model_name,
      "Labels for generated images: ",
      np.argmax(noise_label, axis=1))

for i in range(train_steps):
    # train the discriminator for 1 batch
    # 1 batch of real (label=1.0) and fake images (label=0.0)
    # randomly pick real images and corresponding labels
    # from dataset
    rand_indexes = np.random.randint(0,
                                     train_size,
```

```
                                         size=batch_size)
        real_images = x_train[rand_indexes]
        real_labels = y_train[rand_indexes]
        # generate fake images from noise using generator
        # generate noise using uniform distribution
        noise = np.random.uniform(-1.0,
                                  1.0,
                                  size=[batch_size, latent_size])
        # randomly pick one-hot labels
        fake_labels = np.eye(num_labels)[np.random.choice(num_labels,
                                                   batch_size)]
        # generate fake images
        fake_images = generator.predict([noise, fake_labels])
        # real + fake images = 1 batch of train data
        x = np.concatenate((real_images, fake_images))
        # real + fake labels = 1 batch of train data labels
        labels = np.concatenate((real_labels, fake_labels))


        # label real and fake images
        # real images label is 1.0
        y = np.ones([2 * batch_size, 1])
        # fake images label is 0.0
        y[batch_size:, :] = 0
        # train discriminator network, log the loss and accuracy
        # ['loss', 'activation_1_loss', 'label_loss',
        # 'activation_1_acc', 'label_acc']
        metrics  = discriminator.train_on_batch(x, [y, labels])
        fmt = "%d: [disc loss: %f, srcloss: %f, lblloss: %f, srcacc:
%f, lblacc: %f]"
        log = fmt % (i, metrics[0], metrics[1], metrics[2],
metrics[3], metrics[4])


        # train the adversarial network for 1 batch
        # 1 batch of fake images with label=1.0 and
        # corresponding one-hot label or class
        # since the discriminator weights are frozen
        # in adversarial network
        # only the generator is trained
        # generate noise using uniform distribution
        noise = np.random.uniform(-1.0,
                                  1.0,
                                  size=[batch_size, latent_size])
        # randomly pick one-hot labels
        fake_labels = np.eye(num_labels)[np.random.choice(num_labels,
```

```
                                               batch_size)]
        # label fake images as real
        y = np.ones([batch_size, 1])
        # train the adversarial network
        # note that unlike in discriminator training,
        # we do not save the fake images in a variable
        # the fake images go to the discriminator input
        # of the adversarial
        # for classification
        # log the loss and accuracy
        metrics  = adversarial.train_on_batch([noise, fake_labels],
                                [y, fake_labels])
        fmt = "%s [advr loss: %f, srcloss: %f, lblloss: %f, srcacc:
%f, lblacc: %f]"
        log = fmt % (log, metrics[0], metrics[1], metrics[2],
metrics[3], metrics[4])
        print(log)
        if (i + 1) % save_interval == 0:
            if (i + 1) == train_steps:
                show = True
            else:
                show = False

            # plot generator images on a periodic basis
            gan.plot_images(generator,
                        noise_input=noise_input,
                        noise_label=noise_label,
                        show=show,
                        step=(i + 1),
                        model_name=model_name)

    # save the model after training the generator
    # the trained generator can be reloaded for
    # future MNIST digit generation
    generator.save(model_name + ".h5")
```

In turned out that with the additional task, the performance improvement in ACGAN is significant compared to all GANs that we have discussed previously. ACGAN training is stable as shown in *Figure 5.3.3* sample outputs of ACGAN for the following labels:

```
[0 1 2 3
 4 5 6 7
 8 9 0 1
 2 3 4 5]
```

Unlike CGAN, the sample outputs appearance does not vary widely during training. The MNIST digit image perceptive quality is also better. *Figure 5.3.4* shows a side by side comparison of every MNIST digit produced by both CGAN and ACGAN. Digits 2-6 are of better quality in ACGAN than in CGAN.

I encourage you to run the trained generator model to see new synthesized MNIST digits images:

```
python3 acgan-mnist-5.3.1.py --generator=acgan_mnist.h5
```

Alternatively, a specific digit (for example, 3) to be generated can also be requested:

```
python3 acgan-mnist-5.3.1.py --generator=acgan_mnist.h5 --digit=3
```

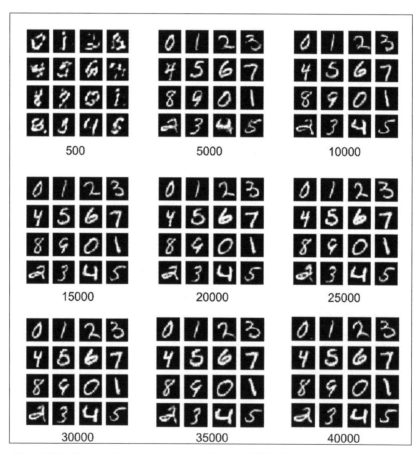

Figure 5.3.3: The sample outputs generated by the ACGAN as a function of train steps for labels [0 1 2 3 4 5 6 7 8 9 0 1 2 3 4 5]

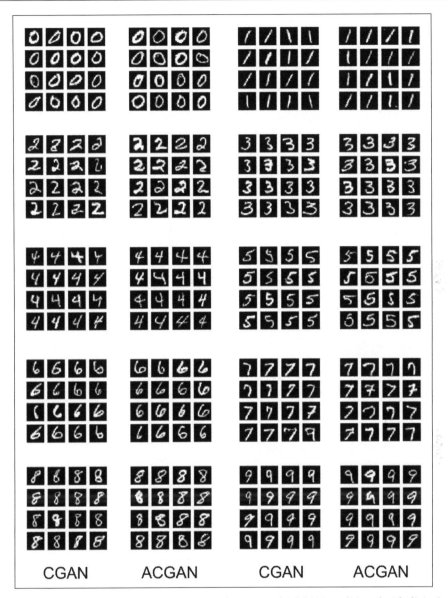

Figure 5.3.4: A side by side comparison of outputs of CGAN and ACGAN conditioned with digits 0 to 9

Conclusion

In this chapter, we've presented various improvements in the original algorithm of GAN, first introduced in the previous chapter. WGAN proposed an algorithm to improve the stability of training by using the EMD or Wassertein 1 loss. LSGAN argued that the original cross-entropy function of GAN is prone to vanishing gradients, unlike least squares loss. LSGAN proposed an algorithm to achieve stable training and quality outputs. ACGAN convincingly improved the quality of the conditional generation of MNIST digits by requiring the discriminator to perform classification task on top of determining whether the input image is fake or real.

In the next chapter, we'll study how to control the attributes of generator outputs. Whilst CGAN and ACGAN are able to indicate the desired digits to produce; we have not analyzed GANs that can specify the attributes of outputs. For example, we may want to control the writing style of the MNIST digits such as roundness, tilt angle, and thickness. Therefore, the goal will be to introduce GANs with disentangled representations to control the specific attributes of the generator outputs.

References

1. Ian Goodfellow and others. *Generative Adversarial Nets*. Advances in neural information processing systems, 2014(http://papers.nips.cc/paper/5423-generative-adversarial-nets.pdf).

2. Martin Arjovsky, Soumith Chintala, and Léon Bottou, *Wasserstein GAN*. arXiv preprint, 2017(https://arxiv.org/pdf/1701.07875.pdf).

3. Xudong Mao and others. *Least Squares Generative Adversarial Networks*. 2017 IEEE International Conference on Computer Vision (ICCV). IEEE 2017(http://openaccess.thecvf.com/content_ICCV_2017/papers/Mao_Least_Squares_Generative_ICCV_2017_paper.pdf).

4. Augustus Odena, Christopher Olah, and Jonathon Shlens. *Conditional Image Synthesis with Auxiliary Classifier GANs*. ICML, 2017(http://proceedings.mlr.press/v70/odena17a/odena17a.pdf).

6
Disentangled Representation GANs

As we've explored, GANs can generate meaningful outputs by learning the data distribution. However, there was no control over the attributes of the outputs generated. Some variations of GANs like **Conditional GAN (CGAN)** and **Auxiliary Classifier GAN (ACGAN)**, as discussed in the previous chapter are able to train a generator that is conditioned to synthesize specific outputs. For example, both CGAN and ACGAN can induce the generator to produce a specific MNIST digit. This is achieved by using both a 100-dim noise code and the corresponding one-hot label as inputs. However, other than the one-hot label, we have no other ways to control the properties of generated outputs.

For a review on CGAN and ACGAN, please see *Chapter 4, Generative Adversarial Networks (GANs),* and *Chapter 5, Improved GANs.*

In this chapter, we will be covering the variations of GANs that enable us to modify the generator outputs. In the context of the MNIST dataset, apart from which number to produce, we may find that we want to control the writing style. This could involve the tilt or the width of the desired digit. In other words, GANs can also learn disentangled latent codes or representations that we can use to vary the attributes of the generator outputs. A disentangled code or representation is a tensor that can change a specific feature or attribute of the output data while not affecting the other attributes.

In the first section of this chapter, we will be discussing **InfoGAN**: *Interpretable Representation Learning by Information Maximizing Generative Adversarial Nets* [1], an extension to GANs. InfoGAN learns the disentangled representations in an unsupervised manner by maximizing the mutual information between the input codes and the output observation. On the MNIST dataset, InfoGAN disentangles the writing styles from digits dataset.

In the following part of the chapter, we'll also be discussing the **Stacked Generative Adversarial Networks** or **StackedGAN** [2], another extension to GANs. StackedGAN uses a pretrained encoder or classifier in order to aid in disentangling the latent codes. StackedGAN can be viewed as a stack of models, with each being made of an encoder and a GAN. Each GAN is trained in an adversarial manner by using the input and output data of the corresponding encoder.

In summary, the goal of this chapter is to present:

- The concepts of disentangled representations
- The principles of both InfoGAN and StackedGAN
- Implementation of both InfoGAN and StackedGAN using Keras

Disentangled representations

The original GAN was able to generate meaningful outputs, but the downside was that it couldn't be controlled. For example, if we trained a GAN to learn the distribution of celebrity faces, the generator would produce new images of celebrity-looking people. However, there is no way to influence the generator on the specific attributes of the face that we want. For example, we're unable to ask the generator for a face of a female celebrity with long black hair, a fair complexion, brown eyes, and whose smiling. The fundamental reason for this is because the 100-dim noise code that we use entangles all of the salient attributes of the generator outputs. We can recall that in Keras, the 100-dim code was generated by random sampling of uniform noise distribution:

```
# generate 64 fake images from 64 x 100-dim uniform noise
noise = np.random.uniform(-1.0, 1.0, size=[64, 100])
fake_images = generator.predict(noise)
```

If we are able to modify the original GAN, such that we were able to separate the code or representation into entangled and disentangled interpretable latent codes, we would be able to tell the generator what to synthesize.

Following figure shows us a GAN with an entangled code and its variation with a mixture of entangled and disentangled representations. In the context of the hypothetical celebrity face generation, with the disentangled codes, we are able to indicate the gender, hairstyle, facial expression, skin complexion and eye color of the face we wish to generate. The *n–dim* entangled code is still needed to represent all the other facial attributes that we have not disentangled like the face shape, facial hair, eye-glasses, as just three examples. The concatenation of entangled and disentangled codes serves as the new input to the generator. The total dimension of the concatenated code may not be necessarily 100:

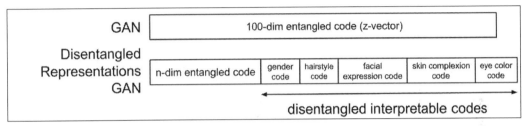

Figure 6.1.1: The GAN with the entangled code and its variation with both entangled and disentangled codes. This example is shown in the context of celebrity face generation.

Looking at preceding figure, it appears that GANs with disentangled representations can also be optimized in the same way as a vanilla GAN can be. This is because the generator output can be represented as:

$$G(z,c) = G(\mathbf{z}) \qquad \text{(Equation 6.1.1)}$$

The code $\mathbf{z} = (z,c)$ is made of two elements:

1. Incompressible entangled noise code similar to GANs z or noise vector.
2. Latent codes, $c_1, c_2, \ldots, c_L$, which represent the interpretable disentangled codes of the data distribution. Collectively all latent codes are represented by c.

For simplicity, all the latent codes are assumed to be independent:

$$p(c_1, c_2, \ldots, c_L) = \prod_{i=1}^{L} p(c_i) \qquad \text{(Equation 6.1.2)}$$

The generator function $x = G(z,c) = G(\mathbf{z})$ is provided with both the incompressible noise code and the latent codes. From the point of view of the generator, optimizing $\mathbf{z} = (z,c)$ is the same as optimizing z. The generator network will simply ignore the constraint imposed by the disentangled codes when coming up with a solution. The generator learns the distribution $p_g(x|c) = p_g(x)$. This will practically defeat the objective of disentangled representations.

InfoGAN

To enforce the disentanglement of codes, InfoGAN proposed a regularizer to the original loss function that maximizes the mutual information between the latent codes c and $G(z,c)$:

$$I\big(c;G(z,c)\big) = I\big(c;G(\mathbf{z})\big) \qquad \text{(Equation 6.1.3)}$$

The regularizer forces the generator to consider the latent codes when it formulates a function that synthesizes the fake images. In the field of information theory, the mutual information between latent codes c and $G(z,c)$ is defined as:

$$I\big(c;G(z,c)\big) = H\big(c\big) - H\big(c\,|\,G(z,c)\big) \qquad \text{(Equation 6.1.4)}$$

Where $H(c)$ is the entropy of the latent code c and $H\big(c\,|\,G(z,c)\big)$ is the conditional entropy of c, after observing the output of the generator, $G(z,c)$. Entropy is a measure of uncertainty of a random variable or an event. For example, information like, *the sun rises in the east*, has low entropy. Whereas, *winning the jackpot in the lottery* has high entropy.

In *Equation 6.1.4*, maximizing the mutual information means minimizing $H\big(c\,|\,G(z,c)\big)$ or decreasing the uncertainty in the latent code upon observing the generated output. This makes sense since, for example, in the MNIST dataset, the generator becomes more confident in synthesizing the digit 8 if the GAN sees that it observed the digit 8.

However, it is hard to estimate $H\big(c\,|\,G(z,c)\big)$ since it requires knowledge of the posterior $P\big(c\,|\,G(z,c)\big) = P(c\,|\,x)$, which is something that we don't have access to. The workaround is to estimate the lower bound of mutual information by estimating the posterior with an auxiliary distribution $Q(c\,|\,x)$. InfoGAN estimates the lower bound of mutual information as:

$$I\big(c;G(z,c)\big) \geq L_I\big(G,Q\big) = E_{c\sim P(c),x\sim G(z,c)}\Big[\log Q\big(c\,|\,x\big)\Big] + H\big(c\big) \qquad \text{(Equation 6.1.5)}$$

In InfoGAN, $H(c)$ is assumed to be a constant. Therefore, maximizing the mutual information is a matter of maximizing the expectation. The generator must be confident that it has generated an output with the specific attributes. We should note that the maximum value of this expectation is zero. Therefore, the maximum of the lower bound of the mutual information is $H(c)$. In InfoGAN, $Q(c\,|\,x)$ for discrete latent codes can be represented by *softmax* nonlinearity. The expectation is the negative `categorical_crossentropy` loss in Keras.

For continuous codes of a single dimension, the expectation is a double integral over c and x. This is due to the expectation that samples from both disentangled code distribution and generator distribution. One way of estimating the expectation is by assuming the samples as a good measure of continuous data. Therefore, the loss is estimated as $c \log Q(c \mid x)$.

To complete the network of InfoGAN, we should have an implementation of $Q(c \mid x)$. For simplicity, the network Q is an auxiliary network attached to the second to last layer of the discriminator. Therefore, this has a minimal impact on the training of the original GAN. Following figure shows InfoGAN network diagram:

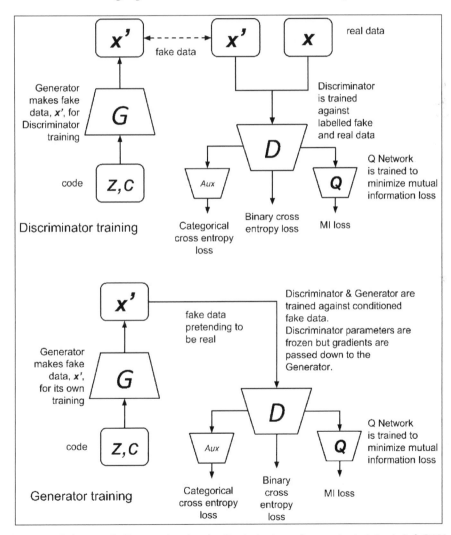

Figure 6.1.2: A network diagram showing the discriminator and generator training in InfoGAN

Following table shows the loss functions of InfoGAN as compared to the original GAN. The loss functions of InfoGAN differ from the original GAN by an additional term $-\lambda I\big(c;\mathcal{G}(z,c)\big)$ where λ is a small positive constant. Minimizing the loss function of InfoGAN translates to minimizing the loss of the original GAN and maximizing the mutual information $I\big(c;\mathcal{G}(z,c)\big)$.

Network	Loss Functions	Number
GAN	$\mathcal{L}^{(D)} = -\mathbb{E}_{x \sim p_{data}} \log \mathcal{D}(x) - \mathbb{E}_z \log\big(1 - \mathcal{D}\big(\mathcal{G}(z)\big)\big)$	4.1.1
	$\mathcal{L}^{(G)} = -\mathbb{E}_z \log \mathcal{D}\big(\mathcal{G}(z)\big)$	4.1.5
InfoGAN	$\mathcal{L}^{(D)} = -\mathbb{E}_{x \sim p_{data}} \log \mathcal{D}(x) - \mathbb{E}_{z,c} \log\big(1 - \mathcal{D}\big(\mathcal{G}(z,c)\big)\big) - \lambda I\big(c;\mathcal{G}(z,c)\big)$	6.1.1
	$\mathcal{L}^{(G)} = -\mathbb{E}_{z,c} \log \mathcal{D}\big(\mathcal{G}(z,c)\big) - \lambda I\big(c;\mathcal{G}(z,c)\big)$	6.1.2
	For continuous codes, InfoGAN recommends a value of $\lambda < 1$. In our example, we set $\lambda = 0.5$. For discrete codes, InfoGAN recommends $\lambda = 1$.	

Table 6.1.1: A comparison between the loss functions of GAN and InfoGAN

If applied on the MNIST dataset, InfoGAN can learn the disentangled discrete and continuous codes in order to modify the generator output attributes. For example, like CGAN and ACGAN, the discrete code in the form of a 10-dim one-hot label will be used to specify the digit to generate. However, we can add two continuous codes, one for controlling the angle of writing style and another for adjusting the stroke width. Following figure shows the codes for the MNIST digit in InfoGAN. We retain the entangled code with a smaller dimensionality to represent all other attributes:

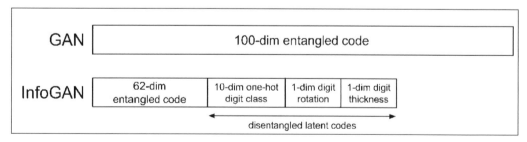

Figure 6.1.3: The codes for both GAN and InfoGAN in the context of MNIST dataset

Implementation of InfoGAN in Keras

To implement InfoGAN on MNIST dataset, there are some changes that need to be made in the base code of ACGAN. As highlighted in following listing, the generator concatenates both entangled (z noise code) and disentangled codes (one-hot label and continuous codes) to serve as input. The builder functions for the generator and discriminator are also implemented in gan.py in the lib folder.

 The complete code is available on GitHub:

https://github.com/PacktPublishing/Advanced-Deep-Learning-with-Keras

Listing 6.1.1, infogan-mnist-6.1.1.py shows us how the InfoGAN generator concatenates both entangled and disentangled codes to serve as input:

```
def generator(inputs,
              image_size,
              activation='sigmoid',
              labels=None,
              codes=None):
    """Build a Generator Model

    Stack of BN-ReLU-Conv2DTranpose to generate fake images.
    Output activation is sigmoid instead of tanh in [1].
    Sigmoid converges easily.

    # Arguments
        inputs (Layer): Input layer of the generator (the z-vector)
        image_size (int): Target size of one side (assuming square
image)
        activation (string): Name of output activation layer
        labels (tensor): Input labels
        codes (list): 2-dim disentangled codes for InfoGAN

    # Returns
        Model: Generator Model
    """
    image_resize = image_size // 4
    # network parameters
    kernel_size = 5
    layer_filters = [128, 64, 32, 1]

    if labels is not None:
        if codes is None:
```

```
                    # ACGAN labels
                    # concatenate z noise vector and one-hot labels
                    inputs = [inputs, labels]
                else:
                    # infoGAN codes
                    # concatenate z noise vector, one-hot labels,
                    # and codes 1 & 2
                    inputs = [inputs, labels] + codes
            x = concatenate(inputs, axis=1)
        elif codes is not None:
            # generator 0 of StackedGAN
            inputs = [inputs, codes]
            x = concatenate(inputs, axis=1)
        else:
            # default input is just 100-dim noise (z-code)
            x = inputs

    x = Dense(image_resize * image_resize * layer_filters[0])(x)
    x = Reshape((image_resize, image_resize, layer_filters[0]))(x)

    for filters in layer_filters:
        # first two convolution layers use strides = 2
        # the last two use strides = 1
        if filters > layer_filters[-2]:
            strides = 2
        else:
            strides = 1
        x = BatchNormalization()(x)
        x = Activation('relu')(x)
        x = Conv2DTranspose(filters=filters,
                            kernel_size=kernel_size,
                            strides=strides,
                            padding='same')(x)

    if activation is not None:
        x = Activation(activation)(x)

    # generator output is the synthesized image x
    return Model(inputs, x, name='generator')
```

The preceding listing shows the discriminator and *Q*-Network with the original default GAN output. The three auxiliary outputs corresponding to discrete code (for one-hot label) softmax prediction and the continuous codes probabilities given the input MNIST digit image are highlighted.

Listing 6.1.2, `infogan-mnist-6.1.1.py`. InfoGAN discriminator and *Q*-Network:

```python
def discriminator(inputs,
                  activation='sigmoid',
                  num_labels=None,
                  num_codes=None):
    """Build a Discriminator Model

    Stack of LeakyReLU-Conv2D to discriminate real from fake
    The network does not converge with BN so it is not used here
    unlike in [1]

    # Arguments
        inputs (Layer): Input layer of the discriminator (the image)
        activation (string): Name of output activation layer
        num_labels (int): Dimension of one-hot labels for ACGAN &
InfoGAN
        num_codes (int): num_codes-dim Q network as output
                    if StackedGAN or 2 Q networks if InfoGAN


    # Returns
        Model: Discriminator Model
    """
    kernel_size = 5
    layer_filters = [32, 64, 128, 256]

    x = inputs
    for filters in layer_filters:
        # first 3 convolution layers use strides = 2
        # last one uses strides = 1
        if filters == layer_filters[-1]:
            strides = 1
        else:
            strides = 2
        x = LeakyReLU(alpha=0.2)(x)
        x = Conv2D(filters=filters,
                   kernel_size=kernel_size,
                   strides=strides,
                   padding='same')(x)

    x = Flatten()(x)
    # default output is probability that the image is real
    outputs = Dense(1)(x)
```

```
        if activation is not None:
            print(activation)
            outputs = Activation(activation)(outputs)

    if num_labels:
        # ACGAN and InfoGAN have 2nd output
        # 2nd output is 10-dim one-hot vector of label
        layer = Dense(layer_filters[-2])(x)
        labels = Dense(num_labels)(layer)
        labels = Activation('softmax', name='label')(labels)
        if num_codes is None:
            outputs = [outputs, labels]
        else:
            # InfoGAN have 3rd and 4th outputs
            # 3rd output is 1-dim continous Q of 1st c given x
            code1 = Dense(1)(layer)
            code1 = Activation('sigmoid', name='code1')(code1)

            # 4th output is 1-dim continuous Q of 2nd c given x
            code2 = Dense(1)(layer)
            code2 = Activation('sigmoid', name='code2')(code2)

            outputs = [outputs, labels, code1, code2]
    elif num_codes is not None:
        # StackedGAN Q0 output
        # z0_recon is reconstruction of z0 normal distribution
        z0_recon =  Dense(num_codes)(x)
        z0_recon = Activation('tanh', name='z0')(z0_recon)
        outputs = [outputs, z0_recon]

    return Model(inputs, outputs, name='discriminator')
```

Figure 6.1.4 shows the InfoGAN model in Keras. Building the discriminator and adversarial models also requires a number of changes. The changes are on the loss functions used. The original discriminator loss function `binary_crossentropy`, the `categorical_crossentropy` for discrete code, and the `mi_loss` function for each continuous code comprise the overall loss function. Each loss function is given a weight of 1.0, except for the `mi_loss` function which is given 0.5 corresponding to $\lambda = 0.5$ for the continuous code.

Listing 6.1.3 highlights the changes made. However, we should note that by using the builder function, the discriminator is instantiated as:

```
# call discriminator builder with 4 outputs: source, label,
# and 2 codes
discriminator = gan.discriminator(inputs, num_labels=num_labels, with_
codes=True)
```

The generator is created by:

```
# call generator with inputs, labels and codes as total inputs
# to generator
generator = gan.generator(inputs, image_size, labels=labels,
codes=[code1, code2])
```

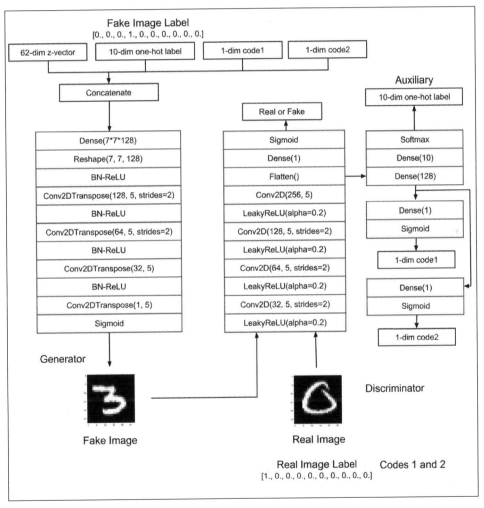

Figure 6.1.4: The InfoGAN Keras model

Listing 6.1.3, `infogan-mnist-6.1.1.py` shows us the mutual Information loss function as used in building the InfoGAN discriminator and adversarial networks:

```python
def mi_loss(c, q_of_c_given_x):
    """ Mutual information, Equation 5 in [2], assuming H(c) is
constant"""
    # mi_loss = -c * log(Q(c|x))
    return K.mean(-K.sum(K.log(q_of_c_given_x + K.epsilon()) * c,
axis=1))


def build_and_train_models(latent_size=100):
    # load MNIST dataset
    (x_train, y_train), (_, _) = mnist.load_data()

    # reshape data for CNN as (28, 28, 1) and normalize
    image_size = x_train.shape[1]
    x_train = np.reshape(x_train, [-1, image_size, image_size, 1])
    x_train = x_train.astype('float32') / 255

    # train labels
    num_labels = len(np.unique(y_train))
    y_train = to_categorical(y_train)

    model_name = "infogan_mnist"
    # network parameters
    batch_size = 64
    train_steps = 40000
    lr = 2e-4
    decay = 6e-8
    input_shape = (image_size, image_size, 1)
    label_shape = (num_labels, )
    code_shape = (1, )

    # build discriminator model
    inputs = Input(shape=input_shape, name='discriminator_input')
    # call discriminator builder with 4 outputs:
    # source, label, and 2 codes
    discriminator = gan.discriminator(inputs,
                                      num_labels=num_labels,
                                      num_codes=2)
    # [1] uses Adam, but discriminator converges easily with RMSprop
    optimizer = RMSprop(lr=lr, decay=decay)
    # loss functions: 1) probability image is real (binary
crossentropy)
```

```
    # 2) categorical cross entropy image label,
    # 3) and 4) mutual information loss
    loss = ['binary_crossentropy', 'categorical_crossentropy', mi_
loss, mi_loss]
    # lamda or mi_loss weight is 0.5
    loss_weights = [1.0, 1.0, 0.5, 0.5]
    discriminator.compile(loss=loss,
                          loss_weights=loss_weights,
                          optimizer=optimizer,
                          metrics=['accuracy'])
    discriminator.summary()


    # build generator model
    input_shape = (latent_size, )
    inputs = Input(shape=input_shape, name='z_input')
    labels = Input(shape=label_shape, name='labels')
    code1 = Input(shape=code_shape, name="code1")
    code2 = Input(shape=code_shape, name="code2")
    # call generator with inputs,
    # labels and codes as total inputs to generator
    generator = gan.generator(inputs,
                              image_size,
                              labels=labels,
                              codes=[code1, code2])
    generator.summary()

    # build adversarial model = generator + discriminator
    optimizer = RMSprop(lr=lr*0.5, decay=decay*0.5)
    discriminator.trainable = False
    # total inputs = noise code, labels, and codes
    inputs = [inputs, labels, code1, code2]
    adversarial = Model(inputs,
                        discriminator(generator(inputs)),
                        name=model_name)
    # same loss as discriminator
    adversarial.compile(loss=loss,
                        loss_weights=loss_weights,
                        optimizer=optimizer,
                        metrics=['accuracy'])
    adversarial.summary()

    # train discriminator and adversarial networks
    models = (generator, discriminator, adversarial)
```

```
        data = (x_train, y_train)
        params = (batch_size, latent_size, train_steps, num_labels,
    model_name)
        train(models, data, params)
```

As far as the training is concerned, we can see that InfoGAN is similar to ACGAN except that we need to supply *c* for the continuous code. *c* is drawn from normal distribution with a standard deviation of 0.5 and mean of 0.0. We'll use randomly sampled labels for the fake data and dataset class labels for the real data to represent discrete latent code. Following listing highlights the changes made on the training function. Similar to all previous GANs, the discriminator and generator (through adversarial) are trained alternately. During adversarial training, the discriminator weights are frozen. Sample generator output images are saved every 500 interval steps by using the `gan.py plot_images()` function.

Listing 6.1.4, `infogan-mnist-6.1.1.py` shows us how the training function for InfoGAN is similar to ACGAN. The only difference is that we supply continuous codes sampled from a normal distribution:

```
def train(models, data, params):
    """Train the Discriminator and Adversarial networks

    Alternately train discriminator and adversarial networks by batch.
    Discriminator is trained first with real and fake images,
    corresponding one-hot labels and continuous codes.
    Adversarial is trained next with fake images pretending to be
real,
    corresponding one-hot labels and continous codes.
    Generate sample images per save_interval.

    # Arguments
        models (Models): Generator, Discriminator, Adversarial models
        data (tuple): x_train, y_train data
        params (tuple): Network parameters
    """
    # the GAN models
    generator, discriminator, adversarial = models
    # images and their one-hot labels
    x_train, y_train = data
    # network parameters
    batch_size, latent_size, train_steps, num_labels, model_name =
params
    # the generator image is saved every 500 steps
    save_interval = 500
    # noise vector to see how the generator output evolves
```

```
    # during training
    noise_input = np.random.uniform(-1.0, 1.0, size=[16, latent_size])
    # random class labels and codes
    noise_label = np.eye(num_labels)[np.arange(0, 16) % num_labels]
    noise_code1 = np.random.normal(scale=0.5, size=[16, 1])
    noise_code2 = np.random.normal(scale=0.5, size=[16, 1])
    # number of elements in train dataset
    train_size = x_train.shape[0]
    print(model_name,
          "Labels for generated images: ",
          np.argmax(noise_label, axis=1))


    for i in range(train_steps):
        # train the discriminator for 1 batch
        # 1 batch of real (label=1.0) and fake images (label=0.0)
        # randomly pick real images and corresponding labels from
dataset
        rand_indexes = np.random.randint(0, train_size, size=batch_
size)
        real_images = x_train[rand_indexes]
        real_labels = y_train[rand_indexes]
        # random codes for real images
        real_code1 = np.random.normal(scale=0.5, size=[batch_size, 1])
        real_code2 = np.random.normal(scale=0.5, size=[batch_size, 1])
        # generate fake images, labels and codes
        noise = np.random.uniform(-1.0, 1.0, size=[batch_size, latent_
size])
        fake_labels = np.eye(num_labels)[np.random.choice(num_labels,
                                               batch_size)]
        fake_code1 = np.random.normal(scale=0.5, size=[batch_size, 1])
        fake_code2 = np.random.normal(scale=0.5, size=[batch_size, 1])
        inputs = [noise, fake_labels, fake_code1, fake_code2]
        fake_images = generator.predict(inputs)

        # real + fake images = 1 batch of train data
        x = np.concatenate((real_images, fake_images))
        labels = np.concatenate((real_labels, fake_labels))
        codes1 = np.concatenate((real_code1, fake_code1))
        codes2 = np.concatenate((real_code2, fake_code2))

        # label real and fake images
        # real images label is 1.0
        y = np.ones([2 * batch_size, 1])
        # fake images label is 0.0
```

```
        y[batch_size:, :] = 0

        # train discriminator network, log the loss and label accuracy
        outputs = [y, labels, codes1, codes2]
        # metrics = ['loss', 'activation_1_loss', 'label_loss',
        # 'code1_loss', 'code2_loss', 'activation_1_acc',
        # 'label_acc', 'code1_acc', 'code2_acc']
        # from discriminator.metrics_names
        metrics = discriminator.train_on_batch(x, outputs)
        fmt = "%d: [discriminator loss: %f, label_acc: %f]"
        log = fmt % (i, metrics[0], metrics[6])

        # train the adversarial network for 1 batch
        # 1 batch of fake images with label=1.0 and
        # corresponding one-hot label or class + random codes
        # since the discriminator weights are frozen in
        # adversarial network only the generator is trained
        # generate fake images, labels and codes
        noise = np.random.uniform(-1.0, 1.0, size=[batch_size, latent_
size])
        fake_labels = np.eye(num_labels)[np.random.choice(num_labels,
                                                        batch_size)]
        fake_code1 = np.random.normal(scale=0.5, size=[batch_size, 1])
        fake_code2 = np.random.normal(scale=0.5, size=[batch_size, 1])
        # label fake images as real
        y = np.ones([batch_size, 1])

        # note that unlike in discriminator training,
        # we do not save the fake images in a variable
        # the fake images go to the discriminator input of the
        # adversarial for classification
        # log the loss and label accuracy
        inputs = [noise, fake_labels, fake_code1, fake_code2]
        outputs = [y, fake_labels, fake_code1, fake_code2]
        metrics = adversarial.train_on_batch(inputs, outputs)
        fmt = "%s [adversarial loss: %f, label_acc: %f]"
        log = fmt % (log, metrics[0], metrics[6])

        print(log)
        if (i + 1) % save_interval == 0:
            if (i + 1) == train_steps:
                show = True
            else:
                show = False
```

```
# plot generator images on a periodic basis
gan.plot_images(generator,
                noise_input=noise_input,
                noise_label=noise_label,
                noise_codes=[noise_code1, noise_code2],
                show=show,
                step=(i + 1),
                model_name=model_name)

# save the model after training the generator
# the trained generator can be reloaded for
# future MNIST digit generation
generator.save(model_name + ".h5")
```

Generator outputs of InfoGAN

Similar to all previous GANs that have been presented to us, we've trained InfoGAN for 40,000 steps. After the training is completed, we're able to run the InfoGAN generator to generate new outputs using the model saved on the infogan_mnist.h5 file. The following validations are conducted:

1. Generate digits 0 to 9 by varying the discrete labels from 0 to 9. Both continuous codes are set to zero. The results are shown in *Figure 6.1.5*. We can see that the InfoGAN discrete code can control the digits produced by the generator:

   ```
   python3 infogan-mnist-6.1.1.py --generator=infogan_mnist.h5
   --digit=0 --code1=0 --code2=0
   ```

   to

   ```
   python3 infogan-mnist-6.1.1.py --generator=infogan_mnist.h5
   --digit=9 --code1=0 --code2=0
   ```

2. Examine the effect of the first continuous code to understand which attribute has been affected. We vary the first continuous code from -2.0 to 2.0 for digits 0 to 9. The second continuous code is set to 0.0. *Figure 6.1.6* shows that the first continuous code controls the thickness of the digit:

   ```
   python3 infogan-mnist-6.1.1.py --generator=infogan_mnist.h5
   --digit=0 --code1=0 --code2=0 --p1
   ```

3. Similar to the previous step, but instead focusing more on the second continuous code. *Figure 6.1.7* shows that the second continuous code controls the rotation angle (tilt) of the writing style:

```
python3 infogan-mnist-6.1.1.py --generator=infogan_mnist.h5
--digit=0 --code1=0 --code2=0 --p2
```

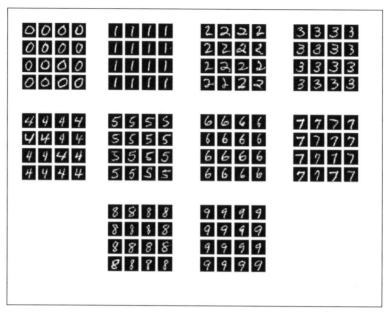

Figure 6.1.5: The images generated by the InfoGAN as the discrete code is varied from 0 to 9. Both continuous codes are set to zero.

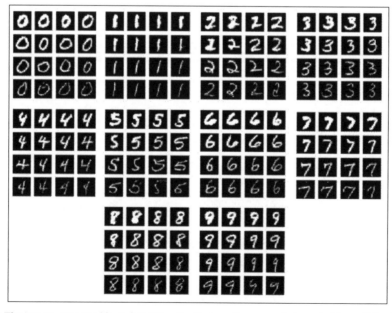

Figure 6.1.6: The images generated by InfoGAN as the first continuous code is varied from -2.0 to 2.0 for digits 0 to 9. The second continuous code is set to zero. The first continuous code controls the thickness of the digit.

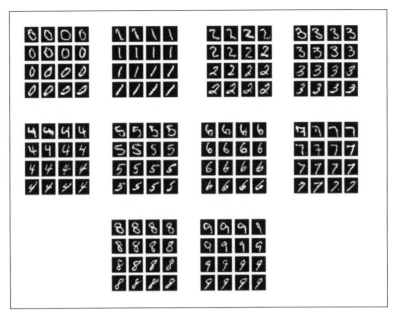

Figure 6.1.7: The images generated by InfoGAN as the second continuous code is varied from -2.0 to 2.0 for digits 0 to 9. The first continuous code is set to zero. The second continuous code controls the rotation angle (tilt) of the writing style.

From these validation results, we can see that apart from the ability to generate MNIST looking digits, InfoGAN expanded the ability of conditional GANs such as CGAN and ACGAN. The network automatically learned two arbitrary codes that can control the specific attributes of the generator output. It would be interesting to see what additional attributes could be controlled if we increased the number of continuous codes beyond 2.

StackedGAN

In the same spirit as InfoGAN, StackedGAN proposes a method for disentangling latent representations for conditioning generator outputs. However, StackedGAN uses a different approach to the problem. Instead of learning how to condition the noise to produce the desired output, StackedGAN breaks down a GAN into a stack of GANs. Each GAN is trained independently in the usual discriminator-adversarial manner with its own latent code.

Figure 6.2.1 shows us how StackedGAN works in the context of the hypothetical celebrity face generation. Assuming that the *Encoder* network is trained to classify celebrity faces.

The *Encoder* network is made of a stack of simple encoders, *Encoder*$_i$ *where i = 0 ...*
n - 1 corresponding to *n* features. Each encoder extracts certain facial features. For
example, *Encoder*$_0$ may be the encoder for hairstyle features, *Features*$_1$. All the simple
encoders contribute to making the overall *Encoder* perform correct predictions.

The idea behind StackedGAN is that if we would like to build a GAN that generates
fake celebrity faces, we should simply invert the *Encoder*. StackedGAN are made
of a stack of simpler GANs, GAN$_i$ where i = 0 ... *n* - 1 corresponding to *n* features.
Each GAN$_i$ learns to invert the process of its corresponding encoder, *Encoder*$_i$. For
example, *GAN*$_0$ generates fake celebrity faces from fake hairstyle features which is
the inverse of the *Encoder*$_0$ process.

Each *GAN*$_i$ uses a latent code, z_i, that conditions its generator output. For example,
the latent code, z_0, can alter the hairstyle from curly to wavy. The stack of GANs
can also act as one to synthesize fake celebrity faces, completing the inverse process
of the whole *Encoder*. The latent code of each *GAN*$_i$, z_i, can be used to alter specific
attributes of fake celebrity faces:

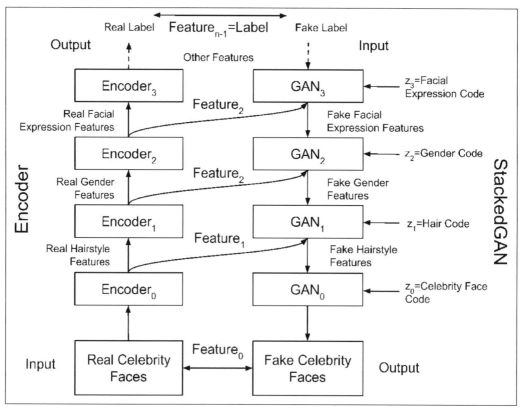

Figure 6.2.1: The basic idea of StackedGAN in the context of celebrity faces generation. Assuming that there is
a hypothetical deep encoder network that can perform classification on celebrity faces, a StackedGAN simply
inverts the process of the encoder.

Implementation of StackedGAN in Keras

The detailed network model of StackedGAN can be seen in the following figure. For conciseness, only two encoder-GANs per stack are shown. The figure may initially appear complex, but it is just a repetition of an encoder-GAN. Meaning that if we understood how to train one encoder-GAN, the rest uses the same concept. In the following section, we assume that the StackedGAN is designed for the MNIST digit generation:

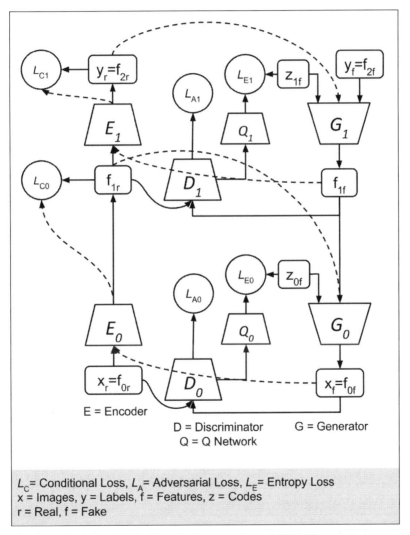

Figure 6.2.2: A StackedGAN is made of a stack of an encoder and GAN. The encoder is pre-trained to perform classification. *Generator₁, G_1, learns to synthesize f_{1f} features conditioned on the fake label, y_f, and latent code, z_{1f}. Generator₀, G_0, produces fake images using both the fake features, f_{1f} and latent code, z_{0f}.*

StackedGAN starts with an *Encoder*. It could be a trained classifier that predicts the correct labels. The intermediate features vector, f_{1r}, is made available for GAN training. For MNIST, we can use a CNN-based classifier similar to what we discussed in *Chapter 1, Introducing Advanced Deep Learning with Keras*. Following figure shows the *Encoder* and its network model implementation in Keras:

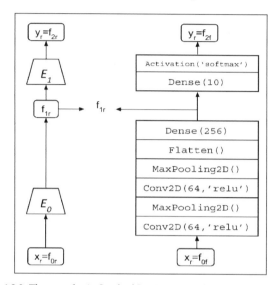

Figure 6.2.3: The encoder in StackedGAN is a simple CNN-based classifier

Listing 6.2.1 shows the Keras code for preceding figure. It is similar to the CNN-based classifier in *Chapter 1, Introducing Advanced Deep Learning with Keras* except that we use a Dense layer to extract the 256-dim feature. There are two output models, *Encoder$_0$* and *Encoder$_1$*. Both will be used to train the StackedGAN.

The *Encoder$_0$* output, f_{1r}, is the 256-dim feature vector that we want *Generator$_1$* to learn to synthesize. It is available as an auxiliary output of *Encoder$_0$*, E_0. The overall *Encoder* is trained to classify MNIST digits, x_r. The correct labels, y_r, are predicted by *Encoder$_1$*, E_1. In the process, the intermediate set of features, f_{1r}, is learned and made available for *Generator$_0$* training. Subscript r is used to emphasize and distinguish real data from fake data when the GAN is trained against this encoder.

Listing 6.2.1, stackedgan-mnist-6.2.1.py shows encoder implementation in Keras:

```
def build_encoder(inputs, num_labels=10, feature1_dim=256):
    """ Build the Classifier (Encoder) Model sub networks

    Two sub networks:
    1) Encoder0: Image to feature1 (intermediate latent feature)
    2) Encoder1: feature1 to labels
```

```
    # Arguments
        inputs (Layers): x - images, feature1 - feature1 layer output
        num_labels (int): number of class labels
        feature1_dim (int): feature1 dimensionality

    # Returns
        enc0, enc1 (Models): Description below
    """
    kernel_size = 3
    filters = 64

    x, feature1 = inputs
    # Encoder0 or enc0
    y = Conv2D(filters=filters,
               kernel_size=kernel_size,
               padding='same',
               activation='relu')(x)
    y = MaxPooling2D()(y)
    y = Conv2D(filters=filters,
               kernel_size=kernel_size,
               padding='same',
               activation='relu')(y)
    y = MaxPooling2D()(y)
    y = Flatten()(y)
    feature1_output = Dense(feature1_dim, activation='relu')(y)
    # Encoder0 or enc0: image to feature1
    enc0 = Model(inputs=x, outputs=feature1_output, name="encoder0")

    # Encoder1 or enc1
    y = Dense(num_labels)(feature1)
    labels = Activation('softmax')(y)
    # Encoder1 or enc1: feature1 to class labels
    enc1 = Model(inputs=feature1, outputs=labels, name="encoder1")

    # return both enc0 and enc1
    return enc0, enc1
```

Network	Loss Functions	Number
GAN	$\mathcal{L}^{(D)} = -\mathbb{E}_{x \sim p_{data}} \log \mathcal{D}(\boldsymbol{x}) - \mathbb{E}_z \log\left(1 - \mathcal{D}\left(\mathcal{G}(\boldsymbol{z})\right)\right)$	4.1.1
	$\mathcal{L}^{(G)} = -\mathbb{E}_z \log \mathcal{D}\left(\mathcal{G}(z)\right)$	4.1.5

StackedGAN	$\mathcal{L}_i^{(D)} = -\mathbb{E}_{f_i \sim p_{data}} \log \mathcal{D}(f_i) - \mathbb{E}_{f_{i+1} \sim p_{data}, z_i} \log\left(1 - \mathcal{D}\left(\mathcal{G}\left(f_{i+1}, z_i\right)\right)\right)$	6.2.1
	$\mathcal{L}_i^{(G)_{adv}} = -\mathbb{E}_{f_{i+1} \sim p_{data}, z_i} \log \mathcal{D}\left(\mathcal{G}\left(f_{i+1}, z_i\right)\right)$	6.2.2
	$\mathcal{L}_i^{(G)_{cond}} = \| \mathbb{E}_{f_{i+1} \sim p_{data}, z_i} \left(\mathcal{G}\left(f_{i+1}, z_i\right)\right), f_{i+1} \|_2$	6.2.3
	$\mathcal{L}_i^{(G)_{ent}} = \| \mathbb{E}_{f_{i+1}, z_i} \left(\mathcal{G}\left(f_{i+1}, z_i\right)\right), z_i \|_2$	6.2.4
	$\mathcal{L}_i^{(G)} = \lambda_1 \mathcal{L}_i^{(G)_{adv}} + \lambda_2 \mathcal{L}_i^{(G)_{cond}} + \lambda_3 \mathcal{L}_i^{(G)_{ent}}$	6.2.5
	where $\lambda_1, \lambda_2, and \lambda_3$ are weights and $i = Encoder\ and\ GAN\ id$	

Table 6.2.1: A comparison between the loss functions of GAN and StackedGAN.
$\sim p_{data}$ means sampling from the corresponding encoder data (input, feature or output).

Given the *Encoder* inputs (x_r) intermediate features (f_{1r}) and labels (y_r), each GAN is trained in the usual discriminator–adversarial manner. The loss functions are given by *Equation 6.2.1* to *6.2.5* in *Table 6.2.1*. Equations *6.2.1* and *6.2.2* are the usual loss functions of the generic GAN. StackedGAN has two additional loss functions, **Conditional** and **Entropy**.

The conditional loss function, $\mathcal{L}_i^{(G)_{cond}}$ in *Equation 6.2.3*, ensures that the generator does not ignore the input, f_{i+1}, when synthesizing the output, f_i, from input noise code z_i. The encoder, *Encoder$_i$*, must be able to recover the generator input by inverting the process of the generator, *Generator$_i$*. The difference between the generator input and the recovered input using the encoder is measured by *L2* or Euclidean distance **Mean Squared Error** (**MSE**). *Figure 6.2.4* shows the network elements involved in the computation of $\mathcal{L}_0^{(G)_{cond}}$:

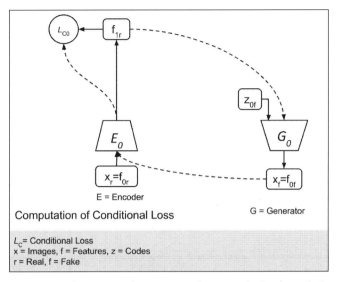

Figure 6.2.4: A simpler version of Figure 6.2.3 showing only the network elements involved in the computation of $\mathcal{L}_0^{(G)}{}_{cond}$

The conditional loss function, however, introduces a new problem for us. The generator ignores the input noise code, z_i and simply relies on f_{i+1}. Entropy loss function, $\mathcal{L}_0^{(G)}{}_{cond}$ in *Equation 6.2.4*, ensures that the generator does not ignore the noise code, z_i. The Q-Network recovers the noise code from the output of the generator. The difference between the recovered noise and the input noise is also measured by *L2* or the MSE. Following figure shows the network elements involved in the computation of $\mathcal{L}_0^{(G)}{}_{ent}$:

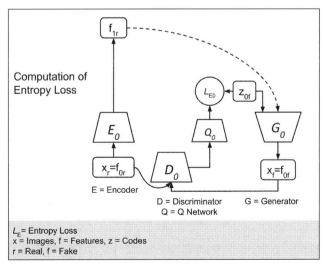

Figure 6.2.5: A simpler version of Figure 6.2.3 only showing us the network elements involved in the computation of $\mathcal{L}_0^{(G)}{}_{ent}$

The last loss function is similar to the usual GAN loss. It's made of a discriminator loss $\mathcal{L}_i^{(D)}$ and a generator (through adversarial) loss $\mathcal{L}_i^{(G)_{adv}}$. Following figure shows us the elements involved in the GAN loss:

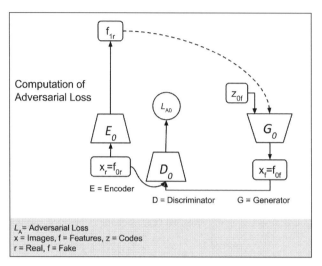

Figure 6.2.6: A simpler version of Figure 6.2.3 showing only the network elements involved in the computation of $\mathcal{L}_i^{(D)}$ and $\mathcal{L}_i^{(G)_{adv}}$

In *Equation 6.2.5*, the weighted sum of the three generator loss functions is the final generator loss function. In the Keras code that we will present, all the weights are set to 1.0, except for the entropy loss which is set to 10.0. In *Equation 6.2.1* to *Equation 6.2.5, i* refers to the encoder and GAN group id or level. In the original paper, the network is first trained independently and then jointly. During independent training, the encoder is trained first. During joint training, both real and fake data are used.

The implementation of the StackedGAN generator and discriminator in Keras requires few changes to provide auxiliary points to access the intermediate features. *Figure 6.2.7* shows the generator Keras model. *Listing 6.2.2* illustrates the function that builds two generators (gen0 and gen1) corresponding to *Generator_0* and *Generator_1*. The gen1 generator is made of three Dense layers with label and the noise code z_{1f} as inputs. The third layer generates the fake f_{1f} feature. The gen0 generator is similar to other GAN generators that we've presented and can be instantiated using the generator builder in gan.py:

```
# gen0: feature1 + z0 to feature0 (image)
gen0 = gan.generator(feature1, image_size, codes=z0)
```

The gen0 input is f_1 features and the noise code z_0. The output is the generated fake image, x_f:

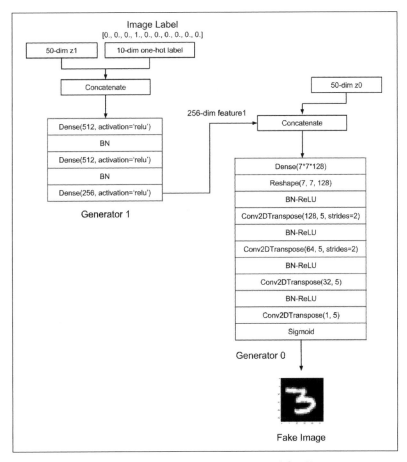

Figure 6.2.7: A StackedGAN Generator model in Keras

Listing 6.2.2, `stackedgan-mnist-6.2.1.py` shows us generator implementation in Keras:

```
def build_generator(latent_codes, image_size, feature1_dim=256):
    """Build Generator Model sub networks

    Two sub networks: 1) Class and noise to feature1 (intermediate
feature)
    2) feature1 to image

    # Arguments
        latent_codes (Layers): discrete code (labels), noise and
feature1 features
        image_size (int): Target size of one side (assuming square
image)
```

```
        feature1_dim (int): feature1 dimensionality

    # Returns
        gen0, gen1 (Models): Description below
    """

    # Latent codes and network parameters
    labels, z0, z1, feature1 = latent_codes
    # image_resize = image_size // 4
    # kernel_size = 5
    # layer_filters = [128, 64, 32, 1]

    # gen1 inputs
    inputs = [labels, z1]        # 10 + 50 = 62-dim
    x = concatenate(inputs, axis=1)
    x = Dense(512, activation='relu')(x)
    x = BatchNormalization()(x)
    x = Dense(512, activation='relu')(x)
    x = BatchNormalization()(x)
    fake_feature1 = Dense(feature1_dim, activation='relu')(x)
    # gen1: classes and noise (feature2 + z1) to feature1
    gen1 = Model(inputs, fake_feature1, name='gen1')

    # gen0: feature1 + z0 to feature0 (image)
    gen0 = gan.generator(feature1, image_size, codes=z0)

    return gen0, gen1
```

Figure 6.2.8 shows the discriminator Keras model. We provide the functions to build *Discriminator*$_0$ and *Discriminator*$_1$ (dis0 and dis1).The dis0 discriminator is similar to a GAN discriminator except for the feature vector input and the auxiliary network Q_0 that recovers z_0. The builder function in gan.py is used to create dis0:

```
    dis0 = gan.discriminator(inputs, num_codes=z_dim)
```

The dis1 discriminator is made of a three-layer MLP as shown in *Listing 6.2.3*. The last layer discriminates between the real and fake f_1. Q_1 network shares the first two layers of dis1. Its third layer recovers z_1:

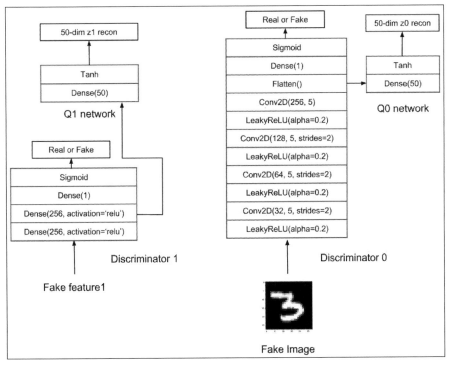

Figure 6.2.8: A StackedGAN Discriminator model in Keras

Listing 6.2.3, `stackedgan-mnist-6.2.1.py` shows the *Discriminator*₁ implementation in Keras:

```
def build_discriminator(inputs, z_dim=50):
    """Build Discriminator 1 Model

    Classifies feature1 (features) as real/fake image and recovers
    the input noise or latent code (by minimizing entropy loss)

    # Arguments
        inputs (Layer): feature1
        z_dim (int): noise dimensionality

    # Returns
        dis1 (Model): feature1 as real/fake and recovered latent code
    """

    # input is 256-dim feature1
    x = Dense(256, activation='relu')(inputs)
    x = Dense(256, activation='relu')(x)
```

```
    # first output is probability that feature1 is real
    f1_source = Dense(1)(x)
    f1_source = Activation('sigmoid', name='feature1_source')
(f1_source)

    # z1 reonstruction (Q1 network)
    z1_recon = Dense(z_dim)(x)
    z1_recon = Activation('tanh', name='z1')(z1_recon)

    discriminator_outputs = [f1_source, z1_recon]
    dis1 = Model(inputs, discriminator_outputs, name='dis1')
    return dis1
```

With all builder functions available, StackedGAN is assembled in *Listing 6.2.4*. Before training StackedGAN, the encoder is pretrained. Note that we already incorporated the three generator loss functions (adversarial, conditional, and entropy) in the adversarial model training. The *Q*-Network shares some common layers with the discriminator model. Therefore, its loss function is also incorporated in the discriminator model training.

Listing 6.2.4, `stackedgan-mnist-6.2.1.py`. Building StackedGAN in Keras:

```
def build_and_train_models():
    # load MNIST dataset
    (x_train, y_train), (x_test, y_test) = mnist.load_data()

    # reshape and normalize images
    image_size = x_train.shape[1]
    x_train = np.reshape(x_train, [-1, image_size, image_size, 1])
    x_train = x_train.astype('float32') / 255

    x_test = np.reshape(x_test, [-1, image_size, image_size, 1])
    x_test = x_test.astype('float32') / 255

    # number of labels
    num_labels = len(np.unique(y_train))
    # to one-hot vector
    y_train = to_categorical(y_train)
    y_test = to_categorical(y_test)

    model_name = "stackedgan_mnist"
    # network parameters
    batch_size = 64
    train_steps = 40000
```

```
lr = 2e-4
decay = 6e-8
input_shape = (image_size, image_size, 1)
label_shape = (num_labels, )
z_dim = 50
z_shape = (z_dim, )
feature1_dim = 256
feature1_shape = (feature1_dim, )

# build discriminator 0 and Q network 0 models
inputs = Input(shape=input_shape, name='discriminator0_input')
dis0 = gan.discriminator(inputs, num_codes=z_dim)
# [1] uses Adam, but discriminator converges easily with RMSprop
optimizer = RMSprop(lr=lr, decay=decay)
# loss fuctions: 1) probability image is real (adversarial0 loss)
# 2) MSE z0 recon loss (Q0 network loss or entropy0 loss)
loss = ['binary_crossentropy', 'mse']
loss_weights = [1.0, 10.0]
dis0.compile(loss=loss,
             loss_weights=loss_weights,
             optimizer=optimizer,
             metrics=['accuracy'])
dis0.summary() # image discriminator, z0 estimator

# build discriminator 1 and Q network 1 models
input_shape = (feature1_dim, )
inputs = Input(shape=input_shape, name='discriminator1_input')
dis1 = build_discriminator(inputs, z_dim=z_dim )
# loss fuctions: 1) probability feature1 is real (adversarial1
loss)
# 2) MSE z1 recon loss (Q1 network loss or entropy1 loss)
loss = ['binary_crossentropy', 'mse']
loss_weights = [1.0, 1.0]
dis1.compile(loss=loss,
             loss_weights=loss_weights,
             optimizer=optimizer,
             metrics=['accuracy'])
dis1.summary() # feature1 discriminator, z1 estimator

# build generator models
feature1 = Input(shape=feature1_shape, name='feature1_input')
labels = Input(shape=label_shape, name='labels')
z1 = Input(shape=z_shape, name="z1_input")
z0 = Input(shape=z_shape, name="z0_input")
```

```
latent_codes = (labels, z0, z1, feature1)
gen0, gen1 = build_generator(latent_codes, image_size)
gen0.summary() # image generator
gen1.summary() # feature1 generator

# build encoder models
input_shape = (image_size, image_size, 1)
inputs = Input(shape=input_shape, name='encoder_input')
enc0, enc1 = build_encoder((inputs, feature1), num_labels)
enc0.summary() # image to feature1 encoder
enc1.summary() # feature1 to labels encoder (classifier)
encoder = Model(inputs, enc1(enc0(inputs)))
encoder.summary() # image to labels encoder (classifier)

data = (x_train, y_train), (x_test, y_test)
train_encoder(encoder, data, model_name=model_name)

# build adversarial0 model =
# generator0 + discriminator0 + encoder0
optimizer = RMSprop(lr=lr*0.5, decay=decay*0.5)
# encoder0 weights frozen
enc0.trainable = False
# discriminator0 weights frozen
dis0.trainable = False
gen0_inputs = [feature1, z0]
gen0_outputs = gen0(gen0_inputs)
adv0_outputs = dis0(gen0_outputs) + [enc0(gen0_outputs)]
# feature1 + z0 to prob feature1 is
# real + z0 recon + feature0/image recon
adv0 = Model(gen0_inputs, adv0_outputs, name="adv0")
# loss functions: 1) prob feature1 is real (adversarial0 loss)
# 2) Q network 0 loss (entropy0 loss)
# 3) conditional0 loss
loss = ['binary_crossentropy', 'mse', 'mse']
loss_weights = [1.0, 10.0, 1.0]
adv0.compile(loss=loss,
             loss_weights=loss_weights,
             optimizer=optimizer,
             metrics=['accuracy'])
adv0.summary()

# build adversarial1 model =
# generator1 + discriminator1 + encoder1
# encoder1 weights frozen
```

```
enc1.trainable = False
# discriminator1 weights frozen
dis1.trainable = False
gen1_inputs = [labels, z1]
gen1_outputs = gen1(gen1_inputs)
adv1_outputs = dis1(gen1_outputs) + [enc1(gen1_outputs)]
# labels + z1 to prob labels are real + z1 recon + feature1 recon
adv1 = Model(gen1_inputs, adv1_outputs, name="adv1")
# loss functions: 1) prob labels are real (adversarial1 loss)
# 2) Q network 1 loss (entropy1 loss)
# 3) conditional1 loss (classifier error)
loss_weights = [1.0, 1.0, 1.0]
loss = ['binary_crossentropy', 'mse', 'categorical_crossentropy']
adv1.compile(loss=loss,
             loss_weights=loss_weights,
             optimizer=optimizer,
             metrics=['accuracy'])
adv1.summary()

# train discriminator and adversarial networks
models = (enc0, enc1, gen0, gen1, dis0, dis1, adv0, adv1)
params = (batch_size, train_steps, num_labels, z_dim, model_name)
train(models, data, params)
```

Finally, the training function bears a resemblance to a typical GAN training except that we only train one GAN at a time (that is, GAN_1 then GAN_0). The code is shown in *Listing 6.2.5*. It's worth noting that the training sequence is:

1. *Discriminator*$_1$ and Q_1 networks by minimizing the discriminator and entropy losses

2. *Discriminator*$_0$ and Q_0 networks by minimizing the discriminator and entropy losses

3. *Adversarial*$_1$ network by minimizing the adversarial, entropy, and conditional losses

4. *Adversarial*$_0$ network by minimizing the adversarial, entropy, and conditional losses

Listing 6.2.5, `stackedgan-mnist-6.2.1.py` shows us training the StackedGAN in Keras:

```
def train(models, data, params):
    """Train the discriminator and adversarial Networks

    Alternately train discriminator and adversarial networks by batch.
```

Discriminator is trained first with real and fake images,
corresponding one-hot labels and latent codes.
Adversarial is trained next with fake images pretending
to be real,
corresponding one-hot labels and latent codes.
Generate sample images per save_interval.

```
# Arguments
    models (Models): Encoder, Generator, Discriminator,
Adversarial models
    data (tuple): x_train, y_train data
    params (tuple): Network parameters

"""
# the StackedGAN and Encoder models
enc0, enc1, gen0, gen1, dis0, dis1, adv0, adv1 = models
# network parameters
batch_size, train_steps, num_labels, z_dim, model_name = params
# train dataset
(x_train, y_train), (_, _) = data
# the generator image is saved every 500 steps
save_interval = 500

# label and noise codes for generator testing
z0 = np.random.normal(scale=0.5, size=[16, z_dim])
z1 = np.random.normal(scale=0.5, size=[16, z_dim])
noise_class = np.eye(num_labels)[np.arange(0, 16) % num_labels]
noise_params = [noise_class, z0, z1]
# number of elements in train dataset
train_size = x_train.shape[0]
print(model_name,
    "Labels for generated images: ",
    np.argmax(noise_class, axis=1))

for i in range(train_steps):
    # train the discriminator1 for 1 batch
    # 1 batch of real (label=1.0) and fake feature1 (label=0.0)
    # randomly pick real images from dataset
    rand_indexes = np.random.randint(0, train_size,
size=batch_size)
    real_images = x_train[rand_indexes]
    # real feature1 from encoder0 output
    real_feature1 = enc0.predict(real_images)
    # generate random 50-dim z1 latent code
```

```
        real_z1 = np.random.normal(scale=0.5, size=[batch_size,
z_dim])
        # real labels from dataset
        real_labels = y_train[rand_indexes]

        # generate fake feature1 using generator1 from
        # real labels and 50-dim z1 latent code
        fake_z1 = np.random.normal(scale=0.5, size=[batch_size,
z_dim])
        fake_feature1 = gen1.predict([real_labels, fake_z1])

        # real + fake data
        feature1 = np.concatenate((real_feature1, fake_feature1))
        z1 = np.concatenate((fake_z1, fake_z1))

        # label 1st half as real and 2nd half as fake
        y = np.ones([2 * batch_size, 1])
        y[batch_size:, :] = 0

        # train discriminator1 to classify feature1
        # as real/fake and recover
        # latent code (z1). real = from encoder1,
        # fake = from genenerator1
        # joint training using discriminator part of advseria1 loss
        # and entropy1 loss
        metrics = dis1.train_on_batch(feature1, [y, z1])
        # log the overall loss only (fr dis1.metrics_names)
        log = "%d: [dis1_loss: %f]" % (i, metrics[0])



        # train the discriminator0 for 1 batch
        # 1 batch of real (label=1.0) and fake images (label=0.0)
        # generate random 50-dim z0 latent code
        fake_z0 = np.random.normal(scale=0.5, size=[batch_size,
z_dim])
        # generate fake images from real feature1 and fake z0
        fake_images = gen0.predict([real_feature1, fake_z0])

        # real + fake data
        x = np.concatenate((real_images, fake_images))
        z0 = np.concatenate((fake_z0, fake_z0))

        # train discriminator0 to classify image as real/fake
and recover
        # latent code (z0)
```

```
        # joint training using discriminator part of advserial0 loss
        # and entropy0 loss
        metrics = dis0.train_on_batch(x, [y, z0])
        # log the overall loss only (fr dis0.metrics_names)
        log = "%s [dis0_loss: %f]" % (log, metrics[0])


        # adversarial training
        # generate fake z1, labels
        fake_z1 = np.random.normal(scale=0.5, size=[batch_size,
    z_dim])
        # input to generator1 is sampling fr real labels and
        # 50-dim z1 latent code
        gen1_inputs = [real_labels, fake_z1]

        # label fake feature1 as real
        y = np.ones([batch_size, 1])

        # train generator1 (thru adversarial) by
        # fooling the discriminator
        # and approximating encoder1 feature1 generator
        # joint training: adversarial1, entropy1, conditional1
        metrics = adv1.train_on_batch(gen1_inputs, [y, fake_z1,
    real_labels])
        fmt = "%s [adv1_loss: %f, enc1_acc: %f]"
        # log the overall loss and classification accuracy
        log = fmt % (log, metrics[0], metrics[6])


        # input to generator0 is real feature1 and
        # 50-dim z0 latent code
        fake_z0 = np.random.normal(scale=0.5, size=[batch_size,
    z_dim])
        gen0_inputs = [real_feature1, fake_z0]

        # train generator0 (thru adversarial) by
        # fooling the discriminator
        # and approximating encoder1 image source generator
        # joint training: adversarial0, entropy0, conditional0
        metrics = adv0.train_on_batch(gen0_inputs, [y, fake_z0,
    real_feature1])
        # log the overall loss only
        log = "%s [adv0_loss: %f]" % (log, metrics[0])


        print(log)
```

```
    if (i + 1) % save_interval == 0:
        if (i + 1) == train_steps:
            show = True
        else:
            show = False
        generators = (gen0, gen1)
        plot_images(generators,
                    noise_params=noise_params,
                    show=show,
                    step=(i + 1),
                    model_name=model_name)

# save the modelis after training generator0 & 1
# the trained generator can be reloaded for
# future MNIST digit generation
gen1.save(model_name + "-gen1.h5")
gen0.save(model_name + "-gen0.h5")
```

Generator outputs of StackedGAN

After training the StackedGAN for 10,000 steps, the $Generator_0$ and $Generator_1$ models are saved on files. Stacked together, $Generator_0$ and $Generator_1$ can synthesize fake images conditioned on label and noise codes, z_0 and z_1.

The StackedGAN generator can be qualitatively validated by:

1. Varying the discrete labels from 0 to 9 with both noise codes, z_0 and z_1 sampled from a normal distribution with a mean of 0.5 and standard -deviation of 1.0. The results are shown in *Figure 6.2.9*. We're able to see that the StackedGAN discrete code can control the digits produced by the generator:

    ```
    python3 stackedgan-mnist-6.2.1.py

    --generator0=stackedgan_mnist-gen0.h5

    --generator1=stackedgan_mnist-gen1.h5 --digit=0
    ```

    to

    ```
    python3 stackedgan-mnist-6.2.1.py

    --generator0=stackedgan_mnist-gen0.h5

    --generator1=stackedgan_mnist-gen1.h5 --digit=9
    ```

2. Varying the first noise code, z_0, as a constant vector from -4.0 to 4.0 for digits 0 to 9 as shown as follows. The second noise code, z_0, is set to zero vector. *Figure 6.2.10* shows that the first noise code controls the thickness of the digit. For example, for digit 8:

```
python3 stackedgan-mnist-6.2.1.py

--generator0=stackedgan_mnist-gen0.h5

--generator1=stackedgan_mnist-gen1.h5 --z0=0 --z1=0 -p0

--digit=8
```

3. Varying the second noise code, z_1, as a constant vector from -1.0 to 1.0 for digits 0 to 9 shown as follows. The first noise code, z_0, is set to zero vector. *Figure 6.2.11* shows that the second noise code controls the rotation (tilt) and to a certain extent the thickness of the digit. For example, for digit 8:

```
python3 stackedgan-mnist-6.2.1.py

--generator0=stackedgan_mnist-gen0.h5

--generator1=stackedgan_mnist-gen1.h5 --z0=0 --z1=0 -p1

--digit=8
```

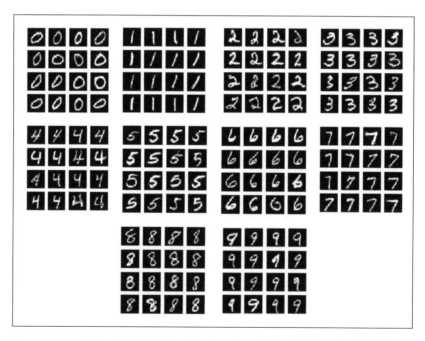

Figure 6.2.9: Images generated by StackedGAN as the discrete code is varied from 0 to 9. Both $\mathbf{z_0}$ and $\mathbf{z_1}$ have been sampled from a normal distribution with zero mean and 0.5 standard deviation.

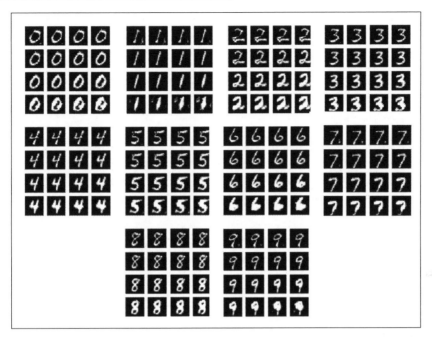

Figure 6.2.10: Images generated by using a StackedGAN as the first noise code, z_0, varies from constant vector -4.0 to 4.0 for digits 0 to 9. z_0 appears to control the thickness of each digit.

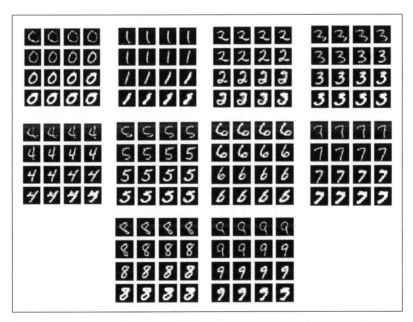

Figure 6.2.11: The images generated by StackedGAN as the second noise code, z_1, varies from constant vector -1.0 to 1.0 for digits 0 to 9. z_1 appears to control the rotation (tilt) and the thickness of stroke of each digit.

Figures 6.2.9 to *6.2.11* demonstrate that the StackedGAN has provided additional control on the attributes of the generator outputs. The control and attributes are (label, which digit), ($z0$, digit thickness), and ($z1$, digit tilt). From this example, there are other possible experiments that we can control such as:

- Increasing the number of elements of the stack from the current 2
- Decreasing the dimension of codes $z0$ and $z1$, like in InfoGAN

Following figure shows the differences between the latent codes of InfoGAN and StackedGAN. The basic idea of disentangling codes is to put a constraint on the loss functions such that only specific attributes are affected by a code. Structure-wise, InfoGAN are easier to implement when compared to StackedGAN. InfoGAN is also faster to train:

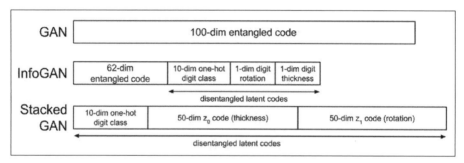

Figure 6.2.12: Latent representations for different GANs

Conclusion

In this chapter, we've discussed how to disentangle the latent representations of GANs. Earlier on in the chapter, we discussed how InfoGAN maximizes the mutual information in order to force the generator to learn disentangled latent vectors. In the MNIST dataset example, InfoGAN uses three representations and a noise code as inputs. The noise represents the rest of the attributes in the form of an entangled representation. StackedGAN approaches the problem in a different way. It uses a stack of encoder-GANs to learn how to synthesize fake features and images. The encoder is first trained to provide a dataset of features. Then, the encoder-GANs are trained jointly to learn how to use the noise code to control attributes of the generator output.

In the next chapter, we will embark on a new type of GAN that is able to generate new data in another domain. For example, given an image of a horse, the GAN can perform an automatic transformation to an image of a zebra. The interesting feature of this type of GAN is that it can be trained without supervision.

Reference

1. Xi Chen and others. *InfoGAN: Interpretable Representation Learning by Information Maximizing Generative Adversarial Nets.* Advances in Neural Information Processing Systems, 2016(`http://papers.nips.cc/ paper/6399-infogan-interpretable-representation-learning-by- information-maximizing-generative-adversarial-nets.pdf`).

2. Xun Huang and others. *Stacked Generative Adversarial Networks.* IEEE Conference on Computer Vision and Pattern Recognition (CVPR). Vol. 2, 2017(`http://openaccess.thecvf.com/content_cvpr_2017/papers/ Huang_Stacked_Generative_Adversarial_CVPR_2017_paper.pdf`).

7
Cross-Domain GANs

In computer vision, computer graphics, and image processing a number of tasks involve translating an image from one form to another. As an example, colorization of grayscale images, converting satellite images to maps, changing the artwork style of one artist to another, making night-time images into daytime, and summer photos to winter, are just a few examples. These tasks are referred to as **cross-domain transfer and will be the focus of this chapter**. An image in the source domain is transferred to a target domain resulting in a new translated image.

A cross-domain transfer has a number of practical applications in the real world. As an example, in autonomous driving research, collecting road scene driving data is both time-consuming and expensive. In order to cover as many scene variations as possible in that example, the roads would be traversed during different weather conditions, seasons, and times giving us a large and varied amount of data. With the use of a cross-domain transfer, it's possible to generate new synthetic scenes that look real by translating existing images. For example, we may just need to collect road scenes in the summer from one area and gather road scenes in the winter from another place. Then, we can transform the summer images to winter and the winter images to summer. In this case, it reduces the number of tasks having to be done by half.

Generation of realistic synthesized images is an area that GANs excel at. Therefore, cross-domain translation is one of the applications of GANs. In this chapter, we're going to focus on a popular cross-domain GAN algorithm called **CycleGAN** [2]. Unlike other cross-domain transfer algorithms, such as a **pix2pix** [3], CycleGAN doesn't require aligned training images to work. In aligned images, the training data should be a pair of images made up of the source image and its corresponding target image. For example, a satellite image and the corresponding map derived from this image. CycleGAN only requires the satellite data images and maps. The maps may be from another satellite data and are not necessarily previously generated from the training data.

In this chapter, we will explore the following:

- The principles of CycleGAN, including its implementation in Keras
- Example applications of CycleGAN, including the colorization of grayscale images using the CIFAR10 dataset and style transfer as applied on MNIST digits and **Street View House Numbers (SVHN)** [1] datasets

Principles of CycleGAN

Figure 7.1.1: Example of aligned image pair: left, original image and right, transformed image using a Canny edge detector. Original photos were taken by the author.

Translating an image from one domain to another is a common task in computer vision, computer graphics, and image processing. The preceding figure shows edge detection which is a common image translation task. In this example, we can consider the real photo (left) as an image in the source domain and the edge detected photo (right) as a sample in the target domain. There are many other cross-domain translation procedures that have practical applications such as:

- Satellite image to map
- Face image to emoji, caricature or anime
- Body image to the avatar
- Colorization of grayscale photos
- Medical scan to a real photo
- Real photo to an artist's painting

There are many more examples of this in different fields. In computer vision and image processing, for example, we can perform the translation by inventing an algorithm that extracts features from the source image to translate it into the target image. Canny edge operator is an example of such an algorithm. However, in many cases, the translation is very complex to hand-engineer that it is almost impossible to find a suitable algorithm. Both the source and target domain distributions are high-dimensional and complex:

Figure 7.1.2: Example of not aligned image pair: left, a photo of real sunflowers along University Avenue, University of the Philippines and right, Sunflowers by Vincent Van Gogh at the National Gallery, London, UK. Original photos were taken by the author.

A workaround on the image translation problem is to use deep learning techniques. If we have a sufficiently large dataset from both the source and target domains, we can train a neural network to model the translation. Since the images in the target domain must be automatically generated given a source image, they must look like real samples from the target domain. GANs are a suitable network for such cross-domain tasks. The pix2pix [3] algorithm is an example of a cross-domain algorithm.

The pix2pix bears a resemblance to **Conditional GAN (CGAN)** [4] that we discussed in *Chapter 4, Generative Adversarial Networks (GANs)*. We can recall, that in conditional GANs, on top of the noise input, z, a condition such as in the form of a one-hot vector constrains the generator's output. For example, in the MNIST digit, if we want the generator to output the digit 8, the condition is the one-hot vector [0, 0, 0, 0, 0, 0, 0, 0, 1, 0]. In pix2pix, the condition is the image to be translated. The generator's output is the translated image. The pix2pix is trained by optimizing the conditional GAN loss. To minimize blurring in the generated images, the *L1* loss is also included.

The main disadvantage of neural networks similar to pix2pix is the training input, and output images must be aligned. *Figure 7.1.1* is an example of an aligned image pair. The sample target image is generated from the source. In most occasions, aligned image pairs are not available or expensive to generate from the source images, or we have no idea on how to generate the target image from the given source image. What we have are sample data from the source and target domains. *Figure 7.1.2* is an example of data from the source domain (real photo) and the target domain (Van Gogh's art style) on the same sunflower subject. The source and target images are not necessarily aligned.

Unlike pix2pix, CycleGAN learns image translation as long as there are a sufficient amount and variation of source and target data. No alignment is needed. CycleGAN learns the source and target distributions and how to translate from source to target distribution from given sample data. No supervision is needed. In the context of *Figure 7.1.2*, we just need thousands of photos of real sunflowers and thousands of photos of Van Gogh's paintings of sunflowers. After training the CycleGAN, we're able to translate a photo of sunflowers to a Van Gogh's painting:

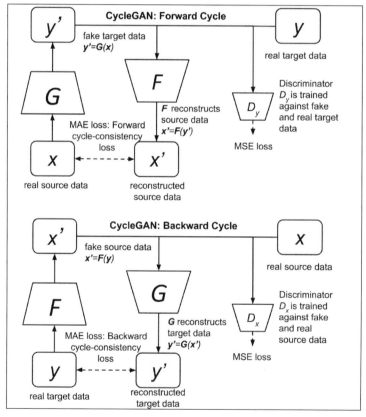

Figure 7.1.3: The CycleGAN model is made of four networks: Generator G, Generator F, Discriminator D_y, and Discriminator D_x

The CycleGAN Model

Figure 7.1.3 shows the network model of the CycleGAN. The objective of the CycleGAN is to learn the function:

$$y' = G(x) \qquad \text{(Equation 7.1.1)}$$

That generates fake images, y', in the target domain as a function of the real source image, x. Learning is unsupervised by capitalizing only on the available real images, x, in the source domain and real images, y, in the target domain.

Unlike regular GANs, CycleGAN imposes the cycle-consistency constraint. The forward cycle-consistency network ensures that the real source data can be reconstructed from the fake target data:

$$x' = F(G(x)) \qquad \text{(Equation 7.1.2)}$$

This is done by minimizing the forward cycle-consistency *L1* loss:

$$\mathcal{L}_{forward-cyc} = \mathbb{E}_{x \sim p_{data}(x)} \left[\left\| F\left(G(x)\right) - x \right\|_1 \right] \qquad \text{(Equation 7.1.3)}$$

The network is symmetric. The backward cycle-consistency network also attempts to reconstruct the real target data from the fake source data:

$$y' = G(F(y)) \qquad \text{(Equation 7.1.4)}$$

This is done by minimizing the backward cycle-consistency *L1* loss:

$$\mathcal{L}_{backward-cyc} = \mathbb{E}_{y \sim p_{data}(y)} \left[\left\| G\left(F(y)\right) - y \right\|_1 \right] \qquad \text{(Equation 7.1.5)}$$

The sum of these two losses is known as cycle-consistency loss:

$$\mathcal{L}_{cyc} = \mathcal{L}_{forward-cyc} + \mathcal{L}_{backward-cyc}$$

$$\mathcal{L}_{cyc} = \mathbb{E}_{x \sim p_{data}(x)} \left[\left\| F\left(G(x)\right) - x \right\|_1 \right] + \mathbb{E}_{y \sim p_{data}(y)} \left[\left\| G\left(F(y)\right) - y \right\|_1 \right] \qquad \text{(Equation 7.1.6)}$$

The cycle-consistency loss uses *L1* or **Mean Absolute Error (MAE)** since it generally results in less blurry image reconstruction compared to *L2* or **Mean Square Error (MSE)**.

Similar to other GANs, the ultimate objective of CycleGAN is for the generator G to learn how to synthesize fake target data, y', that can fool the discriminator, D_y, in the forward cycle. Since the network is symmetric, CycleGAN also wants the generator F to learn how to synthesize fake source data, x', that can fool the discriminator, D_x, in the backward cycle. Inspired by the better perceptual quality of **Least Squares GAN (LSGAN)** [5], as described in *Chapter 5, Improved GANs*, CycleGAN also uses MSE for the discriminator and generator losses. Recall that the difference of LSGAN from the original GAN is that the use of the MSE loss instead of a binary cross-entropy loss. CycleGAN expresses the generator-discriminator loss functions as:

$$\mathcal{L}_{forward-GAN}^{(D)} = \mathbb{E}_{y \sim p_{data}(y)} \left(D_y(y) - 1 \right)^2 + \mathbb{E}_{x \sim p_{data}(x)} D_y \left(G(x) \right)^2 \qquad \text{(Equation 7.1.7)}$$

$$\mathcal{L}_{forward-GAN}^{(G)} = \mathbb{E}_{x \sim p_{data}(x)} \left(D_y \left(G(x) \right) - 1 \right)^2 \qquad \text{(Equation 7.1.8)}$$

$$\mathcal{L}_{backward-GAN}^{(D)} = \mathbb{E}_{x \sim p_{data}(x)} \left(D_x(x) - 1 \right)^2 + \mathbb{E}_{y \sim p_{data}(y)} D_x \left(F(y) \right)^2 \qquad \text{(Equation 7.1.9)}$$

$$\mathcal{L}_{backward-GAN}^{(G)} = \mathbb{E}_{y \sim p_{data}(y)} \left(D_x \left(F(y) \right) - 1 \right)^2 \qquad \text{(Equation 7.1.10)}$$

$$\mathcal{L}_{GAN}^{(D)} = \mathcal{L}_{forward-GAN}^{(D)} + \mathcal{L}_{backward-GAN}^{(D)} \qquad \text{(Equation 7.1.11)}$$

$$\mathcal{L}_{GAN}^{(D)} = \mathcal{L}_{forward-GAN}^{(D)} + \mathcal{L}_{backward-GAN}^{(D)} \qquad \text{(Equation 7.1.12)}$$

The total loss of CycleGAN is shown as:

$$\mathcal{L} = \lambda_1 \mathcal{L}_{GAN} + \lambda_2 \mathcal{L}_{cyc} \qquad \text{(Equation 7.1.13)}$$

CycleGAN recommends the following weight values: $\lambda_1 = 1.0$ and $\lambda_2 = 10.0$ to give more importance to the cyclic consistency check.

The training strategy is similar to the vanilla GAN. *Algorithm 7.1.1* summarizes the CycleGAN training procedure.

Repeat for *n* training steps:

1. Minimize $\mathcal{L}_{forward-GAN}^{(D)}$ by training the forward-cycle discriminator using real source and target data. A minibatch of real target data, y, is labeled 1.0. A minibatch of fake target data, $y' = G(x)$, is labelled 0.0.

2. Minimize $\mathcal{L}_{backward-GAN}^{(D)}$ by training the backward-cycle discriminator using real source and target data. A minibatch of real source data, x, is labeled 1.0. A minibatch of fake source data, $x' = F(y)$, is labeled 0.0.

3. Minimize $\mathcal{L}_{GAN}^{(G)}$ and $\mathcal{L}_{cyc}$ by training the forward-cycle and backward-cycle generators in the adversarial networks. A minibatch of fake target data, $y' = G(x)$, is labeled 1.0. A minibatch of fake source data, $x' = F(y)$, is labeled 1.0. The weights of discriminators are frozen.

| Source Domain: Real Sunflower | Target Domain: Van Gogh's Sunflower Style | Predicted Target Domain: Van Gogh's Sunflower Style w/o the right color composition |

Figure 7.1.4: During style transfer, the color composition may not be transferred successfully. To address this issue, the identity loss is added to the total loss function.

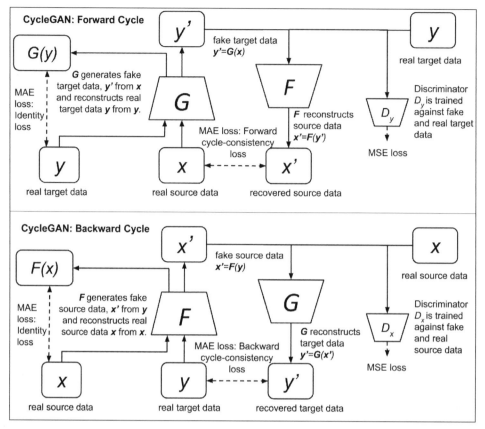

Figure 7.1.5: The CycleGAN model with identity loss as shown on the left side of the image

In neural style transfer problems, the color composition may not be successfully transferred from source image to the fake target image. This problem is shown in *Figure 7.1.4*. To address this problem, CycleGAN proposes to include the forward and backward-cycle identity loss function:

$$\mathcal{L}_{identity} = \mathbb{E}_{x \sim p_{data}(x)}\left[\left\|F(x) - x\right\|_1\right] + \mathbb{E}_{y \sim p_{data}(y)}\left[\left\|G(y) - y\right\|_1\right] \qquad \text{(Equation 7.1.14)}$$

The total loss of CycleGAN becomes:

$$\mathcal{L} = \lambda_1 \mathcal{L}_{GAN} + \lambda_2 \mathcal{L}_{cyc} + \lambda_3 \mathcal{L}_{identity} \qquad \text{(Equation 7.1.15)}$$

with $\lambda_3 = 0.5$. The identity loss is also optimized during adversarial training. *Figure 7.1.5* shows CycleGAN with identity loss.

Implementing CycleGAN using Keras

Let us tackle a simple problem that CycleGAN can address. In *Chapter 3, Autoencoders*, we used an autoencoder to colorize grayscale images from the CIFAR10 dataset. We can recall that the CIFAR10 dataset is made of 50,000 trained data and 10,000 test data samples of 32 × 32 RGB images belonging to ten categories. We can convert all color images into grayscale using `rgb2gray(RGB)` as discussed in *Chapter 3, Autoencoders*.

Following on from that, we can use the grayscale train images as source domain images and the original color images as the target domain images. It's worth noting that although the dataset is aligned, the input to our CycleGAN is a random sample of color images and a random sample of grayscale images. Thus, our CycleGAN will not see the train data as aligned. After training, we'll use the test grayscale images to observe the performance of the CycleGAN:

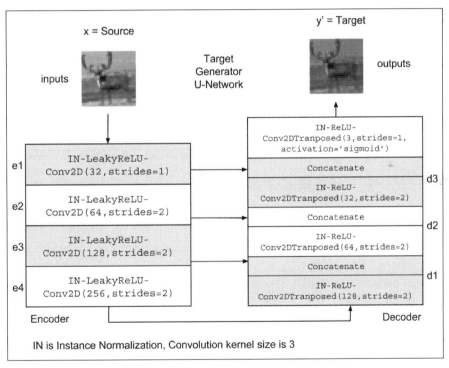

Figure 7.1.6: The forward cycle generator G, implementation in Keras.
The generator is a U-Network made of encoder and decoder.

As discussed in the previous section, to implement the CycleGAN, we need to build two generators and two discriminators. The generator of CycleGAN learns the latent representation of the source input distribution and translates this representation into target output distribution. This is exactly what autoencoders do. However, typical autoencoders similar to the ones discussed in *Chapter 3, Autoencoders,* use an encoder that downsamples the input until the bottleneck layer at which point the process is reversed in the decoder. This structure is not suitable in some image translation problems since many low-level features are shared between the encoder and decoder layers. For example, in colorization problems, the form, structure, and edges of the grayscale image are the same as in the color image. To circumvent this problem, the CycleGAN generators use a **U-Net** [7] structure as shown in *Figure 7.1.6.*

In a U-Net structure, the output of the encoder layer e_{n-i} is concatenated with the output of the decoder layer d_i, where $n = 4$ is the number of encoder/decoder layers and $i = 1, 2$ and 3 are layer numbers that share information.

We should note that although the example uses $n = 4$, problems with a higher input/output dimensions may require deeper encoder/decoder. The U-Net structure enables a free flow of feature-level information between encoder and decoder. An encoder layer is made of `Instance Normalization(IN)-LeakyReLU-Conv2D` while the decoder layer is made of `IN-ReLU-Conv2D`. The encoder/decoder layer implementation is shown in *Listing 7.1.1* while the generator implementation is shown in *Listing 7.1.2.*

The complete code is available on GitHub:

`https://github.com/PacktPublishing/Advanced-Deep-Learning-with-Keras`

Instance Normalization (IN) is **Batch Normalization (BN)** per sample of data (that is, IN is BN per image or per feature). In style transfer, it's important to normalize the contrast per sample not per batch. Instance normalization is equivalent to contrast normalization. Meanwhile, Batch normalization breaks contrast normalization.

Remember to install `keras-contrib` before using instance normalization:

`$ sudo pip3 install git+https://www.github.com/keras-team/keras-contrib.git`

Listing 7.1.1, `cyclegan-7.1.1.py` shows us the encoder and decoder layers implementation in Keras:

```
def encoder_layer(inputs,
```

```
                        filters=16,
                        kernel_size=3,
                        strides=2,
                        activation='relu',
                        instance_norm=True):
    """Builds a generic encoder layer made of Conv2D-IN-LeakyReLU
    IN is optional, LeakyReLU may be replaced by ReLU

    """

    conv = Conv2D(filters=filters,
                  kernel_size=kernel_size,
                  strides=strides,
                  padding='same')

    x = inputs
    if instance_norm:
        x = InstanceNormalization()(x)
    if activation == 'relu':
        x = Activation('relu')(x)
    else:
        x = LeakyReLU(alpha=0.2)(x)
    x = conv(x)
    return x


def decoder_layer(inputs,
                  paired_inputs,

                        filters=16,
                        kernel_size=3,
                        strides=2,
                        activation='relu',
                        instance_norm=True):
    """Builds a generic decoder layer made of Conv2D-IN-LeakyReLU
    IN is optional, LeakyReLU may be replaced by ReLU
    Arguments: (partial)
    inputs (tensor): the decoder layer input
    paired_inputs (tensor): the encoder layer output
        provided by U-Net skip connection &
        concatenated to inputs.
    """

    conv = Conv2DTranspose(filters=filters,
```

```
                        kernel_size=kernel_size,
                        strides=strides,
                        padding='same')

    x = inputs
    if instance_norm:
        x = InstanceNormalization()(x)
    if activation == 'relu':
        x = Activation('relu')(x)
    else:
        x = LeakyReLU(alpha=0.2)(x)
    x = conv(x)
    x = concatenate([x, paired_inputs])
    return x
```

Listing 7.1.2, `cyclegan-7.1.1.py`. Generator implementation in Keras:

```
def build_generator(input_shape,
                    output_shape=None,
                    kernel_size=3,
                    name=None):
    """The generator is a U-Network made of a 4-layer encoder
    and a 4-layer decoder. Layer n-i is connected to layer i.

    Arguments:
    input_shape (tuple): input shape
    output_shape (tuple): output shape
    kernel_size (int): kernel size of encoder & decoder layers
    name (string): name assigned to generator model

    Returns:
    generator (Model):

    """

    inputs = Input(shape=input_shape)
    channels = int(output_shape[-1])
    e1 = encoder_layer(inputs,
                       32,
                       kernel_size=kernel_size,
                       activation='leaky_relu',
                       strides=1)
    e2 = encoder_layer(e1,
                       64,
                       activation='leaky_relu',
```

```
                               kernel_size=kernel_size)
    e3 = encoder_layer(e2,
                       128,
                       activation='leaky_relu',
                       kernel_size=kernel_size)
    e4 = encoder_layer(e3,
                       256,
                       activation='leaky_relu',
                       kernel_size=kernel_size)

    d1 = decoder_layer(e4,
                       e3,
                       128,
                       kernel_size=kernel_size)
    d2 = decoder_layer(d1,
                       e2,
                       64,
                       kernel_size=kernel_size)
    d3 = decoder_layer(d2,
                       e1,
                       32,
                       kernel_size=kernel_size)
    outputs = Conv2DTranspose(channels,
                              kernel_size=kernel_size,
                              strides=1,
                              activation='sigmoid',
                              padding='same')(d3)

    generator = Model(inputs, outputs, name=name)

    return generator
```

The discriminator of CycleGAN is similar to vanilla GAN discriminator. The input image is downsampled several times (in this example, three times). The final layer is a `Dense(1)` layer which predicts the probability that the input is real. Each layer is similar to the encoder layer of the generator except that no IN is used. However, in large images, computing the image as real or fake with a single number turns out to be parameter inefficient and results in poor image quality for the generator.

The solution is to use PatchGAN [6] which divides the image into a grid of patches and use a grid of scalar values to predict the probability that the patches are real. The comparison between the vanilla GAN discriminator and a 2 × 2 PatchGAN discriminator is shown in *Figure 7.1.7*. In this example, the patches do not overlap and meet at their boundaries. However, in general, patches may overlap.

We should note that PatchGAN is not introducing a new type of GAN in CycleGAN. To improve the generated image quality, instead of having one output to discriminate, we have four outputs to discriminate if we used a 2 × 2 PatchGAN. There are no changes in the loss functions. Intuitively, this makes sense since the whole image will look more real if every patch or section of the image looks real:

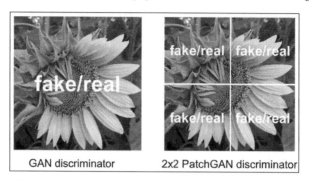

Figure 7.1.7: A comparison between GAN and PatchGAN discriminators

Following figure shows the discriminator network as implemented in Keras. The illustration shows the discriminator determining how likely the input image or a patch is a color CIFAR10 image. Since the output image is small at only 32 × 32 RGB, a single scalar representing that the image is real is sufficient. However, we also evaluate the results when PatchGAN is used. *Listing 7.1.3* shows the function builder for the discriminator:

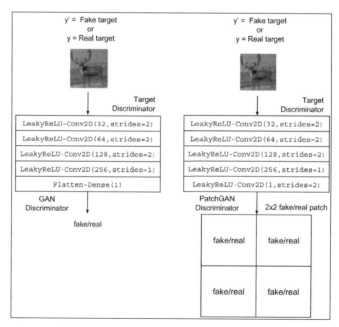

Figure 7.1.8: The target discriminator, D_y, implementation in Keras. The PatchGAN discriminator is shown on the right.

Listing 7.1.3, `cyclegan-7.1.1.py` shows discriminator implementation in Keras:

```
def build_discriminator(input_shape,
                        kernel_size=3,
                        patchgan=True,
                        name=None):
    """The discriminator is a 4-layer encoder that outputs either
    a 1-dim or a n x n-dim patch of probability that input is real

    Arguments:
    input_shape (tuple): input shape
    kernel_size (int): kernel size of decoder layers
    patchgan (bool): whether the output is a patch or just a 1-dim
    name (string): name assigned to discriminator model

    Returns:
    discriminator (Model):

    """

    inputs = Input(shape=input_shape)
    x = encoder_layer(inputs,
                      32,
                      kernel_size=kernel_size,
                      activation='leaky_relu',
                      instance_norm=False)
    x = encoder_layer(x,
                      64,
                      kernel_size=kernel_size,
                      activation='leaky_relu',
                      instance_norm=False)
    x = encoder_layer(x,
                      128,
                      kernel_size=kernel_size,
                      activation='leaky_relu',
                      instance_norm=False)
    x = encoder_layer(x,
                      256,
                      kernel_size=kernel_size,
                      strides=1,
                      activation='leaky_relu',
                      instance_norm=False)

    # if patchgan=True use nxn-dim output of probability
```

```
        # else use 1-dim output of probability
        if patchgan:
            x = LeakyReLU(alpha=0.2)(x)
            outputs = Conv2D(1,
                             kernel_size=kernel_size,
                             strides=1,
                             padding='same')(x)
        else:
            x = Flatten()(x)
            x = Dense(1)(x)
            outputs = Activation('linear')(x)


        discriminator = Model(inputs, outputs, name=name)

        return discriminator
```

Using the generator and discriminator builders, we are now able to build the CycleGAN. *Listing 7.1.4* shows the builder function. In line with our discussion in the previous section, two generators, g_source = *F* and g_target = *G*, and two discriminators, d_source = D_x and d_target = D_y are instantiated. The forward cycle is $x' = F(G(x)) = $ reco_source = g_source(g_target(source_input)). The backward cycle is $y' = G(F(y)) = $ reco_target = g_target(g_source (target_input)).

The inputs to the adversarial model are the source and target data while the outputs are the outputs of D_x and D_y and the reconstructed inputs, *x'* and *y.'* The identity network is not used in this example due to the difference between the number of channels of the grayscale image and color image. We use the recommended loss weights of $\lambda_1 = 1.0$ and $\lambda_2 = 10.0$ for the GAN and cyclic consistency losses respectively. Similar to GANs in the previous chapters, we use RMSprop with a learning rate of 2e-4 and decay rate of 6e-8 for the optimizer of the discriminators. The learning and decay rate for the adversarial is half of the discriminator's.

Listing 7.1.4, cyclegan-7.1.1.py shows us the CycleGAN builder in Keras:

```
def build_cyclegan(shapes,
                   source_name='source',
                   target_name='target',
                   kernel_size=3,
                   patchgan=False,
                   identity=False
                   ):
    """Build the CycleGAN
```

```
1) Build target and source discriminators
2) Build target and source generators
3) Build the adversarial network

Arguments:
shapes (tuple): source and target shapes
source_name (string): string to be appended on dis/gen models
target_name (string): string to be appended on dis/gen models
kernel_size (int): kernel size for the encoder/decoder or dis/gen
                   models
patchgan (bool): whether to use patchgan on discriminator
identity (bool): whether to use identity loss

Returns:
(list): 2 generator, 2 discriminator, and 1 adversarial models

"""

source_shape, target_shape = shapes
lr = 2e-4
decay = 6e-8
gt_name = "gen_" + target_name
gs_name = "gen_" + source_name
dt_name = "dis_" + target_name
ds_name = "dis_" + source_name

# build target and source generators
g_target = build_generator(source_shape,
                           target_shape,
                           kernel_size=kernel_size,
                           name=gt_name)
g_source = build_generator(target_shape,
                           source_shape,
                           kernel_size=kernel_size,
                           name=gs_name)
print('---- TARGET GENERATOR ----')
g_target.summary()
print('---- SOURCE GENERATOR ----')
g_source.summary()


# build target and source discriminators
d_target = build_discriminator(target_shape,
                               patchgan=patchgan,
```

```
                                        kernel_size=kernel_size,
                                        name=dt_name)
        d_source = build_discriminator(source_shape,
                                        patchgan=patchgan,
                                        kernel_size=kernel_size,
                                        name=ds_name)
        print('---- TARGET DISCRIMINATOR ----')
        d_target.summary()
        print('---- SOURCE DISCRIMINATOR ----')
        d_source.summary()

        optimizer = RMSprop(lr=lr, decay=decay)
        d_target.compile(loss='mse',
                         optimizer=optimizer,
                         metrics=['accuracy'])
        d_source.compile(loss='mse',
                         optimizer=optimizer,
                         metrics=['accuracy'])
        # freeze the discriminator weights in the adversarial model
        d_target.trainable = False
        d_source.trainable = False

        # build the computational graph for the adversarial model
        # forward cycle network and target discriminator
        source_input = Input(shape=source_shape)
        fake_target = g_target(source_input)
        preal_target = d_target(fake_target)
        reco_source = g_source(fake_target)

        # backward cycle network and source discriminator
        target_input = Input(shape=target_shape)
        fake_source = g_source(target_input)
        preal_source = d_source(fake_source)
        reco_target = g_target(fake_source)

        # if we use identity loss, add 2 extra loss terms
        # and outputs
        if identity:
            iden_source = g_source(source_input)
            iden_target = g_target(target_input)
            loss = ['mse', 'mse', 'mae', 'mae', 'mae', 'mae']
            loss_weights = [1., 1., 10., 10., 0.5, 0.5]
            inputs = [source_input, target_input]
            outputs = [preal_source,
```

```
                    preal_target,
                    reco_source,
                    reco_target,
                    iden_source,
                    iden_target]
    else:
        loss = ['mse', 'mse', 'mae', 'mae']
        loss_weights = [1., 1., 10., 10.]
        inputs = [source_input, target_input]
        outputs = [preal_source,
                    preal_target,
                    reco_source,
                    reco_target]

    # build adversarial model
    adv = Model(inputs, outputs, name='adversarial')
    optimizer = RMSprop(lr=lr*0.5, decay=decay*0.5)
    adv.compile(loss=loss,
                loss_weights=loss_weights,
                optimizer=optimizer,
                metrics=['accuracy'])
    print('---- ADVERSARIAL NETWORK ----')
    adv.summary()

    return g_source, g_target, d_source, d_target, adv
```

We follow the training procedure in *Algorithm 7.1.1* from the previous section. Following listing shows the CycleGAN training. The minor difference between this training from the vanilla GAN is there are two discriminators to be optimized. However, there is only one adversarial model to optimize. For every 2000 steps, the generators save the predicted source and target images. We'll use a batch size of 32. We also tried a batch size of one, but the output quality is almost the same and takes a longer amount of time to train (43 ms/image for a batch size of one vs. 3.6 ms/image for a batch size of 32 on an NVIDIA GTX 1060).

Listing 7.1.5, `cyclegan-7.1.1.py` shows us the CycleGAN training routine in Keras:

```
def train_cyclegan(models, data, params, test_params, test_generator):
    """ Trains the CycleGAN.

    1) Train the target discriminator
    2) Train the source discriminator
    3) Train the forward and backward cyles of adversarial networks

    Arguments:
```

```
        models (Models): Source/Target Discriminator/Generator,
                    Adversarial Model
        data (tuple): source and target training data
        params (tuple): network parameters
        test_params (tuple): test parameters
        test_generator (function): used for generating predicted target
                    and source images
        """

        # the models
        g_source, g_target, d_source, d_target, adv = models
        # network parameters
        batch_size, train_steps, patch, model_name = params
        # train dataset
        source_data, target_data, test_source_data, test_target_data =
data

        titles, dirs = test_params

        # the generator image is saved every 2000 steps
        save_interval = 2000
        target_size = target_data.shape[0]
        source_size = source_data.shape[0]

        # whether to use patchgan or not
        if patch > 1:
            d_patch = (patch, patch, 1)
            valid = np.ones((batch_size,) + d_patch)
            fake = np.zeros((batch_size,) + d_patch)
        else:
            valid = np.ones([batch_size, 1])
            fake = np.zeros([batch_size, 1])

        valid_fake = np.concatenate((valid, fake))
        start_time = datetime.datetime.now()

        for step in range(train_steps):
            # sample a batch of real target data
            rand_indexes = np.random.randint(0, target_size,
size=batch_size)
            real_target = target_data[rand_indexes]

            # sample a batch of real source data
            rand_indexes = np.random.randint(0, source_size,
```

```
size=batch_size)
        real_source = source_data[rand_indexes]
        # generate a batch of fake target data fr real source data
        fake_target = g_target.predict(real_source)

        # combine real and fake into one batch
        x = np.concatenate((real_target, fake_target))
        # train the target discriminator using fake/real data
        metrics = d_target.train_on_batch(x, valid_fake)
        log = "%d: [d_target loss: %f]" % (step, metrics[0])

        # generate a batch of fake source data fr real target data
        fake_source = g_source.predict(real_target)
        x = np.concatenate((real_source, fake_source))
        # train the source discriminator using fake/real data
        metrics = d_source.train_on_batch(x, valid_fake)
        log = "%s [d_source loss: %f]" % (log, metrics[0])

        # train the adversarial network using forward and backward
        # cycles. the generated fake source and target data attempts
        # to trick the discriminators
        x = [real_source, real_target]
        y = [valid, valid, real_source, real_target]
        metrics = adv.train_on_batch(x, y)
        elapsed_time = datetime.datetime.now() - start_time
        fmt = "%s [adv loss: %f] [time: %s]"
        log = fmt % (log, metrics[0], elapsed_time)
        print(log)
        if (step + 1) % save_interval == 0:
            if (step + 1) == train_steps:
                show = True
            else:
                show = False

            test_generator((g_source, g_target),
                           (test_source_data, test_target_data),
                           step=step+1,
                           titles=titles,
                           dirs=dirs,
                           show=show)

    # save the models after training the generators
    g_source.save(model_name + "-g_source.h5")
    g_target.save(model_name + "-g_target.h5")
```

Finally, before we can use the CycleGAN to build and train functions, we have to perform some data preparation. The modules `cifar10_utils.py` and `other_utils.py` load the CIFAR10 train and test data. Please refer to the source code for details of these two files. After loading, the train and test images are converted to grayscale to generate the source data and test source data.

Following listing shows how the CycleGAN is used to build and train a generator network (`g_target`) for colorization of grayscale images. Since CycleGAN is symmetric, we also build and train a second generator network (`g_source`) that converts from color to grayscale. Two CycleGAN colorization networks were trained. The first use discriminators with a scalar output similar to vanilla GAN. The second uses a 2 × 2 PatchGAN.

Listing 7.1.6, `cyclegan-7.1.1.py` shows us the CycleGAN for colorization problem:

```python
def graycifar10_cross_colorcifar10(g_models=None):
    """Build and train a CycleGAN that can do grayscale <--> color
       cifar10 images
    """

    model_name = 'cyclegan_cifar10'
    batch_size = 32
    train_steps = 100000
    patchgan = True
    kernel_size = 3
    postfix = ('%dp' % kernel_size) if patchgan else
('%d' % kernel_size)

    data, shapes = cifar10_utils.load_data()
    source_data, _, test_source_data, test_target_data = data
    titles = ('CIFAR10 predicted source images.',
              'CIFAR10 predicted target images.',
              'CIFAR10 reconstructed source images.',
              'CIFAR10 reconstructed target images.')
    dirs = ('cifar10_source-%s' % postfix, 'cifar10_target-%s'
% postfix)

    # generate predicted target(color) and source(gray) images
    if g_models is not None:
        g_source, g_target = g_models
        other_utils.test_generator((g_source, g_target),
                                   (test_source_data, test_target_
data),
                                   step=0,
                                   titles=titles,
```

```
                                    dirs=dirs,
                                    show=True)
        return


    # build the cyclegan for cifar10 colorization
    models = build_cyclegan(shapes,
                            "gray-%s" % postfix,
                            "color-%s" % postfix,
                            kernel_size=kernel_size,
                            patchgan=patchgan)
    # patch size is divided by 2^n since we downscaled the input
    # in the discriminator by 2^n (ie. we use strides=2 n times)
    patch = int(source_data.shape[1] / 2**4) if patchgan else 1
    params = (batch_size, train_steps, patch, model_name)
    test_params = (titles, dirs)
    # train the cyclegan
    train_cyclegan(models,
                    data,
                    params,
                    test_params,
                    other_utils.test_generator)
```

Generator outputs of CycleGAN

Figure 7.1.9 shows the colorization results of CycleGAN. The source images are from the test dataset. For comparison, we show the ground truth and the colorization results using a plain autoencoder described in *Chapter 3, Autoencoders*. Generally, all colorized images are perceptually acceptable. Overall, it seems that each colorization technique has both its own pros and cons. All colorization methods are not consistent with the right color of the sky and vehicle.

For example, the sky in the background of the plane (3rd row, 2nd column) is white. The autoencoder got it right, but the CycleGAN thinks it is light brown or blue. For the 6th row, 6th column, the boat on the dark sea had an overcast sky but was colorized with blue sky and blue sea by autoencoder and blue sea and white sky by CycleGAN without PatchGAN. Both predictions make sense in the real world. Meanwhile, the prediction of CycleGAN with PatchGAN is similar to the ground truth. On 2nd to the last row and 2nd column, no method was able to predict the red color of the car. On animals, both flavors of CycleGAN have closer colors to the ground truth.

Since CycleGAN is symmetric, it also predicts the grayscale image given a color image. *Figure 7.1.10* shows the color to grayscale conversion performed by the two CycleGAN variations. The target images are from the test dataset. Except for minor differences in the grayscale shades of some images, the predictions are generally accurate:

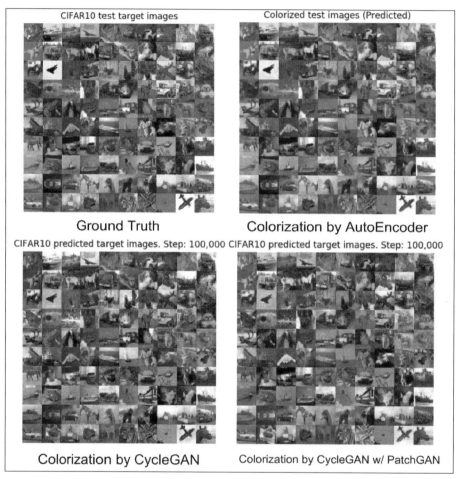

Figure 7.1.9: Colorization using different techniques. Shown are the ground truth, colorization using autoencoder (Chapter 3, Autoencoders,), colorization using CycleGAN with a vanilla GAN discriminator, and colorization using CycleGAN with PatchGAN discriminator. Best viewed in color. Original color photo can be found on the book GitHub repository, https://github.com/PacktPublishing/Advanced-Deep-Learning-with-Keras/blob/master/chapter7-cross-domain-gan/README.md.

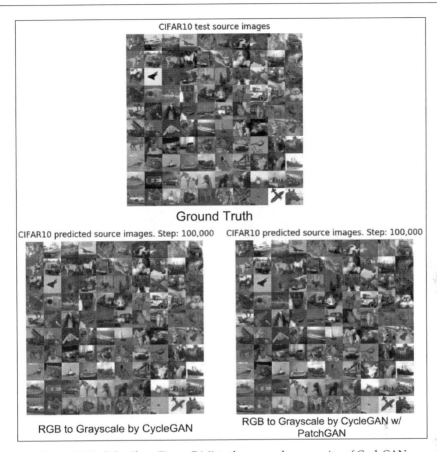

Figure 7.1.10: Color (from Figure 7.1.9) to the grayscale conversion of CycleGAN

The reader can run the image translation by using the pretrained models for CycleGAN with PatchGAN:

```
python3 cyclegan-7.1.1.py --cifar10_g_source=cyclegan_cifar10-g_source.h5
--cifar10_g_target=cyclegan_cifar10-g_target.h5
```

CycleGAN on MNIST and SVHN datasets

We're now going to tackle a more challenging problem. Suppose we use MNIST digits in grayscale as our source data, and we want to borrow style from SVHN [1] which is our target data. The sample data in each domain are shown in *Figure 7.1.11*. We can reuse all the build and train functions for CycleGAN that were discussed in the previous section to perform style transfer. The only difference is we have to add routines for loading MNIST and SVHN data. SVHN dataset can be found at http://ufldl.stanford.edu/housenumbers/.

We introduce module `mnist_svhn_utils.py` to help us with this task. *Listing 7.1.7* shows the initialization and training of the CycleGAN for cross-domain transfer. The CycleGAN structure is same as in the previous section except that we use a kernel size of 5 since the two domains are drastically different:

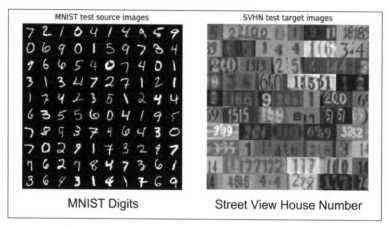

Figure 7.1.11: Two different domains with data that are not aligned. Original color photo can be found on the book GitHub repository, https://github.com/PacktPublishing/Advanced-Deep-Learning-with-Keras/blob/master/chapter7-cross-domain-gan/README.md.

Remember to install `keras-contrib` before using instance normalization:

`$ sudo pip3 install git+https://www.github.com/keras-team/keras-contrib.git`

Listing 7.1.7, `cyclegan-7.1.1.py` shows us the CycleGAN for cross-domain style transfer between MNIST and SVHN:

```
def mnist_cross_svhn(g_models=None):
    """Build and train a CycleGAN that can do mnist <--> svhn
    """

    model_name = 'cyclegan_mnist_svhn'
    batch_size = 32
    train_steps = 100000
    patchgan = True
    kernel_size = 5
    postfix = ('%dp' % kernel_size) if patchgan else ('%d' % kernel_
size)

    data, shapes = mnist_svhn_utils.load_data()
    source_data, _, test_source_data, test_target_data = data
```

```
        titles = ('MNIST predicted source images.',
                  'SVHN predicted target images.',
                  'MNIST reconstructed source images.',
                  'SVHN reconstructed target images.')
        dirs = ('mnist_source-%s' % postfix, 'svhn_target-%s' % postfix)

        # genrate predicted target(svhn) and source(mnist) images
        if g_models is not None:
            g_source, g_target = g_models
            other_utils.test_generator((g_source, g_target),
                                       (test_source_data, test_
target_data),
                                       step=0,
                                       titles=titles,
                                       dirs=dirs,
                                       show=True)

        return

    # build the cyclegan for mnist cross svhn
    models = build_cyclegan(shapes,
                            "mnist-%s" % postfix,
                            "svhn-%s" % postfix,
                            kernel_size=kernel_size,
                            patchgan=patchgan)
    # patch size is divided by 2^n since we downscaled the input
    # in the discriminator by 2^n (ie. we use strides=2 n times)
    patch = int(source_data.shape[1] / 2**4) if patchgan else 1
    params = (batch_size, train_steps, patch, model_name)
    test_params = (titles, dirs)
    # train the cyclegan
    train_cyclegan(models,
                   data,
                   params,
                   test_params,
                   other_utils.test_generator)
```

The results for transferring the MNIST from the test dataset to SVHN are shown in *Figure 7.1.12*. The generated images have the style of SVHN, but the digits are not completely transferred. For example, on the 4th row, digits 3, 1, and 3 are stylized by CycleGAN. However, on the 3rd row, digits 9, 6, and 6 are stylized as 0, 6, 01, 0, 65, and 68 for the CycleGAN without and with PatchGAN respectively.

The results of the backward cycle are shown in *Figure 7.1.13*. In this case, the target images are from the SVHN test dataset. The generated images have the style of MNIST, but the digits are not correctly translated. For example, on the 1st row, the digits 5, 2, and 210 are stylized as 7, 7, 8, 3, 3, and 1 for the CycleGAN without and with PatchGAN respectively.

In the case of PatchGAN, the output 1 is understandable given the predicted MNIST digit is constrained to one digit. There are somehow correct predictions like in 2nd row last 3 columns of the SVHN digits, 6, 3, and 4 are converted to 6, 3, and 6 by CycleGAN without PatchGAN. However, the outputs on both flavors of CycleGAN are consistently single digit and recognizable.

The problem exhibited in the conversion from MNIST to SVHN where a digit in the source domain is translated to another digit in the target domain is called **label flipping** [8]. Although the predictions of CycleGAN are cycle-consistent, they are not necessarily semantic consistent. The meaning of digits is lost during translation. To address this problem, Hoffman [8] introduced an improved CycleGAN called **CyCADA (Cycle-Consistent Adversarial Domain Adaptation)**. The difference is the additional semantic loss term ensures that the prediction is not only cycle-consistent but also sematic-consistent:

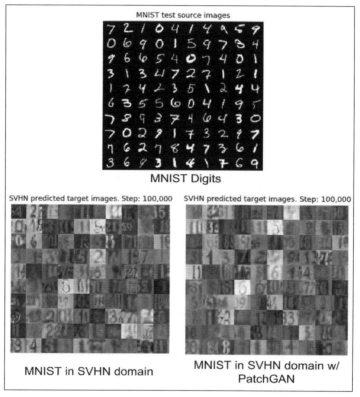

Figure 7.1.12: Style transfer of test data from the MNIST domain to SVHN. Original color photo can be found on the book GitHub repository, https://github.com/PacktPublishing/Advanced-Deep-Learning-with-Keras/blob/master/chapter7-cross-domain-gan/README.md.

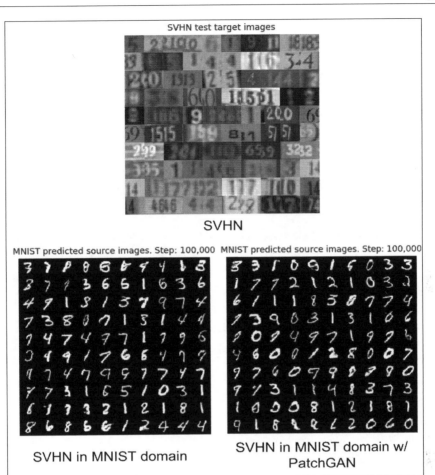

Figure 7.1.13: Style transfer of test data from SVHN domain to MNIST. Original color photo can be found on the book GitHub repository, https://github.com/PacktPublishing/Advanced-Deep-Learning-with-Keras/blob/master/chapter7-cross-domain-gan/README.md.

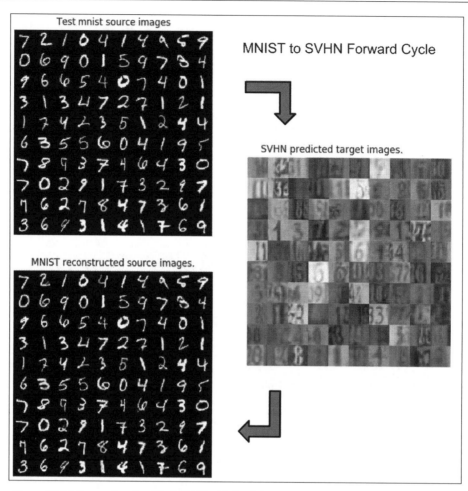

Figure 7.1.14: Forward cycle of CycleGAN with PatchGAN on MNIST (source) to SVHN (target).
The reconstructed source is similar to the original source. Original color photo can be found on the book
GitHub repository, https://github.com/PacktPublishing/Advanced-Deep-Learning-with-Keras/blob/
master/chapter7-cross-domain-gan/README.md.

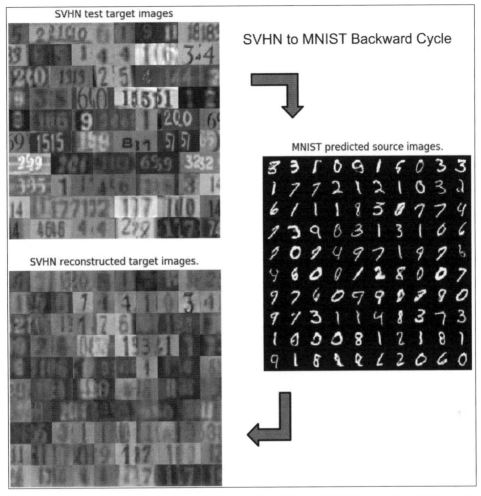

Figure 7.1.15: The backward cycle of CycleGAN with PatchGAN on MNIST (source) to SVHN (target). The reconstructed target is not entirely similar to the original target. Original color photo can be found on the book GitHub repository, https://github.com/PacktPublishing/Advanced-Deep-Learning-with-Keras/blob/master/chapter7-cross-domain-gan/README.md.

In *Figure 7.1.3*, CycleGAN is described to be cycle consistent. In other words, given source x, CycleGAN reconstructs the source in the forward cycle as x'. In addition, given target y, CycleGAN reconstructs the target in the backward cycle as y'.

Figure 7.1.14 shows CycleGAN reconstructing MNIST digits in the forward cycle. The reconstructed MNIST digits are almost identical with the source MNIST digits. *Figure 7.1.15* shows the CycleGAN reconstructing SVHN digits in the backward cycle. Many target images are reconstructed. Some digits are clearly the same such as the 2nd row last 2 columns (3 and 4). While some are the same but blurred like 1st row first 2 columns (5 and 2). Some digits are transformed to another digit although the style remains like 2nd row first two columns (from 33 and 6 to 1 and an unrecognizable digit).

On a personal note, I encourage you to run the image translation by using the pretrained models of CycleGAN with PatchGAN:

```
python3 cyclegan-7.1.1.py --mnist_svhn_g_source=cyclegan_mnist_svhn-g_
source.h5 --mnist_svhn_g_target=cyclegan_mnist_svhn-g_target.h5
```

Conclusion

In this chapter, we've discussed CycleGAN as an algorithm that can be used for image translation. In CycleGAN, the source and target data are not necessarily aligned. We demonstrated two examples, *grayscale* ↔ *color,* and *MNIST* ↔ *SVHN.* Though there are many other possible image translations that CycleGAN can perform.

In the next chapter, we'll embark on another type of generative model, **Variational AutoEncoders (VAEs)**. VAEs have a similar objective of learning how to generate new images (data). They focus on learning the latent vector modeled as a Gaussian distribution. We'll demonstrate other similarities in the problem being addressed by GANs in the form of conditional VAEs and the disentangling of latent representations in VAEs.

References

1. Yuval Netzer and others. *Reading Digits in Natural Images with Unsupervised Feature Learning*. NIPS workshop on deep learning and unsupervised feature learning. Vol. 2011. No. 2. 2011(`https://www-cs.stanford.edu/~twangcat/papers/nips2011_housenumbers.pdf`).

2. Zhu, Jun-Yan and others. *Unpaired Image-to-Image Translation Using Cycle-Consistent Adversarial Networks*. 2017 IEEE International Conference on Computer Vision (ICCV). IEEE, 2017 (`http://openaccess.thecvf.com/content_ICCV_2017/papers/Zhu_Unpaired_Image-To-Image_Translation_ICCV_2017_paper.pdf`).

3. Phillip Isola and others. *Image-to-Image Translation with Conditional Adversarial Networks*. 2017 IEEE Conference on Computer Vision and Pattern Recognition (CVPR). IEEE, 2017 (`http://openaccess.thecvf.com/content_cvpr_2017/papers/Isola_Image-To-Image_Translation_With_CVPR_2017_paper.pdf`).

4. Mehdi Mirza and Simon Osindero. *Conditional Generative Adversarial Nets*. arXiv preprint arXiv:1411.1784, 2014(`https://arxiv.org/pdf/1411.1784.pdf`).

5. Xudong Mao and others. *Least Squares Generative Adversarial Networks*. 2017 IEEE International Conference on Computer Vision (ICCV). IEEE, 2017(`http://openaccess.thecvf.com/content_ICCV_2017/papers/Mao_Least_Squares_Generative_ICCV_2017_paper.pdf`).

6. Chuan Li and Michael Wand. *Precomputed Real-Time Texture Synthesis with Markovian Generative Adversarial Networks*. European Conference on Computer Vision. Springer, Cham, 2016(`https://arxiv.org/pdf/1604.04382.pdf`).

7. Olaf Ronneberger, Philipp Fischer, and Thomas Brox. *U-Net: Convolutional Networks for Biomedical Image Segmentation*. International Conference on Medical image computing and computer-assisted intervention. Springer, Cham, 2015(`https://arxiv.org/pdf/1505.04597.pdf`).

8. Judy Hoffman and others. *CyCADA: Cycle-Consistent Adversarial Domain Adaptation*. arXiv preprint arXiv:1711.03213, 2017(`https://arxiv.org/pdf/1711.03213.pdf`).

8
Variational Autoencoders (VAEs)

Similar to **Generative Adversarial Networks (GANs)** that we've discussed in the previous chapters, **Variational Autoencoders (VAEs)** [1] belong to the family of generative models. The generator of VAE is able to produce meaningful outputs while navigating its continuous latent space. The possible attributes of the decoder outputs are explored through the latent vector.

In GANs, the focus is on how to arrive at a model that approximates the input distribution. VAEs attempt to model the input distribution from a decodable continuous latent space. This is one of the possible underlying reasons why GANs are able to generate more realistic signals when compared to VAEs. For example, in image generation, GANs are able to produce more realistic looking images while VAEs in comparison generate images that are less sharp.

Within VAEs, the focus is on the variational inference of latent codes. Therefore, VAEs provide a suitable framework for both learning and efficient Bayesian inference with latent variables. For example, VAEs with disentangled representations enable latent code reuse for transfer learning.

In terms of structure, VAEs bear a resemblance to an autoencoder. They are also made up of an encoder (also known as recognition or inference model) and a decoder (also known as a generative model). Both VAEs and autoencoders attempt to reconstruct the input data while learning the latent vector. However, unlike autoencoders, the latent space of VAEs is continuous, and the decoder itself is used as a generative model.

In the same line of discussions on GANs that we discussed in the previous chapters, the VAEs decoder can also be conditioned. For example, in the MNIST dataset, we're able to specify the digit to produce given a one-hot vector. This class of conditional VAE is called CVAE [2]. VAE latent vectors can also be disentangled by including a regularizing hyperparameter on the loss function. This is called β-VAE [5]. For example, within MNIST, we're able to isolate the latent vector that determines the thickness or tilt angle of each digit.

The goal of this chapter is to present:

- The principles of VAEs
- An understanding of the reparameterization trick that facilitates the use of stochastic gradient descent on VAE optimization
- The principles of conditional VAE (CVAE) and β-VAE
- An understanding of how to implement VAEs within the Keras library

Principles of VAEs

In a generative model, we're often interested in approximating the true distribution of our inputs using neural networks:

$$x \sim P_\theta(x) \qquad \text{(Equation 8.1.1)}$$

In the preceding equation, θ are the parameters determined during training. For example, in the context of the celebrity faces dataset, this is equivalent to finding a distribution that can draw faces. Similarly, in the MNIST dataset, this distribution can generate recognizable handwritten digits.

In machine learning, to perform a certain level of inference, we're interested in finding $P_\theta(x,z)$, a joint distribution between inputs, x, and the latent variables, z. The latent variables are not part of the dataset but instead encode certain properties observable from inputs. In the context of celebrity faces, these might be facial expressions, hairstyles, hair color, gender, and so on. In the MNIST dataset, the latent variables may represent the digit and writing styles.

$P_\theta(x,z)$ is practically a distribution of input data points and their attributes. $P_\theta(x)$ can be computed from the marginal distribution:

$$P_\theta(x) = \int P_\theta(x,z)dz \qquad \text{(Equation 8.1.2)}$$

In other words, considering all of the possible attributes, we end up with the distribution that describes the inputs. In celebrity faces, if we consider all the facial expressions, hairstyles, hair colors, gender, the distribution describing the celebrity faces is recovered. In the MNIST dataset, if we consider all of the possible digits, writing styles, and so on, we end up with the distribution of handwritten digits.

The problem is *Equation 8.1.2* is *intractable*. the equation does not have an analytic form or an efficient estimator. It cannot be differentiated with respect to its parameters. Therefore, optimization by a neural network is not feasible.

Using Bayes theorem, we can find an alternative expression for *Equation 8.1.2*:

$$P_\theta(x) = \int P_\theta(x \mid z) P(z) \, dz \qquad \text{(Equation 8.1.3)}$$

$P(z)$ is a prior distribution over z. It is not conditioned on any observations. If z is discrete and $P_\theta(x \mid z)$ is a Gaussian distribution, then $P_\theta(x)$ is a mixture of Gaussians. If z is continuous, $P_\theta(x)$ is an infinite mixture of Gaussians.

In practice, if we try to build a neural network to approximate $P_\theta(x \mid z)$ without a suitable loss function, it will just ignore z and arrive at a trivial solution $P_\theta(x \mid z) = P_\theta(x)$. Therefore, *Equation 8.1.3* does not provide us with a good estimate of $P_\theta(x)$.

Alternatively, *Equation 8.1.2* can also be expressed as:

$$P_\theta(x) = \int P_\theta(z \mid x) P(x) \, dz \qquad \text{(Equation 8.1.4)}$$

However, $P_\theta(z \mid x)$ is also intractable. The goal of a VAEs is to find a tractable distribution that closely estimates $P_\theta(z \mid x)$.

Variational inference

In order to make $P_\theta(z \mid x)$ tractable, VAE introduces the variational inference model (an encoder):

$$Q_\phi(z \mid x) \approx P_\theta(z \mid x) \qquad \text{(Equation 8.1.5)}$$

$Q_\phi(z \mid x)$ provides a good estimate of $P_\theta(z \mid x)$. It is both parametric and tractable. $Q_\phi(z \mid x)$ can be approximated by deep neural networks by optimizing the parameters ϕ.

Typically, $Q_\phi(z|x)$ is chosen to be a multivariate Gaussian:

$$Q_\theta(z|x) = \mathcal{N}\left(z; \mu(x), diag\left(\sigma(x)\right)\right) \qquad \text{(Equation 8.1.6)}$$

Both mean, $\mu(x)$, and standard deviation, $\sigma(x)$, are computed by the encoder neural network using the input data points. The diagonal matrix implies that the elements of z are independent.

Core equation

The inference model $Q_\phi(z|x)$ generates latent vector z from input x. $Q_\phi(z|x)$ is like the encoder in an autoencoder model. On the other hand, $P_\theta(x|z)$ reconstructs the input from the latent code z. $P_\theta(x|z)$ acts like the decoder in an autoencoder model. To estimate $P_\theta(x)$, we must identify its relationship with $Q_\phi(z|x)$ and $P_\theta(x|z)$.

If $Q_\phi(z|x)$ is an estimate of $P_\theta(z|x)$, the **Kullback-Leibler (KL)** divergence determines the distance between these two conditional densities:

$$D_{KL}\left(Q_\phi(z|x)\|P_\theta(z|x)\right) = \mathbb{E}_{z\sim Q}\left[\log Q_\phi(z|x) - \log P_\theta(z|x)\right] \qquad \text{(Equation 8.1.7)}$$

Using Bayes theorem,

$$P_\theta(z|x) = \frac{P_\theta(x|z) P_\theta(z)}{P_\theta(x)} \qquad \text{(Equation 8.1.8)}$$

in *Equation 8.1.7*,

$$D_{KL}\left(Q_\phi(z|x)\|P_\theta(z|x)\right) = \mathbb{E}_{z\sim Q}\left[\log Q_\phi(z|x) - \log P_\theta(x|z) - \log P_\theta(z)\right] + \log P_\theta(x) \qquad \text{(Equation 8.1.9)}$$

$\log P_\theta(x)$ can be taken out the expectation since it is not dependent on $z\sim Q$. Rearranging the preceding equation and recognizing that $\mathbb{E}_{z\sim Q}\left[\log Q_\phi(z|x) - \log P_\theta(z)\right] = D_{KL}\left(Q_\phi(z|x)\|P_\theta(z)\right)$:

$$\log P_\theta(x) - D_{KL}\left(Q_\phi(z|x)\|P_\theta(z|x)\right) = \mathbb{E}_{z\sim Q}\left[\log P_\theta(x|z)\right] - D_{KL}\left(Q_\phi(z|x)\|P_\theta(z)\right) \qquad \text{(Equation 8.1.10)}$$

Equation 8.1.10 is the core of VAEs. The left-hand side is the term $P_\theta(x)$ that we are maximizing less the error due to the distance of $Q_\phi(z|x)$ from the true $P_\theta(z|x)$. We can recall that the logarithm does not change the location of maxima (or minima). Given an inference model that provides a good estimate of $P_\theta(z|x)$, $D_{KL}(Q_\phi(z|x) \| P_\theta(z|x))$ is approximately zero. The first term, $P_\theta(x|z)$, on the right-hand side resembles a decoder that takes samples from the inference model to reconstruct the input. The second term is another distance. This time it's between $Q_\phi(z|x)$ and the prior $P_\theta(z)$.

The left side of *Equation 8.1.10* is also known as the **variational lower bound** or **evidence lower bound (ELBO)**. Since the KL is always positive, ELBO is the lower bound of $\log P_\theta(x)$. Maximizing ELBO by optimizing the parameters ϕ and θ of the neural network means that:

- $D_{KL}(Q_\phi(z|x) \| P_\theta(z|x)) \to 0$ or the inference model is getting better in encoding the attributes of x in z

- $\log P_\theta(x|z)$ on the right-hand side of *Equation 8.1.10* is maximized or the decoder model is getting better in reconstructing x from the latent vector z

Optimization

The right-hand side of *Equation 8.1.10* has two important bits of information about the loss function of VAEs. The decoder term $\mathbb{E}_{z \sim Q}[\log P_\theta(x|z)]$ means that the generator takes z samples from the output of the inference model to reconstruct the inputs. Maximizing this term implies that we minimize the **Reconstruction Loss**, $\mathcal{L}_R$. If the image (data) distribution is assumed to be Gaussian, then MSE can be used. If every pixel (data) is considered a Bernoulli distribution, then the loss function is a binary cross entropy.

The second term, $-D_{KL}(Q_\phi(z|x) \| P_\theta(z))$, turns out to be straightforward to evaluate. From *Equation 8.1.6*, Q_ϕ is a Gaussian distribution. Typically, $P_\theta(z) = P(z) = \mathcal{N}(0, I)$ is also a Gaussian with zero mean and standard deviation equal to 1.0. The KL term simplifies to:

$$-D_{KL}(Q_\phi(z|x) \| P_\theta(z)) = \frac{1}{2} \sum_{j=1}^{J} \left(1 + \log(\sigma_j)^2 - (\mu_j)^2 - (\sigma_j)^2\right) \qquad \text{(Equation 8.1.11)}$$

Where J is the dimensionality of z. Both μ_j and σ_j are functions of x computed through the inference model. To maximize $-D_{KL}$, $\sigma_j \to 1$ and $\mu_j \to 0$. The choice of $P(z) = \mathcal{N}(0, I)$ stems from the property of isotropic unit Gaussian which can be morphed to an arbitrary distribution given a suitable function. From *Equation 8.1.11*, the **KL Loss** $\mathcal{L}_{KL}$ is simply D_{KL}.

For example, it was previously [6] demonstrated that an isotropic Gaussian could be morphed into a ring-shaped distribution using the function $g(z) = \frac{z}{10} + \frac{z}{\|z\|}$.

Readers can further explore the theory as presented in Luc Devroye's, *Sample-Based Non-Uniform Random Variate Generation* [7].

In summary, the VAE loss function is defined as:

$$\mathcal{L}_{VAE} = \mathcal{L}_R + \mathcal{L}_{KL} \qquad \text{(Equation 8.1.12)}$$

Reparameterization trick

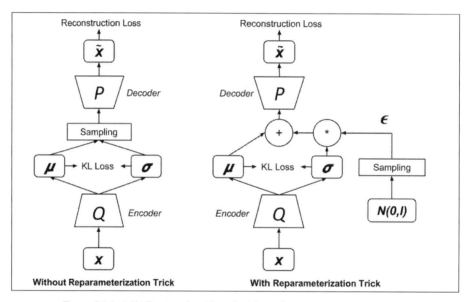

Figure 8.1.1: A VAE network with and without the reparameterization trick

On the left side of the preceding figure shows the VAE network. The encoder takes the input x, and estimates the mean, μ, and the standard deviation, σ, of the multivariate Gaussian distribution of the latent vector z. The decoder takes samples from the latent vector z to reconstruct the input as $\tilde{x}$. This seems straightforward until the gradient updates happen during backpropagation.

Backpropagation gradients will not pass through the stochastic **Sampling** block. While it's fine to have stochastic inputs for neural networks, it's not possible for the gradients to go through a stochastic layer.

The solution to this problem is to push out the **Sampling** process as the input as shown on the right side of *Figure 8.1.1*. Then, compute the sample as:

$$Sample = \mu + \in \sigma \qquad \text{(Equation 8.1.13)}$$

If $\in$ and σ are expressed in vector format, then $\in \sigma$ is element-wise multiplication. Using *Equation 8.1.13*, it appears as if sampling is directly coming from the latent space as originally intended. This technique is better known as the **Reparameterization Trick**.

With *Sampling* now happening at the input, the VAE network can be trained using the familiar optimization algorithms such as SGD, Adam, or RMSProp.

Decoder testing

After training the VAE network, the inference model including the addition and multiplication operator can be discarded. To generate new meaningful outputs, samples are taken from the Gaussian distribution used in generating $\in$. Following figure shows us how to test the decoder:

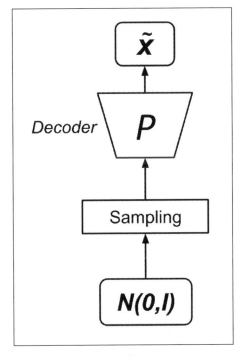

Figure 8.1.2: Decoder testing setup

VAEs in Keras

The structure of VAE bears a resemblance to a typical autoencoder. The difference is mainly on the sampling of the Gaussian random variables in the reparameterization trick. *Listing 8.1.1* shows the encoder, decoder, and VAE which are implemented using MLP. This code has also been contributed to the official Keras GitHub repository. For simplicity of the discussion, the latent vector z is 2-dim.

The encoder is just a two-layer MLP with the second layer generating the mean and log variance. The use of log variance is for simplicity in the computation of *KL Loss* and reparameterization trick. The third output of the encoder is the sampling of z using the reparameterization trick. We should note that in the sampling function, $_e 0.5 \log \sigma^2 = \sqrt{\sigma^2} = \sigma$ since $\sigma > 0$ given that it's the standard deviation of the Gaussian distribution.

The decoder is also a two-layer MLP that takes samples of z to approximate the inputs. Both the encoder and the decoder use an intermediate dimension with a size of 512.

The VAE network is simply both the encoder and the decoder joined together. *Figures 8.1.3* to *8.1.5* show the encoder, decoder, and VAE models. The loss function is the sum of both the *Reconstruction Loss* and *KL Loss*. The VAE network has good results on the default Adam optimizer. The total number of parameters of the VAE network is 807,700.

The Keras code for VAE MLP has pretrained weights. To test, we need to run:

```
$ python3 vae-mlp-mnist-8.1.1.py --weights=vae_mlp_mnist.h5
```

The complete code can be found on the following link: `https://github.com/PacktPublishing/Advanced-Deep-Learning-with-Keras`.

Listing 8.1.1, `vae-mlp-mnist-8.1.1.py` shows us the Keras code of VAE using MLP layers:

```python
# reparameterization trick
# instead of sampling from Q(z|X), sample eps = N(0,I)
# z = z_mean + sqrt(var)*eps
def sampling(args):
    z_mean, z_log_var = args

    batch = K.shape(z_mean)[0]
    # K is the keras backend
    dim = K.int_shape(z_mean)[1]
    # by default, random_normal has mean=0 and std=1.0
```

```
    epsilon = K.random_normal(shape=(batch, dim))
    return z_mean + K.exp(0.5 * z_log_var) * epsilon

# MNIST dataset
(x_train, y_train), (x_test, y_test) = mnist.load_data()

image_size = x_train.shape[1]
original_dim = image_size * image_size
x_train = np.reshape(x_train, [-1, original_dim])
x_test = np.reshape(x_test, [-1, original_dim])
x_train = x_train.astype('float32') / 255
x_test = x_test.astype('float32') / 255

# network parameters
input_shape = (original_dim, )
intermediate_dim = 512
batch_size = 128
latent_dim = 2
epochs = 50

# VAE model = encoder + decoder
# build encoder model
inputs = Input(shape=input_shape, name='encoder_input')
x = Dense(intermediate_dim, activation='relu')(inputs)

z_mean = Dense(latent_dim, name='z_mean')(x)
z_log_var = Dense(latent_dim, name='z_log_var')(x)


# use reparameterization trick to push the sampling out as input
z = Lambda(sampling, output_shape=(latent_dim,), name='z')([z_mean,
z_log_var])
# instantiate encoder model
encoder = Model(inputs, [z_mean, z_log_var, z], name='encoder')
encoder.summary()
plot_model(encoder, to_file='vae_mlp_encoder.png', show_shapes=True)

# build decoder model
latent_inputs = Input(shape=(latent_dim,), name='z_sampling')
x = Dense(intermediate_dim, activation='relu')(latent_inputs)
outputs = Dense(original_dim, activation='sigmoid')(x)

# instantiate decoder model
decoder = Model(latent_inputs, outputs, name='decoder')
decoder.summary()
plot_model(decoder, to_file='vae_mlp_decoder.png', show_shapes=True)

# instantiate vae model
```

```python
outputs = decoder(encoder(inputs)[2])
vae = Model(inputs, outputs, name='vae_mlp')


if __name__ == '__main__':
    parser = argparse.ArgumentParser()
    help_ = "Load h5 model trained weights"
    parser.add_argument("-w", "--weights", help=help_)
    help_ = "Use mse loss instead of binary cross entropy (default)"
    parser.add_argument("-m",
                        "--mse",
                        help=help_, action='store_true')
    args = parser.parse_args()
    models = (encoder, decoder)
    data = (x_test, y_test)
    # VAE loss = mse_loss or xent_loss + kl_loss
    if args.mse:
        reconstruction_loss = mse(inputs, outputs)
    else:
        reconstruction_loss = binary_crossentropy(inputs,
                                                  outputs)
    reconstruction_loss *= original_dim
    kl_loss = 1 + z_log_var - K.square(z_mean) - K.exp(z_log_var)
    kl_loss = K.sum(kl_loss, axis=-1)
    kl_loss *= -0.5
    vae_loss = K.mean(reconstruction_loss + kl_loss)
    vae.add_loss(vae_loss)
    vae.compile(optimizer='adam')
    vae.summary()
    plot_model(vae,
               to_file='vae_mlp.png',
               show_shapes=True)

    if args.weights:
        vae = vae.load_weights(args.weights)
    else:
        # train the autoencoder
        vae.fit(x_train,
                epochs=epochs,
                batch_size=batch_size,
                validation_data=(x_test, None))
        vae.save_weights('vae_mlp_mnist.h5')

    plot_results(models,
                 data,
                 batch_size=batch_size,
                 model_name="vae_mlp")
```

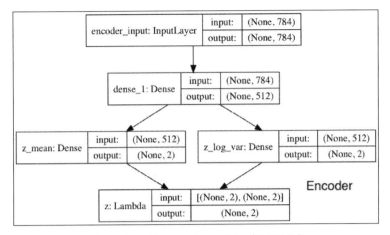

Figure 8.1.3: The encoder models of VAE MLP

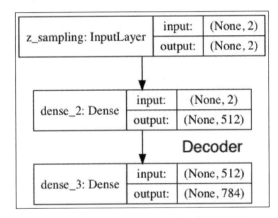

Figure 8.1.4: The decoder model of VAE MLP

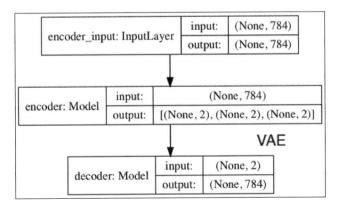

Figure 8.1.5: The VAE model using MLP

Figure 8.1.6 shows the continuous space of latent vector after 50 epochs using `plot_results()`. For simplicity, the function is not shown here but can be found in the rest of the code of `vae-mlp-mnist-8.1.1.py`. The function plots two images, the test dataset labels (*Figure 8.1.6*) and the sample generated digits (*Figure 8.1.7*) both as a function of *z*. Both plots demonstrate how the latent vector determines the attributes of the generated digits.

Navigating through the continuous space will always result in an output that bears a resemblance to the MNIST digits. For example, the region of digit 9 is close to the region of digit 7. Moving from 9 near the center to the left morphs the digit to 7. Moving from the center downward changes the generated digits from 3 to 8 and finally to 1. The morphing of the digits is more evident in *Figure 8.1.7* which is another way of interpreting *Figure 8.1.6*.

In *Figure 8.1.7*, instead of colorbar, the generator output is displayed. The distribution of digits in the latent space is shown. It can be observed that all the digits are represented. Since the distribution is dense near the center, the change is rapid in the middle and slow as the mean values get bigger. We need to remember that *Figure 8.1.7* is a reflection of *Figure 8.1.6*. For example, digit 0 is on the top right quadrant on both figures while digit 1 is on the lower right quadrant.

There are some unrecognizable digits in *Figure 8.1.7*, especially on the top left quadrant. From the following figure, it can be observed that this region is mostly empty and far away from the center:

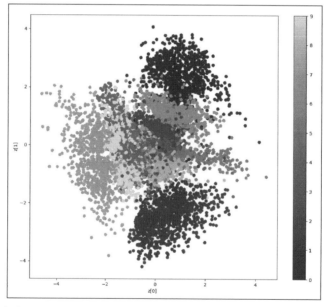

Figure 8.1.6: The latent vector mean values for the test dataset (VAE MLP). The colorbar shows the corresponding MNIST digit as a function of z. Color images can be found on the book GitHub repository: https://github.com/PacktPublishing/Advanced-Deep-Learning-with-Keras/tree/master/chapter8-vae.

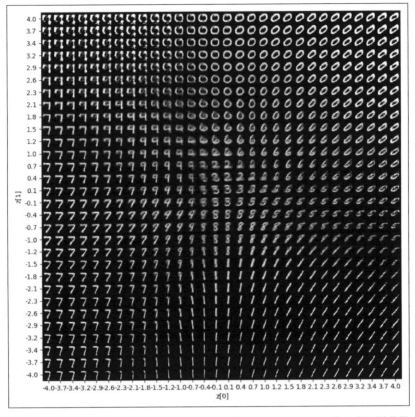

Figure 8.1.7: The digits generated as a function of latent vector mean values (VAE MLP).
For ease of interpretation, the range of values for the mean is similar to Figure 8.1.6.

Using CNNs for VAEs

In the original paper *Auto-encoding Variational Bayes* [1], the VAE network was
implemented using MLP, which is similar to what we covered in the previous
section. In this section, we'll demonstrate that using a CNN will result in a significant
improvement in the quality of the digits produced and a remarkable reduction in the
number of parameters down to 134,165.

Listing 8.1.3 shows the encoder, decoder, and VAE network. This code was also
contributed to the official Keras GitHub repository. For conciseness, some lines
of code that are similar to the MLP are no longer shown. The encoder is made of two
layers of CNNs and two layers of MLPs in order to generate the latent code. The
encoder output structure is similar to the MLP implementation seen in the previous
section. The decoder is made up of one layer of MLP and three layers of transposed
CNNs. *Figures 8.1.8* to *8.1.10* show the encoder, decoder, and VAE models. For VAE
CNN, RMSprop will result in a lower loss than Adam.

The Keras code for VAE CNN has pre-trained weights. To test, we need to run:

```
$ python3 vae-cnn-mnist-8.1.2.py --weights=vae_cnn_mnist.h5
```

Listing 8.1.3, `vae-cnn-mnist-8.1.2.py` shows us the Keras code of VAE using CNN layers:

```
# network parameters
input_shape = (image_size, image_size, 1)
batch_size = 128
kernel_size = 3
filters = 16
latent_dim = 2
epochs = 30


# VAE mode = encoder + decoder
# build encoder model
inputs = Input(shape=input_shape, name='encoder_input')
x = inputs

for i in range(2):
    filters *= 2
    x = Conv2D(filters=filters,
               kernel_size=kernel_size,
               activation='relu',
               strides=2,
               padding='same')(x)


# shape info needed to build decoder model
shape = K.int_shape(x)

# generate latent vector Q(z|X)
x = Flatten()(x)
x = Dense(16, activation='relu')(x)
z_mean = Dense(latent_dim, name='z_mean')(x)
z_log_var = Dense(latent_dim, name='z_log_var')(x)

# use reparameterization trick to push the sampling out as input
# note that "output_shape" isn't necessary with the TensorFlow backend
z = Lambda(sampling, output_shape=(latent_dim,), name='z')([z_mean,
z_log_var])
```

```
# instantiate encoder model
encoder = Model(inputs, [z_mean, z_log_var, z], name='encoder')
encoder.summary()
plot_model(encoder, to_file='vae_cnn_encoder.png', show_shapes=True)

# build decoder model
latent_inputs = Input(shape=(latent_dim,), name='z_sampling')
x = Dense(shape[1]*shape[2]*shape[3], activation='relu')(latent_
inputs)
x = Reshape((shape[1], shape[2], shape[3]))(x)


for i in range(2):
    x = Conv2DTranspose(filters=filters,
                        kernel_size=kernel_size,
                        activation='relu',
                        strides=2,
                        padding='same')(x)

    filters //= 2

outputs = Conv2DTranspose(filters=1,
                    kernel_size=kernel_size,
                    activation='sigmoid',
                    padding='same',
                    name='decoder_output')(x)

# instantiate decoder model
decoder = Model(latent_inputs, outputs, name='decoder')
decoder.summary()
plot_model(decoder, to_file='vae_cnn_decoder.png', show_shapes=True)

# instantiate vae model
outputs = decoder(encoder(inputs)[2])
vae = Model(inputs, outputs, name='vae')
```

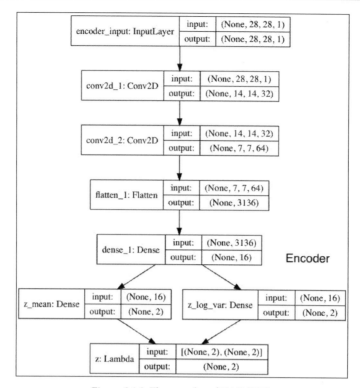

Figure 8.1.8: The encoder of VAE CNN

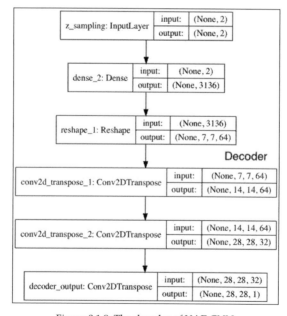

Figure 8.1.9: The decoder of VAE CNN

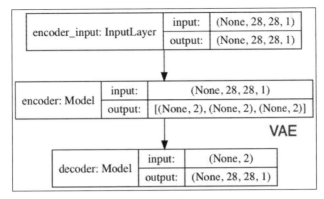

Figure 8.1.10: The VAE model using CNNs

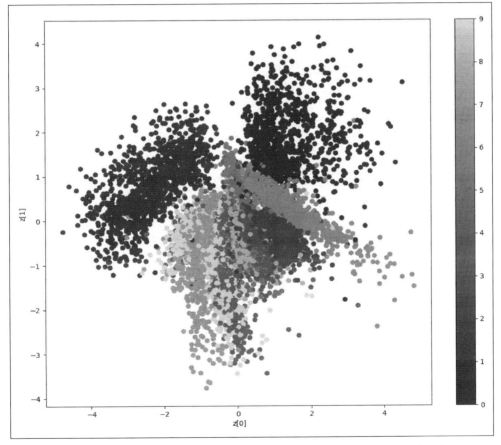

Figure 8.1.11: The latent vector mean values for the test dataset (VAE CNN). The colorbar shows the corresponding MNIST digit as a function of z. Color images can be found on the book GitHub repository: https://github.com/PacktPublishing/Advanced-Deep-Learning-with-Keras/tree/master/chapter8-vae.

Preceding figure shows the continuous latent space of a VAE using the CNN implementation after 30 epochs. The region where each digit is assigned may be different, but the distribution is roughly the same. Following figure shows us the output of the generative model. Qualitatively, there are fewer digits that are ambiguous as compared to *Figure 8.1.7* with the MLP implementation:

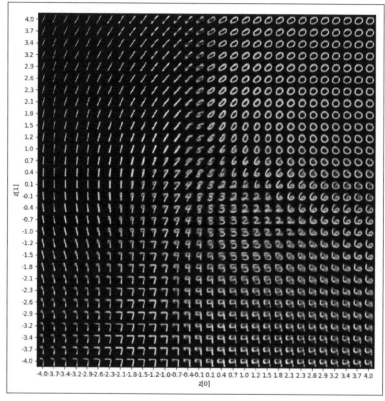

Figure 8.1.12: The digits generated as a function of latent vector mean values (VAE CNN). For ease of interpretation, the range of values for the mean is similar to Figure 8.1.11.

Conditional VAE (CVAE)

Conditional VAE [2] is similar to the idea of CGAN. In the context of the MNIST dataset, if the latent space is randomly sampled, VAE has no control over which digit will be generated. CVAE is able to address this problem by including a condition (a one-hot label) of the digit to produce. The condition is imposed on both the encoder and decoder inputs.

Formally, the core equation of VAE in *Equation 8.1.10* is modified to include the condition c:

$$\log P_\theta(x\,|\,c) - D_{KL}\left(Q_\phi(z\,|\,x,c)\,\|\,P_\theta(z\,|\,x,c)\right) = \mathbb{E}_{z\sim Q}\left[\log P_\theta(x\,|\,z,c)\right] - D_{KL}\left(Q_\phi(z\,|\,x,c)\,\|\,P_\theta(z\,|\,c)\right) \quad \text{(Equation 8.2.1)}$$

Similar to VAEs, *Equation 8.2.1* means that if we want to maximize the output conditioned on c, $P_\theta(x\,|\,c)$, then the two loss terms must be minimized:

- Reconstruction loss of the decoder given both the latent vector and the condition.

- KL loss between the encoder given both the latent vector and the condition and the prior distribution given the condition. Similar to a VAE, we typically choose $P_\theta(z\,|\,c) = P(z\,|\,c) = \mathcal{N}(0,I)$.

Listing 8.2.1, `cvae-cnn-mnist-8.2.1.py` shows us the Keras code of CVAE using CNN layers. In the code that is highlighted showcases the changes made to support CVAE:

```
# compute the number of labels
num_labels = len(np.unique(y_train))

# network parameters
input_shape = (image_size, image_size, 1)
label_shape = (num_labels, )
batch_size = 128
kernel_size = 3
filters = 16
latent_dim = 2
epochs = 30

# VAE model = encoder + decoder
# build encoder model
inputs = Input(shape=input_shape, name='encoder_input')
y_labels = Input(shape=label_shape, name='class_labels')
x = Dense(image_size * image_size)(y_labels)
x = Reshape((image_size, image_size, 1))(x)
x = keras.layers.concatenate([inputs, x])
for i in range(2):
    filters *= 2
    x = Conv2D(filters=filters,
               kernel_size=kernel_size,
               activation='relu',
               strides=2,
               padding='same')(x)


# shape info needed to build decoder model
```

```
    shape = K.int_shape(x)

    # generate latent vector Q(z|X)
    x = Flatten()(x)
    x = Dense(16, activation='relu')(x)
    z_mean = Dense(latent_dim, name='z_mean')(x)
    z_log_var = Dense(latent_dim, name='z_log_var')(x)

    # use reparameterization trick to push the sampling out as input
    # note that "output_shape" isn't necessary with the TensorFlow backend
    z = Lambda(sampling, output_shape=(latent_dim,), name='z')([z_mean,
    z_log_var])

    # instantiate encoder model
    encoder = Model([inputs, y_labels], [z_mean, z_log_var, z],
    name='encoder')
    encoder.summary()
    plot_model(encoder, to_file='cvae_cnn_encoder.png', show_shapes=True)

    # build decoder model
    latent_inputs = Input(shape=(latent_dim,), name='z_sampling')
    x = keras.layers.concatenate([latent_inputs, y_labels])
    x = Dense(shape[1]*shape[2]*shape[3], activation='relu')(x)
    x = Reshape((shape[1], shape[2], shape[3]))(x)
    for i in range(2):
        x = Conv2DTranspose(filters=filters,
                            kernel_size=kernel_size,
                            activation='relu',
                            strides=2,
                            padding='same')(x)
        filters //= 2


    outputs = Conv2DTranspose(filters=1,
                            kernel_size=kernel_size,
                            activation='sigmoid',
                            padding='same',
                            name='decoder_output')(x)

    # instantiate decoder model
    decoder = Model([latent_inputs, y_labels], outputs, name='decoder')
    decoder.summary()
    plot_model(decoder, to_file='cvae_cnn_decoder.png', show_shapes=True)
```

```
# instantiate vae model
outputs = decoder([encoder([inputs, y_labels])[2], y_labels])
cvae = Model([inputs, y_labels], outputs, name='cvae')
if __name__ == '__main__':
    parser = argparse.ArgumentParser()
    help_ = "Load h5 model trained weights"
    parser.add_argument("-w", "--weights", help=help_)
    help_ = "Use mse loss instead of binary cross entropy (default)"
    parser.add_argument("-m", "--mse", help=help_, action='store_
true')
    help_ = "Specify a specific digit to generate"
    parser.add_argument("-d", "--digit", type=int, help=help_)
    help_ = "Beta in Beta-CVAE. Beta > 1. Default is 1.0 (CVAE)"
    parser.add_argument("-b", "--beta", type=float, help=help_)
    args = parser.parse_args()
    models = (encoder, decoder)
    data = (x_test, y_test)

    if args.beta is None or args.beta < 1.0:
        beta = 1.0
        print("CVAE")
        model_name = "cvae_cnn_mnist"
    else:
        beta = args.beta
        print("Beta-CVAE with beta=", beta)
        model_name = "beta-cvae_cnn_mnist"

    # VAE loss = mse_loss or xent_loss + kl_loss
    if args.mse:
        reconstruction_loss = mse(K.flatten(inputs),
K.flatten(outputs))
    else:
        reconstruction_loss = binary_crossentropy(K.flatten(inputs),
                                                   K.flatten(outputs))

    reconstruction_loss *= image_size * image_size
    kl_loss = 1 + z_log_var - K.square(z_mean) - K.exp(z_log_var)
    kl_loss = K.sum(kl_loss, axis=-1)
    kl_loss *= -0.5 * beta
    cvae_loss = K.mean(reconstruction_loss + kl_loss)
    cvae.add_loss(cvae_loss)
    cvae.compile(optimizer='rmsprop')
```

```
cvae.summary()
plot_model(cvae, to_file='cvae_cnn.png', show_shapes=True)

if args.weights:
    cvae = cvae.load_weights(args.weights)
else:
    # train the autoencoder
    cvae.fit([x_train, to_categorical(y_train)],
             epochs=epochs,
             batch_size=batch_size,
             validation_data=([x_test, to_categorical(y_test)],
None))
    cvae.save_weights(model_name + '.h5')

if args.digit in range(0, num_labels):
    digit = np.array([args.digit])
else:
    digit = np.random.randint(0, num_labels, 1)

print("CVAE for digit %d" % digit)
y_label = np.eye(num_labels)[digit]
plot_results(models,
             data,
             y_label=y_label,
             batch_size=batch_size,
             model_name=model_name)
```

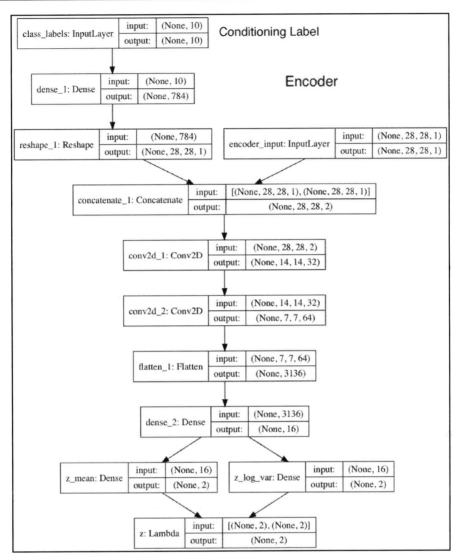

Figure 8.2.1: The encoder in CVAE CNN. The input is now made of the concatenation of the VAE input and a conditioning label.

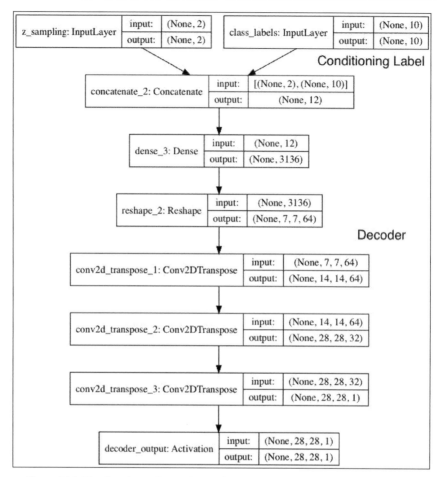

Figure 8.2.2: The decoder in CVAE CNN. The input is now made of the concatenation of the z sampling and a conditioning label.

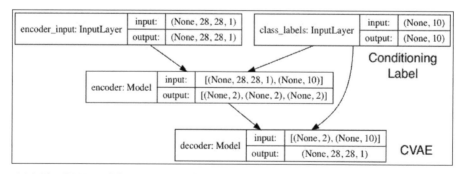

Figure 8.2.3: The CVAE model using a CNN. The input is now made of a VAE input and a conditioning label.

Implementing CVAE requires a few modifications in the code of the VAE. For the CVAE, the VAE CNN implementation is used. *Listing 8.2.1* highlights the changes made to the original code of VAE for MNIST digits. The encoder input is now a concatenation of original input image and its one-hot label. The decoder input is now a combination of the latent space sampling and the one-hot label of the image it should generate. The total number of parameters is 174, 437. The codes related to β -VAE will be discussed in the next section of this chapter.

There are no changes in the loss function. However, the one-hot labels are supplied during training, testing, and plotting of results. *Figures 8.2.1* to *8.2.3* show us the encoder, decoder, and CVAE models. The role of the conditioning label in the form of a one-hot vector is indicated.

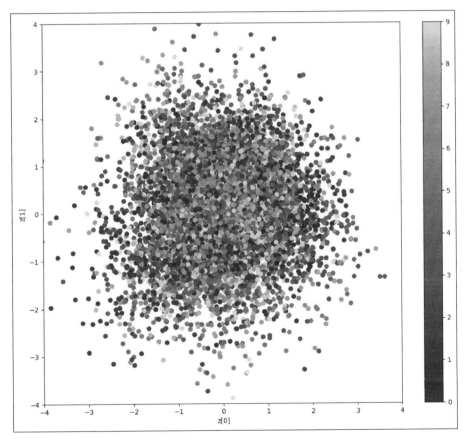

Figure 8.2.4: The latent vector mean values for the test dataset (CVAE CNN). The colorbar shows the corresponding MNIST digit as a function of z. Color images can be found on the book GitHub repository: https://github.com/PacktPublishing/Advanced-Deep-Learning-with-Keras/tree/master/chapter8-vae.

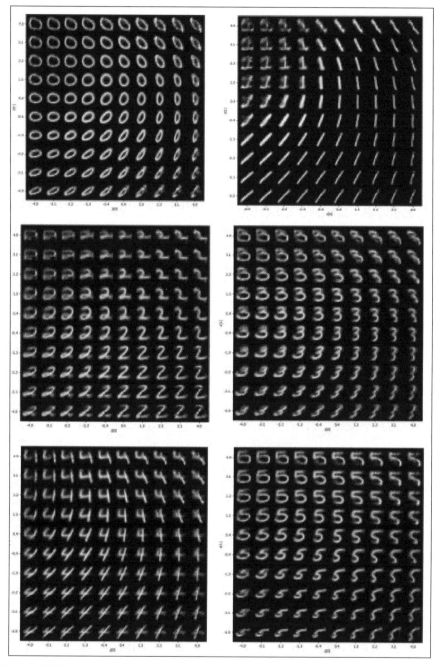

Figure 8.2.5: Digits 0 to 5 generated as a function of latent vector mean values and one-hot label (CVAE CNN). For ease of interpretation, the range of values for the mean is similar to Figure 8.2.4.

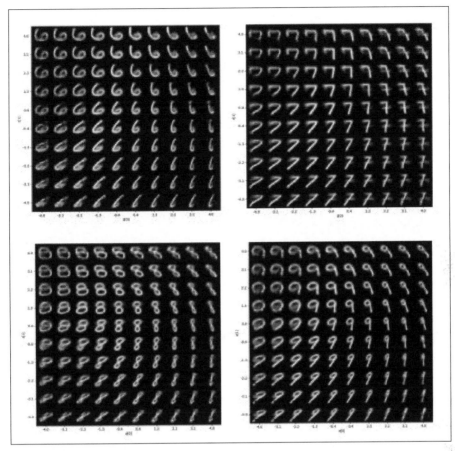

Figure 8.2.6: Digits 6 to 9 generated as a function of latent vector mean values and one-hot label (CVAE CNN). For ease of interpretation, the range of values for the mean is similar to Figure 8.2.4.

In *Figure 8.2.4*, the distribution of mean per label is shown after 30 epochs. Unlike in both *Figures 8.1.6* and *8.1.11* in the previous sections, each label is not concentrated on a region but distributed across the plot. This is expected since every sampling in the latent space should generate a specific digit. Navigating the latent space changes the attribute of that specific digit. For example, if the digit specified is 0, then navigating the latent space will still produce a 0 but the attributes, such as tilt angle, thickness, and other writing style aspects will be different.

These changes are more clearly shown in *Figures 8.2.5* and *8.2.6*. For ease of comparison, the range of values for the latent vector is the same as in *Figure 8.2.4*. Using the pretrained weights, a digit (for example, 0) can be generated by executing the command:

```
$ python3 cvae-cnn-mnist-8.2.1.py --weights=cvae_cnn_mnist.h5 --digit=0
```

In *Figures 8.2.5* and *8.2.6*, it can be noticed that the width and roundness (if applicable) of each digit change as $z[0]$ is traced from left to right. Meanwhile, the tilt angle and roundness (if applicable) of each digit change as $z[1]$ is navigated from top to bottom. As we move away from the center of the distribution, the image of the digit starts to degrade. This is expected since the latent space is a circle.

Other noticeable variations in attributes may be digit specific. For example, the horizontal stroke (arm) for digit 1 becomes visible in the upper left quadrant. The horizontal stroke (crossbar) for digit 7 can be seen in the right quadrants only.

β -VAE: VAE with disentangled latent representations

In *Chapter 6, Disentangled Representation GANs*, the concept, and importance of the disentangled representation of latent codes were discussed. We can recall that a disentangled representation is where single latent units are sensitive to changes in single generative factors while being relatively invariant to changes in other factors [3]. Varying a latent code results to changes in one attribute of the generated output while the rest of the properties remain the same.

In the same chapter, InfoGANs [4] demonstrated to us that in the MNIST dataset, it is possible to control which digit to generate and the tilt and thickness of writing style. Observing the results in the previous section, it can be noticed that the VAE is intrinsically disentangling the latent vector dimensions to a certain extent. For example, looking at digit 8 in *Figure 8.2.6*, navigating $z[1]$ from top to bottom decreases the width and roundness while rotating the digit clockwise. Increasing $z[0]$ from left to right also decreases the width and roundness while rotating the digit counterclockwise. In other words, $z[1]$ controls the clockwise rotation, $z[0]$ affects the counterclockwise rotation, and both of them alter the width and roundness.

In this section, we'll demonstrate that a simple modification in the loss function of VAE forces the latent codes to disentangle further. The modification is the positive constant weight, $\beta > 1$, acting as a regularizer on the KL loss:

$$\mathcal{L}_{\beta-VAE} = \mathcal{L}_{R} + \beta\mathcal{L}_{KL} \qquad \text{(Equation 8.3.1)}$$

This variation of VAE is called β-VAE [5]. The implicit effect of β is a tighter standard deviation. In other words, β forces the latent codes in the posterior distribution, $Q_{\phi}(z\,|\,x)$ to be independent.

It is straightforward to implement β-VAE. For example, for the CVAE from the previous, the required modification is the extra **beta** factor in `kl_loss`.

```
kl_loss = 1 + z_log_var - K.square(z_mean) - K.exp(z_log_var)
kl_loss = K.sum(kl_loss, axis=-1)
kl_loss *= -0.5 * beta
```

CVAE is a special case of β-VAE with $\beta=1$. Everything else is the same. However, determining the value of β requires some trial and error. There must be a careful balance between the reconstruction error and regularization for latent codes independence. The disentanglement is maximized at around $\beta=7$. When the value of $\beta>8$, the β-VAE is forced to learn one disentangled representation only while muting the other latent dimension:

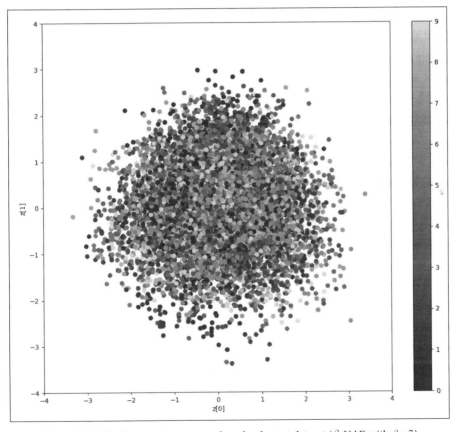

Figure 8.3.1: The latent vector mean values for the test dataset (β-VAE with $\beta=7$)
Color images can be found on the book GitHub repository: https://github.com/PacktPublishing/Advanced-Deep-Learning-with-Keras/tree/master/chapter8-vae.

Figures 8.3.1 and *8.3.2* show the latent vector means for β-VAE with $\beta = 7$ and $\beta = 10$. With $\beta = 7$, the distribution has a smaller standard deviation when compared to CVAE. With $\beta = 10$, there is only the latent code that is learned. The distribution is practically shrunk to 1D with the first latent code $z[0]$ ignored by the encoder and decoder:

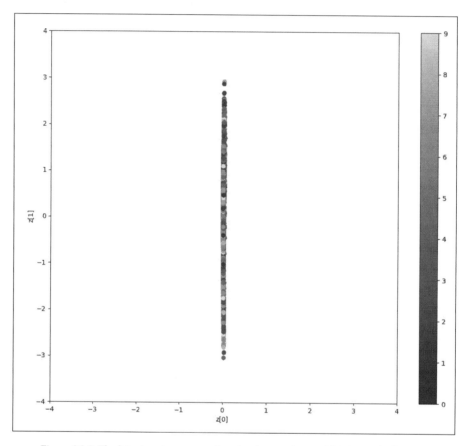

Figure 8.3.2: The latent vector mean values for the test dataset (β-VAE with $\beta = 10$)
Color images can be found on the book GitHub repository: https://github.com/PacktPublishing/Advanced-Deep-Learning-with-Keras/tree/master/chapter8-vae.

These observations are reflected in *Figure 8.3.3*. β-VAE with $\beta = 7$ has two latent codes that are practically independent. $z[0]$ determines the tilt of the writing style. Meanwhile, $z[1]$ specifies the width and roundness (if applicable) of the digits. For β-VAE with $\beta = 10$, $z[0]$ is muted. Increasing $z[0]$ does not alter the digit in a significant way. $z[1]$ determines the tilt angle and width of the writing style.

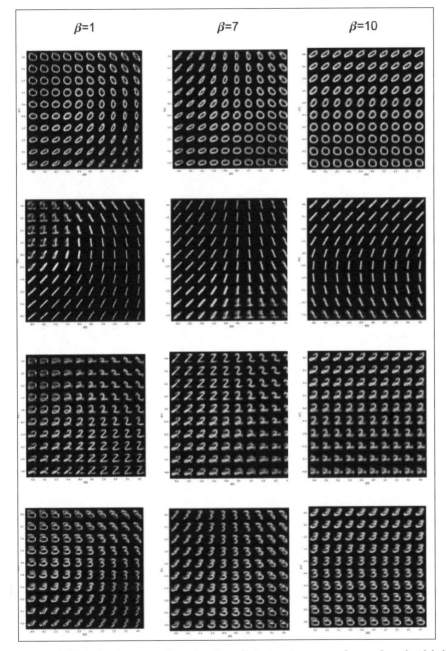

Figure 8.3.3: Digits 0 to 3 generated as a function of latent vector mean values and one-hot label (β-VAE $\beta = 1, 7 \, and \, 10$). For ease of interpretation, the range of values for the mean is similar to Figure 8.3.1.

The Keras code for β-VAE has pre-trained weights. To test β-VAE with $\beta = 7$ generating digit 0, we need to run:

```
$ python3 cvae-cnn-mnist-8.2.1.py --beta=7 --weights=beta-cvae_cnn_mnist.
h5 --digit=0
```

Conclusion

In this chapter, we've covered the principles of variational autoencoders (VAEs). As we learned in the principles of VAEs, they bear a resemblance to GANs in the aspect of both attempt to create synthetic outputs from latent space. However, it can be noticed that the VAE networks are much simpler and easier to train compared to GANs. It's becoming clear how conditional VAE and β-VAE are similar in concept to conditional GAN and disentangled representation GAN respectively.

VAEs have an intrinsic mechanism to disentangle the latent vectors. Therefore, building a β-VAE is straightforward. We should note however that interpretable and disentangled codes are important in building intelligent agents.

In the next chapter, we're going to focus on Reinforcement learning. Without any prior data, an agent learns by interacting with its world. We'll discuss how the agent can be rewarded for correct actions and punished for the wrong ones.

References

1. Diederik P. Kingma and Max Welling. *Auto-encoding Variational Bayes*. arXiv preprint arXiv:1312.6114, 2013(https://arxiv.org/pdf/1312.6114.pdf).

2. Kihyuk Sohn, Honglak Lee, and Xinchen Yan. *Learning Structured Output Representation Using Deep Conditional Generative Models*. Advances in Neural Information Processing Systems, 2015(http://papers.nips.cc/paper/5775-learning-structured-output-representation-using-deep-conditional-generative-models.pdf).

3. Yoshua Bengio, Aaron Courville, and Pascal Vincent. *Representation Learning: A Review and New Perspectives*. IEEE transactions on Pattern Analysis and Machine Intelligence 35.8, 2013: 1798-1828(https://arxiv.org/pdf/1206.5538.pdf).

4. Xi Chen and others. *Infogan: Interpretable Representation Learning by Information Maximizing Generative Adversarial Nets*. Advances in Neural Information Processing Systems, 2016(http://papers.nips.cc/paper/6399-infogan-interpretable-representation-learning-by-information-maximizing-generative-adversarial-nets.pdf).

5. I. Higgins, L. Matthey, A. Pal, C. Burgess, X. Glorot, M. Botvinick, S. Mohamed, and A. Lerchner. *β-VAE: Learning basic visual concepts with a constrained variational framework*. ICLR, 2017(`https://openreview.net/pdf?id=Sy2fzU9gl`).

6. Carl Doersch. *Tutorial on variational autoencoders*. arXiv preprint arXiv:1606.05908, 2016 (`https://arxiv.org/pdf/1606.05908.pdf`).

7. Luc Devroye. *Sample-Based Non-Uniform Random Variate Generation*. Proceedings of the 18th conference on Winter simulation. ACM, 1986(`http://www.eirene.de/Devroye.pdf`).

9

Deep Reinforcement Learning

Reinforcement Learning (**RL**) is a framework that is used by an agent for decision-making. The agent is not necessarily a software entity such as in video games. Instead, it could be embodied in hardware such as a robot or an autonomous car. An embodied agent is probably the best way to fully appreciate and utilize reinforcement learning since a physical entity interacts with the real-world and receives responses.

The agent is situated within an **environment**. The environment has a **state** that can be partially or fully observable. The agent has a set of **actions** that it can use to interact with its environment. The result of an action transitions the environment to a new state. A corresponding scalar **reward** is received after executing an action. The goal of the agent is to maximize the accumulated future reward by learning a **policy** that will decide which action to take given a state.

Reinforcement learning has a strong similarity to human psychology. Humans learn by experiencing the world. Wrong actions result in a certain form of penalty and should be avoided in the future, whilst actions which are right are rewarded and should be encouraged. This strong similarity to human psychology has convinced many researchers to believe that reinforcement learning can lead us towards **Artificial Intelligence** (**AI**).

Reinforcement learning has been around for decades. However, beyond simple world models, RL has struggled to scale. This is where **Deep Learning** (**DL**), came into play. It solved this scalability problem which opened up the era of **Deep Reinforcement Learning** (**DRL**), which is what we are going to focus on in this chapter. One of the notable examples in DRL is the work of DeepMind on agents that were able to surpass the best human performance on different video games. In this chapter, we discuss both RL and DRL.

In summary, the goal of this chapter is to present:

- The principles of RL
- The Reinforcement Learning technique, Q-Learning
- Advanced topics including **Deep Q-Network (DQN)**, and **Double Q-Learning (DDQN)**
- Instructions on how to implement RL on Python and DRL within Keras

Principles of reinforcement learning (RL)

Figure 9.1.1 shows the perception-action-learning loop that is used to describe RL. The environment is a soda can sitting on the floor. The agent is a mobile robot whose goal is to pick up the soda can. It observes the environment around it and tracks the location of the soda can through an onboard camera. The observation is summarized in a form of state which the robot will use to decide which action to take. The actions it takes may pertain to low-level control such as the rotation angle/speed of each wheel, rotation angle/speed of each joint of the arm, and whether the gripper is open or close.

Alternatively, the actions may be high-level control moves such as moving the robot forward/backward, steering with a certain angle, and grab/release. Any action that moves the gripper away from the soda receives a negative reward. Any action that closes the gap between the gripper location and the soda receives a positive reward. When the robot arm successfully picks up the soda can, it receives a big positive reward. The goal of RL is to learn the optimal policy that helps the robot to decide which action to take given a state to maximize the accumulated discounted reward:

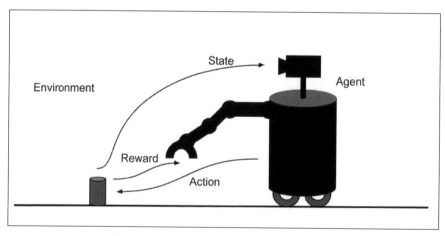

Figure 9.1.1: The perception-action-learning loop in reinforcement learning

Formally, the RL problem can be described as a **Markov Decision Process (MDP)**. For simplicity, we'll assume a *deterministic* environment where a certain action in a given state will consistently result in a known next state and reward. In a later section of this chapter, we'll look at how to consider stochasticity. At timestep t:

- The environment is in a state s_t from the state space $\mathcal{S}$ which may be discrete or continuous. The starting state is s_0 while the terminal state is s_T.

- The agent takes action a_t from the action space $\mathcal{A}$ by obeying the policy, $\pi(a_t \mid s_t)$. $\mathcal{A}$ may be discrete or continuous.

- The environment transitions to a new state s_{t+1} using the state transition dynamics $T(s_{t+1} \mid s_t, a_t)$. The next state is only dependent on the current state and action. T is not known to the agent.

- The agent receives a scalar reward using a reward function, $r_{t+1} = R(s_t, a_t)$ with $r : \mathcal{A} \times \mathcal{S} \to \mathbb{R}$. The reward is only dependent on the current state and action. R is not known to the agent.

- Future rewards are discounted by γ^k where $\gamma \in [0,1]$ and k is the future timestep.

- *Horizon, H,* is the number of timesteps, T, needed to complete one episode from s_0 to s_T.

The environment may be fully or partially observable. The latter is also known as a **partially observable MDP** or **POMDP**. Most of the time, it's unrealistic to fully observe the environment. To improve the observability, past observations are also taken into consideration with the current observation. The state comprises the sufficient observations about the environment for the policy to decide on which action to take. In *Figure 9.1.1*, this could be the 3D position of the soda can with respect to the robot gripper as estimated by the robot camera.

Every time the environment transitions to a new state, the agent receives a scalar reward, r_{t+1}. In *Figure 9.1.1*, the reward could be +1 whenever the robot gets closer to the soda can, -1 whenever it gets farther, and +100 when it closes the gripper and successfully picks up the soda can. The goal of the agent is to learn an optimal policy π^* that maximizes the *return* from all states:

$$\pi^* = argmax_\pi R_t \qquad \text{(Equation 9.1.1)}$$

The return is defined as the discounted cumulative reward, $R_t = \sum_{k=0}^{T} \gamma^k r_{t+k}$. It can be observed from *Equation 9.1.1* that future rewards have lower weights when compared to the immediate rewards since generally $\gamma^k < 1.0$ where $\gamma \in [0,1]$. At the extremes, when $\gamma = 0$, only the immediate reward matters. When $\gamma = 1$ future rewards have the same weight as the immediate reward.

Return can be interpreted as a measure of the *value* of a given state by following an arbitrary policy, π:

$$V^{\pi}(s_t) = R_t = \sum_{k=0}^{T} \gamma^k r_{t+k} \qquad \text{(Equation 9.1.2)}$$

To put the RL problem in another way, the goal of the agent is to learn the optimal policy that maximizes V^{π} for all states s:

$$\pi^* = argmax_{\pi} V^{\pi}(s) \qquad \text{(Equation 9.1.3)}$$

The value function of the optimal policy is simply V^*. In *Figure 9.1.1*, the optimal policy is the one that generates the shortest sequence of actions that brings the robot closer and closer to the soda can until it has been fetched. The closer the state is to the goal state, the higher its value.

The sequence of events leading to the goal (or terminal state) can be modeled as the *trajectory* or *rollout* of the policy:

$$Trajectory = (s_0 a_0 r_1 s_1, s_1 a_1 r_2 s_2, \ldots, s_{T-1} a_{T-1} r_T s_T) \qquad \text{(Equation 9.1.4)}$$

If the MDP is *episodic* when the agent reaches the terminal state, s_T, the state is reset to s_0. If T is finite, we have a finite *horizon*. Otherwise, the horizon is infinite. In *Figure 9.1.1*, if the MDP is episodic, after collecting the soda can, the robot may look for another soda can to pick up and the RL problem repeats.

The Q value

An important question is that if the RL problem is to find π^*, how does the agent learn by interacting with the environment? *Equation 9.1.3* does not explicitly indicate the action to try and the succeeding state to compute the return. In RL, we find that it's easier to learn π^* by using the Q value:

$$\pi^* = argmax_a Q(s,a) \qquad \text{(Equation 9.2.1)}$$

Where:

$$V^*(s) = \max_a Q(s,a) \qquad \text{(Equation 9.2.2)}$$

In other words, instead of finding the policy that maximizes the value for all states, *Equation 9.2.1* looks for the action that maximizes the quality (Q) value for all states. After finding the Q value function, V^* and hence π^* are determined by *Equation 9.2.2* and *9.1.3* respectively.

If for every action, the reward and the next state can be observed, we can formulate the following iterative or trial and error algorithm to learn the Q value:

$$Q(s,a) = r + \gamma \max_{a'} Q(s',a') \qquad \text{(Equation 9.2.3)}$$

For notational simplicity, both s' and a' are the next state and action respectively. *Equation 9.2.3* is known as the **Bellman Equation** which is the core of the Q-Learning algorithm. Q-Learning attempts to approximate the first-order expansion of return or value (*Equation 9.1.2*) as a function of both current state and action.

From zero knowledge of the dynamics of the environment, the agent tries an action a, observes what happens in the form of reward, r, and next state, s'. $\max_{a'} Q(s',a')$ chooses the next logical action that will give the maximum Q value for the next state. With all terms in *Equation 9.2.3* known, the Q value for that current state-action pair is updated. Doing the update iteratively will eventually learn the Q value function.

Q-Learning is an *off-policy* RL algorithm. It learns to improve the policy by not directly sampling experiences from that policy. In other words, the Q values are learned independently of the underlying policy being used by the agent. When the Q value function has converged, only then is the optimal policy determined using *Equation 9.2.1*.

Before giving an example on how to use Q-Learning, we should note that the agent must continually explore its environment while gradually taking advantage of what it has learned so far. This is one of the issues in RL – finding the right balance between *Exploration* and *Exploitation*. Generally, during the start of learning, the action is random (exploration). As the learning progresses, the agent takes advantage of the Q value (exploitation). For example, at the start, 90% of the action is random and 10% from Q value function, and by the end of each episode, this is gradually decreased. Eventually, the action is 10% random and 90% from Q value function.

Q-Learning example

To illustrate the Q-Learning algorithm, we need to consider a simple deterministic environment, as shown in the following figure. The environment has six states. The rewards for allowed transitions are shown. The reward is non-zero in two cases. Transition to the **Goal** (**G**) state has +100 reward while moving into **Hole** (**H**) state has -100 reward. These two states are terminal states and constitute the end of one episode from the **Start** state:

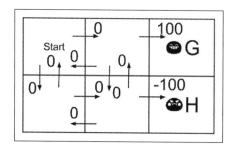

Figure 9.3.1: Rewards in a simple deterministic world

To formalize the identity of each state, we need to use a (*row, column*) identifier as shown in the following figure. Since the agent has not learned anything yet about its environment, the Q-Table also shown in the following figure has zero initial values. In this example, the discount factor, $\gamma = 0.9$. Recall that in the estimate of current Q value, the discount factor determines the weight of future Q values as a function of the number of steps, γ^k. In *Equation 9.2.3*, we only consider the immediate future Q value, $k = 1$:

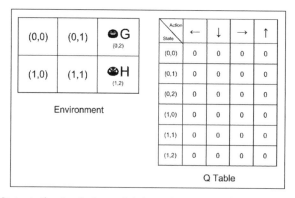

Figure 9.3.2: States in the simple deterministic environment and the agent's initial Q-Table

Initially, the agent assumes a policy that selects a random action 90% of the time and exploits the Q-Table 10% of the time. Suppose the first action is randomly chosen and indicates a move in the right direction. *Figure 9.3.3* illustrates the computation of the new Q value of state $(0, 0)$ for a move to the right action. The next state is $(0, 1)$. The reward is 0, and the maximum of all the next state's Q values is zero. Therefore, the Q value of state $(0, 0)$ for a move to the right action remains 0.

To easily track the initial state and next state, we use different shades of gray on both the environment and the Q-Table–lighter gray for initial state and darker gray for the next state. In choosing the next action for the next state, the candidate actions are in the thicker border:

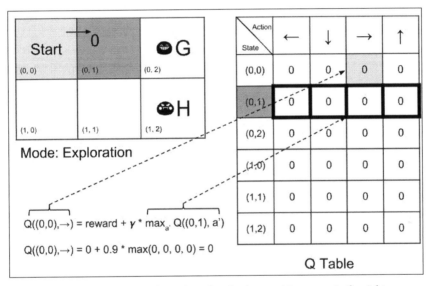

Figure 9.3.3: Assuming the action taken by the agent is a move to the right, the update on Q value of state (0, 0) is shown

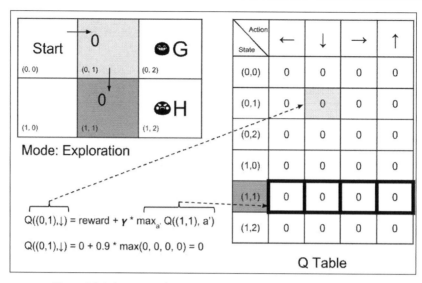

Figure 9.3.4: Assuming the action chosen by the agent is move down,
the update on Q value of state (0, 1) is shown

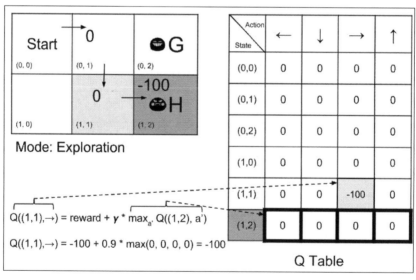

Figure 9.3.5: Assuming the action chosen by the agent is a move to the right,
the update on Q value of state (1, 1) is shown

Let's suppose that the next randomly chosen action is move down. *Figure 9.3.4* shows no change in the Q value of state (0, 1) for the move down action. In *Figure 9.3.5*, the agent's third random action is a move to the right. It encountered the **H** and received a -100 reward. This time, the update is non-zero. The new Q value for the state (1, 1) is -100 for the move to the right direction. One episode has just finished, and the agent returns to the **Start** state.

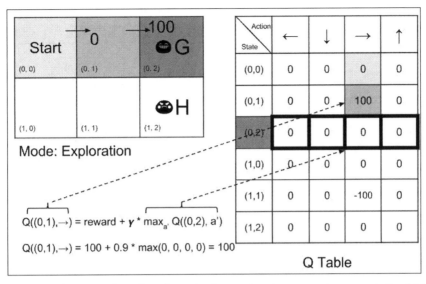

Figure 9.3.6: Assuming the actions chosen by the agent are two successive moves to the right, the update on Q value of state (0, 1) is shown

Let's suppose the agent is still in the exploration mode as shown in *Figure 9.3.6*. The first step it took for the second episode is a move to the right. As expected, the update is 0. However, the second random action it chose is also move to the right. The agent reached the **G** state and received a big +100 reward. The Q value for the state (0, 1) move to the right becomes 100. The second episode is done, and the agent goes back to the **Start** state.

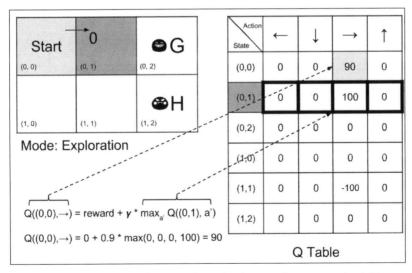

Figure 9.3.7: Assuming the action chosen by the agent is a move to the right, the update on Q value of state (0, 0) is shown

	←	↓	→	↑
(0,0)	0	0	90	0
(0,1)	0	0	100	0
(0,2)	0	0	0	0
(1,0)	0	0	0	0
(1,1)	0	0	-100	0
(1,2)	0	0	0	0

Figure 9.3.8: In this instance, the agent's policy decided to exploit the Q-Table to determine the action at states (0, 0) and (0, 1). The Q-Table suggests to move to the right for both states.

At the beginning of the third episode, the random action taken by the agent is a move to the right. The Q value of state (0, 0) is now updated with a non-zero value because the next state's possible actions have 100 as the maximum Q value. *Figure 9.3.7* shows the computation involved. The Q value of the next state (0, 1) ripples back to the earlier state (0, 0). It is like giving credit to the earlier states that helped in finding the **G** state.

The progress in Q-Table has been substantial. In fact, in the next episode, if for some reason the policy decided to exploit the Q-Table instead of randomly exploring the environment, the first action is to move to the right according to the computation in *Figure 9.3.8*. In the first row of the Q-Table, the action that results in maximum Q value is a move to the right. For the next state (0, 1), the second row of Q-Table suggests that the next action is still to move to the right. The agent has successfully reached the goal. The policy guided the agent on the right set of actions to achieve its goal.

If the Q-Learning algorithm continues to run indefinitely, the Q-Table will converge. The assumptions for convergence are the RL problem must be deterministic MDP with bounded rewards and all states are visited infinitely often.

Q-Learning in Python

The environment and the Q-Learning discussed in the previous section can be implemented in Python. Since the policy is just a simple table, there is, at this point in time no need for Keras. *Listing 9.3.1* shows `q-learning-9.3.1.py`, the implementation of the simple deterministic world (environment, agent, action, and Q-Table algorithms) using the `QWorld` class. For conciseness, the functions dealing with the user interface are not shown.

In this example, the environment dynamics is represented by `self.transition_table`. At every action, `self.transition_table` determines the next state. The reward for executing an action is stored in `self.reward_table`. The two tables are consulted every time an action is executed by the `step()` function. The Q-Learning algorithm is implemented by `update_q_table()` function. Every time the agent needs to decide which action to take, it calls the `act()` function. The action may be randomly drawn or decided by the policy using the Q-Table. The percent chance that the action chosen is random is stored in the `self.epsilon` variable which is updated by `update_epsilon()` function using a fixed `epsilon_decay`.

Before executing the code in *Listing 9.3.1*, we need to run:

```
$ sudo pip3 install termcolor
```

To install `termcolor` package. This package helps in visualizing text outputs on the Terminal.

The complete code can be found on GitHub at: `https://github.com/PacktPublishing/Advanced-Deep-Learning-with-Keras`.

Listing 9.3.1, `q-learning-9.3.1.py`. A simple deterministic MDP with six states:

```python
from collections import deque
import numpy as np
import argparse
import os
import time

from termcolor import colored


class QWorld():
    def __init__(self):
        # 4 actions
        # 0 - Left, 1 - Down, 2 - Right, 3 - Up
```

```
        self.col = 4

        # 6 states
        self.row = 6


        # setup the environment
        self.q_table = np.zeros([self.row, self.col])
        self.init_transition_table()
        self.init_reward_table()

        # discount factor
        self.gamma = 0.9

        # 90% exploration, 10% exploitation
        self.epsilon = 0.9
        # exploration decays by this factor every episode
        self.epsilon_decay = 0.9
        # in the long run, 10% exploration, 90% exploitation
        self.epsilon_min = 0.1

        # reset the environment
        self.reset()
        self.is_explore = True


# start of episode
def reset(self):

    self.state = 0
    return self.state

# agent wins when the goal is reached
def is_in_win_state(self):
    return self.state == 2


def init_reward_table(self):
    """
    0 - Left, 1 - Down, 2 - Right, 3 - Up
    ----------------
    | 0 | 0 | 100  |
    ----------------
    | 0 | 0 | -100 |
```

```
            ----------------
            """
        self.reward_table = np.zeros([self.row, self.col])
        self.reward_table[1, 2] = 100.
        self.reward_table[4, 2] = -100.



    def init_transition_table(self):
        """
        0 - Left, 1 - Down, 2 - Right, 3 - Up
        -------------
        | 0 | 1 | 2 |
        -------------
        | 3 | 4 | 5 |
        -------------
        """
        self.transition_table = np.zeros([self.row, self.col],
dtype=int)

        self.transition_table[0, 0] = 0
        self.transition_table[0, 1] = 3
        self.transition_table[0, 2] = 1
        self.transition_table[0, 3] = 0

        self.transition_table[1, 0] = 0
        self.transition_table[1, 1] = 4
        self.transition_table[1, 2] = 2
        self.transition_table[1, 3] = 1

        # terminal Goal state
        self.transition_table[2, 0] = 2
        self.transition_table[2, 1] = 2
        self.transition_table[2, 2] = 2
        self.transition_table[2, 3] = 2

        self.transition_table[3, 0] = 3
        self.transition_table[3, 1] = 3
        self.transition_table[3, 2] = 4
        self.transition_table[3, 3] = 0

        self.transition_table[4, 0] = 3
        self.transition_table[4, 1] = 4
        self.transition_table[4, 2] = 5
        self.transition_table[4, 3] = 1
```

```
        # terminal Hole state
        self.transition_table[5, 0] = 5
        self.transition_table[5, 1] = 5
        self.transition_table[5, 2] = 5
        self.transition_table[5, 3] = 5


    # execute the action on the environment
    def step(self, action):
        # determine the next_state given state and action
        next_state = self.transition_table[self.state, action]
        # done is True if next_state is Goal or Hole
        done = next_state == 2 or next_state == 5
        # reward given the state and action
        reward = self.reward_table[self.state, action]
        # the enviroment is now in new state
        self.state = next_state
        return next_state, reward, done


    # determine the next action
    def act(self):
        # 0 - Left, 1 - Down, 2 - Right, 3 - Up
        # action is from exploration
        if np.random.rand() <= self.epsilon:
            # explore - do random action
            self.is_explore = True
            return np.random.choice(4,1)[0]

        # or action is from exploitation
        # exploit - choose action with max Q-value
        self.is_explore = False
        return np.argmax(self.q_table[self.state])


    # Q-Learning - update the Q Table using Q(s, a)
    def update_q_table(self, state, action, reward, next_state):
        # Q(s, a) = reward + gamma * max_a' Q(s', a')
        q_value = self.gamma * np.amax(self.q_table[next_state])
        q_value += reward
        self.q_table[state, action] = q_value
```

```
# UI to dump Q Table contents
def print_q_table(self):
    print("Q-Table (Epsilon: %0.2f)" % self.epsilon)
    print(self.q_table)



# update Exploration-Exploitation mix
def update_epsilon(self):
    if self.epsilon > self.epsilon_min:
        self.epsilon *= self.epsilon_decay
```

Listing 9.3.2, `q-learning-9.3.1.py`. The main Q-Learning loop. The agent's Q-Table is updated every state, action, reward, and next state iteration:

```
# state, action, reward, next state iteration
for episode in range(episode_count):
    state = q_world.reset()
    done = False
    print_episode(episode, delay=delay)
    while not done:
        action = q_world.act()
        next_state, reward, done = q_world.step(action)
        q_world.update_q_table(state, action, reward, next_state)
        print_status(q_world, done, step, delay=delay)
        state = next_state
        # if episode is done, perform housekeeping
        if done:
            if q_world.is_in_win_state():
                wins += 1
                scores.append(step)
                if wins > maxwins:
                    print(scores)
                    exit(0)
            # Exploration-Exploitation is updated every episode
            q_world.update_epsilon()
            step = 1
        else:
            step += 1

print(scores)
q_world.print_q_table()
```

The perception-action-learning loop is illustrated in *Listing 9.3.2*. At every episode, the environment resets to the *Start* state. The action to execute is chosen and applied to the environment. The reward and next state are observed and used to update the Q-Table. The episode is completed (`done = True`) upon reaching the *Goal* or *Hole* state. For this example, the Q-Learning runs for 100 episodes or 10 wins, whichever comes first. Due to the decrease in the value of the `self.epsilon` variable at every episode, the agent starts to favor exploitation of Q-Table to determine the action to perform given a state. To see the Q-Learning simulation we simply need to run:

```
$ python3 q-learning-9.3.1.py
```

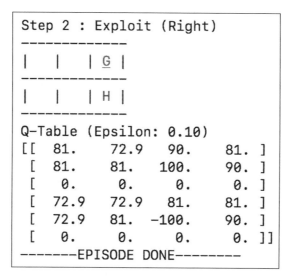

```
Step 2 : Exploit (Right)
--------------
|   |   | G |
--------------
|   |   | H |
--------------
Q-Table (Epsilon: 0.10)
[[  81.    72.9   90.    81. ]
 [  81.    81.   100.    90. ]
 [   0.     0.     0.     0. ]
 [  72.9   72.9   81.    81. ]
 [  72.9   81.  -100.    90. ]
 [   0.     0.     0.     0. ]]
--------EPISODE DONE--------
```

Figure 9.3.9: A screenshot showing the Q-Table after 2000 wins of the agent

The preceding figure shows the screenshot if `maxwins = 2000` (2000x *Goal* state is reached) and `delay = 0` (to see the final Q-Table only) by running:

```
$ python3 q-learning-9.3.1.py --train
```

The Q-Table has converged and shows the logical action that the agent can take given a state. For example, in the first row or state (0, 0), the policy advises move to the right. The same for the state (0, 1) on the second row. The second action reaches the *Goal* state. The `scores` variable dump shows that the minimum number of steps taken decreases as the agent gets correct actions from the policy.

From *Figure 9.3.9*, we can compute the value of each state from *Equation 9.2.2*, $V^*(s) = \max_a Q(s,a)$. For example, for state (0, 0), $V^*(s) = \max(81.0, 72.9, 90.0, 81.0) = 90.0$. Following figure shows the value for each state:

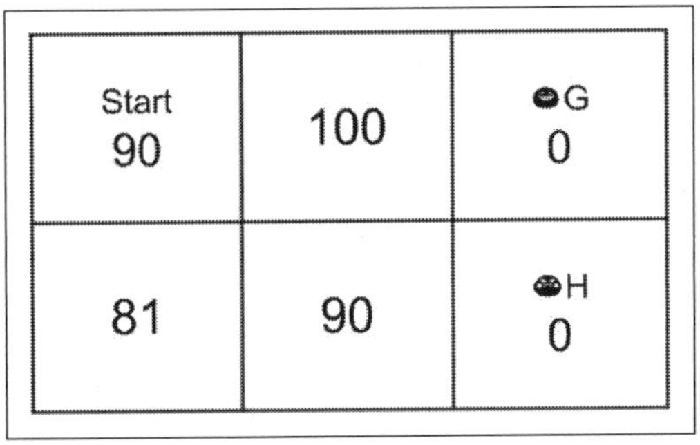

Figure 9.3.10: The value for each state from Figure 9.3.9 and Equation 9.2.2

Nondeterministic environment

In the event that the environment is nondeterministic, both the reward and action are probabilistic. The new system is a stochastic MDP. To reflect the nondeterministic reward the new value function is:

$$V^{\pi}\left(s_{t}\right)=\mathbb{E}\left[R_{t}\right]=\mathbb{E}\left[\sum_{k=0}^{T}\gamma^{k}\mathbf{r}_{t+k}\right] \qquad \text{(Equation 9.4.1)}$$

The Bellman equation is modified as:

$$Q(s,a)=\mathbb{E}_{s'}\left[r+\gamma\max_{a'}Q(s',a')\right] \qquad \text{(Equation 9.4.2)}$$

Temporal-difference learning

Q-Learning is a special case of a more generalized **Temporal-Difference Learning** or **TD-Learning** $TD(\lambda)$. More specifically, it's a special case of one-step TD-Learning $TD(0)$:

$$Q(s,a)=Q(s,a)+\alpha\left(r+\gamma\max_{a'}Q(s',a')-Q(s,a)\right) \qquad \text{(Equation 9.5.1)}$$

In the equation α is the learning rate. We should note that when $\alpha=1$, *Equation 9.5.1* is similar to the Bellman equation. For simplicity, we'll refer to *Equation 9.5.1* as Q-Learning or generalized Q-Learning.

Previously, we referred to Q-Learning as an off-policy RL algorithm since it learns the Q value function without directly using the policy that it is trying to optimize. An example of an *on-policy* one-step TD-learning algorithm is SARSA which similar to *Equation 9.5.1*:

$$Q(s,a) = Q(s,a) + \alpha\left(r + \gamma Q(s',a') - Q(s,a)\right)$$

(Equation 9.5.2)

The main difference is the use of the policy that is being optimized to determine a'. The terms s, a, r, s' and a' (thus the name SARSA) must be known to update the Q value function at every iteration. Both Q-Learning and SARSA use existing estimates in the Q value iteration, a process known as **bootstrapping**. In bootstrapping, we update the current Q value estimate from the reward and the subsequent Q value estimate(s).

Q-Learning on OpenAI gym

Before presenting another example, there appears to be a need for a suitable RL simulation environment. Otherwise, we can only run RL simulations on very simple problems like in the previous example. Fortunately, OpenAI created **Gym**, `https://gym.openai.com`.

The gym is a toolkit for developing and comparing RL algorithms. It works with most deep learning libraries, including Keras. The gym can be installed by running the following command:

```
$ sudo pip3 install gym
```

The gym has several environments where an RL algorithm can be tested against such as toy text, classic control, algorithmic, Atari, and 2D/3D robots. For example, `FrozenLake-v0` (*Figure 9.5.1*) is a toy text environment similar to the simple deterministic world used in the Q-Learning in Python example. `FrozenLake-v0` has 12 states. The state marked **S** is the starting state, **F** is the frozen part of the lake which is safe, **H** is the Hole state that should be avoided, and **G** is the Goal state where the frisbee is. The reward is +1 for transitioning to the Goal state. For all other states, the reward is zero.

In `FrozenLake-v0`, there are also four available actions (Left, Down, Right, Up) known as action space. However, unlike the simple deterministic world earlier, the actual movement direction is only partially dependent on the chosen action. There are two variations of the `FrozenLake-v0` environment, slippery and non-slippery. As expected, the slippery mode is more challenging:

Figure 9.5.1: Frozen lake environment in OpenAI Gym

An action applied on FrozenLake-v0 returns the observation (equivalent to the next state), reward, done (whether the episode is finished), and a dictionary of debugging information. The observable attributes of the environment, known as observation space, are captured by the returned observation object.

The generalized Q-Learning can be applied to the FrozenLake-v0 environment. *Table 9.5.1* shows the improvement in performance of both slippery and non-slippery environments. A method of measuring the performance of the policy is the percent of episodes executed that resulted in reaching the Goal state. The higher is the percentage, the better. From the baseline of pure exploration (random action) of about 1.5%, the policy can achieve ~76% Goal state for non-slippery and ~71% for the slippery environment. As expected, it is harder to control the slippery environment.

The code can still be implemented in Python and NumPy since it only requires a Q-Table. *Listing 9.5.1* shows the implementation of the QAgent class while listing 9.5.2 demonstrates the agent's perception-action-learning loop. Apart from using FrozenLake-v0 environment from OpenAI Gym, the most important change is the implementation of the generalized Q-Learning as defined by *Equation 9.5.1* in the update_q_table() function.

The qagent object can operate in either slippery or non-slippery mode. The agent is trained for 40,000 iterations. After training, the agent can exploit the Q-Table to choose the action to execute given any policy as shown in the test mode of *Table 9.5.1*. There is a huge performance boost in using the learned policy as demonstrated in *Table 9.5.1*. With the use of the gym, a lot of the code in constructing the environment is gone.

This will help us to focus on building a working RL algorithm. To run the code in slow motion or delay of 1 sec per action:

```
$ python3 q-frozenlake-9.5.1.py -d -t=1
```

Mode	Run	Approx % Goal
Train non-slippery	`python3 q-frozenlake-9.5.1.py`	26.0
Test non-slippery	`python3 q-frozenlake-9.5.1.py -d`	76.0
Pure random action non-slippery	`python3 q-frozenlake-9.5.1.py -e`	1.5
Train slippery	`python3 q-frozenlake-9.5.1.py -s`	26
Test slippery	`python3 q-frozenlake-9.5.1.py -s -d`	71.0
Pure random slippery	`python3 q-frozenlake-9.5.1.py -s -e`	1.5

Table 9.5.1: Baseline and performance of generalized Q-Learning on the FrozenLake-v0 environment with learning rate = 0.5

Listing 9.5.1, `q-frozenlake-9.5.1.py` shows the implementation of Q-Learning on FrozenLake-v0 environment:

```python
from collections import deque
import numpy as np
import argparse
import os
import time
import gym
from gym import wrappers, logger


class QAgent():
    def __init__(self,
                 observation_space,
                 action_space,
                 demo=False,
                 slippery=False,
                 decay=0.99):

        self.action_space = action_space
        # number of columns is equal to number of actions
        col = action_space.n
        # number of rows is equal to number of states
        row = observation_space.n
        # build Q Table with row x col dims
        self.q_table = np.zeros([row, col])
```

```
        # discount factor
        self.gamma = 0.9

        # initially 90% exploration, 10% exploitation
        self.epsilon = 0.9
        # iteratively applying decay til 10% exploration/90%
exploitation
        self.epsilon_decay = decay
        self.epsilon_min = 0.1

        # learning rate of Q-Learning
        self.learning_rate = 0.1

        # file where Q Table is saved on/restored fr
        if slippery:
            self.filename = 'q-frozenlake-slippery.npy'
        else:
            self.filename = 'q-frozenlake.npy'

        # demo or train mode
        self.demo = demo
        # if demo mode, no exploration
        if demo:
            self.epsilon = 0

    # determine the next action
    # if random, choose from random action space
    # else use the Q Table
    def act(self, state, is_explore=False):
        # 0 - left, 1 - Down, 2 - Right, 3 - Up
        if is_explore or np.random.rand() < self.epsilon:
            # explore - do random action
            return self.action_space.sample()

        # exploit - choose action with max Q-value
        return np.argmax(self.q_table[state])

    # TD(0) learning (generalized Q-Learning) with learning rate
    def update_q_table(self, state, action, reward, next_state):
        # Q(s, a) += alpha * (reward + gamma * max_a' Q(s', a') - Q
(s, a))
        q_value = self.gamma * np.amax(self.q_table[next_state])
        q_value += reward
        q_value -= self.q_table[state, action]
```

```
            q_value *= self.learning_rate
            q_value += self.q_table[state, action]
            self.q_table[state, action] = q_value


        # dump Q Table
        def print_q_table(self):
            print(self.q_table)
            print("Epsilon : ", self.epsilon)


        # save trained Q Table
        def save_q_table(self):
            np.save(self.filename, self.q_table)


        # load trained Q Table
        def load_q_table(self):
            self.q_table = np.load(self.filename)


        # adjust epsilon
        def update_epsilon(self):
            if self.epsilon > self.epsilon_min:
                self.epsilon *= self.epsilon_decay
```

Listing 9.5.2, `q-frozenlake-9.5.1.py`. The main Q-Learning loop for the `FrozenLake-v0` environment:

```
    # loop for the specified number of episode
    for episode in range(episodes):
        state = env.reset()
        done = False
        while not done:
            # determine the agent's action given state
            action = agent.act(state, is_explore=args.explore)
            # get observable data
            next_state, reward, done, _ = env.step(action)
            # clear the screen before rendering the environment
            os.system('clear')
            # render the environment for human debugging
            env.render()
```

```
# training of Q Table
if done:
    # update exploration-exploitation ratio
    # reward > 0 only when Goal is reached
    # otherwise, it is a Hole
    if reward > 0:
        wins += 1

if not args.demo:
    agent.update_q_table(state, action, reward, next_state)
    agent.update_epsilon()

state = next_state
percent_wins = 100.0 * wins / (episode + 1)
print("-------%0.2f%% Goals in %d Episodes---------"
      % (percent_wins, episode))
if done:
    time.sleep(5 * delay)
else:
    time.sleep(delay)
```

Deep Q-Network (DQN)

Using the Q-Table to implement Q-Learning is fine in small discrete environments. However, when the environment has numerous states or continuous as in most cases, a Q-Table is not feasible or practical. For example, if we are observing a state made of four continuous variables, the size of the table is infinite. Even if we attempt to discretize the four variables into 1000 values each, the total number of rows in the table is a staggering $1000^4 = 1e^{12}$. Even after training, the table is sparse - most of the cells in this table are zero.

A solution to this problem is called DQN [2] which uses a deep neural network to approximate the Q-Table. As shown in *Figure 9.6.1*. There are two approaches to build the Q-network:

1. The input is the state-action pair, and the prediction is the Q value
2. The input is the state, and the prediction is the Q value for each action

The first option is not optimal since the network will be called a number of times equal to the number of actions. The second is the preferred method. The Q-Network is called only once.

The most desirable action is simply the action with the biggest Q value:

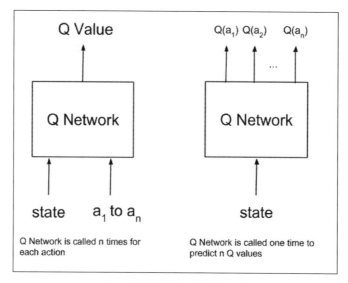

Figure 9.6.1: A Deep Q-Network

The data required to train the Q-Network come from the agent's experiences: $\left(s_0 a_0 r_1 s_1, s_1 a_1 r_2 s_2, \ldots, s_{T-1} a_{T-1} r_T s_T\right)$. Each training sample is a unit of experience $s_t a_t r_{t+1} s_{t+1}$. At a given state at timestep t, $s = s_t$, the action, $a = a_t$, is determined using the Q-Learning algorithm similar to the previous section:

$$\pi(s) = \begin{cases} sample(a) & random < \varepsilon \\ \underset{a}{argmax}\, Q(s, a) & otherwise \end{cases} \qquad \text{(Equation 9.6.1)}$$

For notational simplicity, we omit the subscript and the use of the bold letter. We need to note that $Q(s,a)$ is the Q-Network. Strictly speaking, it is $Q(a \mid s)$ since the action is moved to the prediction as shown on the right of *Figure 9.6.1*. The action with the highest Q value is the action that is applied on the environment to get the reward, $r = r_{t+1}$, the next state, $s' = s_{t+1}$ and a Boolean done indicating if the next state is terminal. From *Equation 9.5.1* on generalized Q-Learning, an MSE loss function can be determined by applying the chosen action:

$$\mathcal{L} = \left(r + \gamma \max_{a'} Q(s', a') - Q(s, a)\right)^2 \qquad \text{(Equation 9.6.2)}$$

Where all terms are familiar from the previous discussion on Q-Learning and $Q(a|s)$ $\rightarrow Q(s,a)$. The term $\max_{a'} Q(s',a') \rightarrow \max_{a'} Q(a'|s')$. In other words, using the Q-Network, predict the Q value of each action given next state and get the maximum among them. Note that at the terminal state s', $\max_{a'} Q(a'|s') = \max_{a'} Q(s'|a') = 0$.

Algorithm 9.6.1, DQN algorithm:

Require: Initialize replay memory D to capacity N

Require: Initialize action-value function Q with random weights θ

Require: Initialize target action-value function Q_{target} with weights $\theta^- = \theta$

Require: Exploration rate, ε and discount factor, γ

1. for *episode* = 1, …,M do:
2.   Given initial state s
3.   for *step* = 1,…, T do:
4.   Choose action $a = \begin{cases} sample(a) & random < \varepsilon \\ \underset{a}{argmax}\, Q(s,a;\theta) & otherwise \end{cases}$
5.   Execute action a, observe reward r and next state s'
6.   Store transition (s, a, r, s') in D
7.   Update the state, $s = s'$
8.   //experience replay
9.   Sample a mini batch of episode experiences $(s_j, a_j, r_{j+1}, s_{j+1})$ from D
10. $Q_{max} = \begin{cases} r_{j+1} & if\ episode\ terminates\ at\ j+1 \\ r_{j+1} + \gamma \max_{a_{j+1}} Q_{target}\left(s_{j+1}, a_{j+1}; \theta^-\right) & otherwise \end{cases}$
11.   Perform gradient descent step on $\left(Q_{max} - Q(s_j, a_j; \theta^-)\right)^2$ with respect to parameters θ
12.   // periodic update of the target network
13.   Every C steps Q_{target} = Q, that is set $\theta^- = \theta$
14.   End

However, it turns out that training the Q-Network is unstable. There are two problems causing the instability:

1. A high correlation between samples
2. A non-stationary target

A high correlation is due to the sequential nature of sampling experiences. DQN addressed this issue by creating a buffer of experiences. The training data are randomly sampled from this buffer. This process is known as **experience replay**.

The issue of the non-stationary target is due to the target network $Q(s',a')$ that is modified after every mini batch of training. A small change in the target network can create a significant change in the policy, the data distribution, and the correlation between the current Q value and target Q value. This is resolved by freezing the weights of the target network for C training steps. In other words, two identical Q-Networks are created. The target Q-Network parameters are copied from the Q-Network under training every C training steps.

The DQN algorithm is summarized in *Algorithm 9.6.1*.

DQN on Keras

To illustrate DQN, the CartPole-v0 environment of the OpenAI Gym is used. CartPole-v0 is a pole balancing problem. The goal is to keep the pole from falling over. The environment is 2D. The action space is made of two discrete actions (left and right movements). However, the state space is continuous and is made of four variables:

1. Linear position
2. Linear velocity
3. Angle of rotation
4. Angular velocity

The CartPole-v0 is shown in *Figure 9.6.1*.

Initially, the pole is upright. A reward of +1 is provided for every timestep that the pole remains upright. The episode ends when the pole exceeds 15 degrees from the vertical or 2.4 units from the center. The CartPole-v0 problem is considered solved if the average reward is 195.0 in 100 consecutive trials:

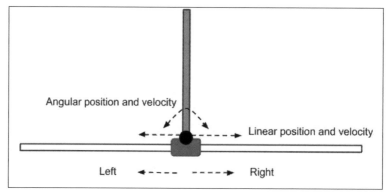

Figure 9.6.1: The CartPole-v0 environment

Listing 9.6.1 shows us the DQN implementation for `CartPole-v0`. The `DQNAgent` class represents the agent using DQN. Two Q-Networks are created:

1. Q-Network or Q in *Algorithm 9.6.1*

2. Target Q-Network or Q_{target} in *Algorithm 9.6.1*

Both networks are MLP with three hidden layers of 256 units each. The Q-Network is trained during experience replay, `replay()`. At a regular interval of $C = 10$ training steps, the Q-Network parameters are copied to the Target Q-Network by `update_weights()`. This implements line *13*, $Q_{target} = Q$, in algorithm *9.6.1*. After every episode, the ratio of exploration-exploitation is decreased by `update_epsilon()` to take advantage of the learned policy.

To implement line *10* in *Algorithm 9.6.1* during experience replay, `replay()`, for each experience unit, $(s_j, a_j, r_{j+1}, s_{j+1})$, the Q value for the action a_j is set to Q_{max}. All other actions have their Q values unchanged.

This is implemented by the following lines:

```
# policy prediction for a given state
q_values = self.q_model.predict(state)

# get Q_max
q_value = self.get_target_q_value(next_state)

# correction on the Q value for the action used
q_values[0][action] = reward if done else q_value
```

Only the action a_j has a non-zero loss equal to $\left(Q_{max} - Q(s_j, a_j; \theta)\right)^2$ as shown by line *11* of *Algorithm 9.6.1*. Note that the experience replay is called by the perception-action-learning loop in *Listing 9.6.2* after the end of each episode assuming that there is sufficient data in the buffer (that is, buffer size, is greater or equal to batch size). During the experience replay, one batch of experience units is randomly sampled and used to train the Q-Network.

Similar to the Q-Table, `act()` implements the ε-greedy policy, *Equation 9.6.1*. Experiences are stored by `remember()` in the replay buffer. The computation of Q is done by the `get_target_q_value()` function. On the average of 10 runs, `CartPole-v0` is solved by DQN within 822 episodes. We need to take note that the results may vary every time the training runs.

Listing 9.6.1, `dqn-cartpole-9.6.1.py` shows us the DQN implementation within Keras:

```
from keras.layers import Dense, Input
```

```python
from keras.models import Model
from keras.optimizers import Adam
from collections import deque
import numpy as np
import random
import argparse
import gym
from gym import wrappers, logger

class DQNAgent():
    def __init__(self, state_space, action_space, args,
episodes=1000):

        self.action_space = action_space

        # experience buffer
        self.memory = []

        # discount rate
        self.gamma = 0.9

        # initially 90% exploration, 10% exploitation
        self.epsilon = 0.9
        # iteratively applying decay til 10% exploration/90%
exploitation
        self.epsilon_min = 0.1
        self.epsilon_decay = self.epsilon_min / self.epsilon
        self.epsilon_decay = self.epsilon_decay ** (1. /
float(episodes))

        # Q Network weights filename
        self.weights_file = 'dqn_cartpole.h5'
        # Q Network for training
        n_inputs = state_space.shape[0]
        n_outputs = action_space.n
        self.q_model = self.build_model(n_inputs, n_outputs)
        self.q_model.compile(loss='mse', optimizer=Adam())
        # target Q Network
        self.target_q_model = self.build_model(n_inputs, n_outputs)
        # copy Q Network params to target Q Network
        self.update_weights()

        self.replay_counter = 0
        self.ddqn = True if args.ddqn else False
```

```python
        if self.ddqn:
            print("---------Double DQN--------")
        else:
            print("------------DQN-----------")


    # Q Network is 256-256-256 MLP
    def build_model(self, n_inputs, n_outputs):
        inputs = Input(shape=(n_inputs, ), name='state')
        x = Dense(256, activation='relu')(inputs)
        x = Dense(256, activation='relu')(x)
      x = Dense(256, activation='relu')(x)
        x = Dense(n_outputs, activation='linear', name='action')(x)
        q_model = Model(inputs, x)
        q_model.summary()
        return q_model


    # save Q Network params to a file
    def save_weights(self):
        self.q_model.save_weights(self.weights_file)


    def update_weights(self):
        self.target_q_model.set_weights(self.q_model.get_weights())


    # eps-greedy policy
    def act(self, state):
        if np.random.rand() < self.epsilon:
            # explore - do random action
            return self.action_space.sample()

        # exploit
        q_values = self.q_model.predict(state)
        # select the action with max Q-value
        return np.argmax(q_values[0])


    # store experiences in the replay buffer
    def remember(self, state, action, reward, next_state, done):
        item = (state, action, reward, next_state, done)
        self.memory.append(item)
```

```
# compute Q_max
# use of target Q Network solves the non-stationarity problem
def get_target_q_value(self, next_state):
    # max Q value among next state's actions
    if self.ddqn:
        # DDQN
        # current Q Network selects the action
        # a'_max = argmax_a' Q(s', a')
        action = np.argmax(self.q_model.predict(next_state)[0])
        # target Q Network evaluates the action
        # Q_max = Q_target(s', a'_max)
        q_value = self.target_q_model.predict(next_state)[0]
[action]
    else:
        # DQN chooses the max Q value among next actions
        # selection and evaluation of action is on the
        # target Q Network
        # Q_max = max_a' Q_target(s', a')
        q_value = np.amax(self.target_q_model.predict(next_state)
[0])

    # Q_max = reward + gamma * Q_max
    q_value *= self.gamma
    q_value += reward
    return q_value


# experience replay addresses the correlation issue between
samples
def replay(self, batch_size):
    # sars = state, action, reward, state' (next_state)
    sars_batch = random.sample(self.memory, batch_size)
    state_batch, q_values_batch = [], []

    # fixme: for speedup, this could be done on the tensor level
    # but easier to understand using a loop
    for state, action, reward, next_state, done in sars_batch:
        # policy prediction for a given state
        q_values = self.q_model.predict(state)

        # get Q_max
        q_value = self.get_target_q_value(next_state)
```

```
            # correction on the Q value for the action used
            q_values[0][action] = reward if done else q_value

            # collect batch state-q_value mapping
            state_batch.append(state[0])
            q_values_batch.append(q_values[0])

        # train the Q-network
        self.q_model.fit(np.array(state_batch),
                         np.array(q_values_batch),
                         batch_size=batch_size,
                         epochs=1,
                         verbose=0)

        # update exploration-exploitation probability
        self.update_epsilon()
        # copy new params on old target after every 10 training
updates
        if self.replay_counter % 10 == 0:
            self.update_weights()

        self.replay_counter += 1



    # decrease the exploration, increase exploitation
    def update_epsilon(self):
        if self.epsilon > self.epsilon_min:
            self.epsilon *= self.epsilon_decay
```

Listing 9.6.2, `dqn-cartpole-9.6.1.py`. Training loop of DQN implementation in Keras:

```
# Q-Learning sampling and fitting
for episode in range(episode_count):
    state = env.reset()
    state = np.reshape(state, [1, state_size])
    done = False
    total_reward = 0
    while not done:
        # in CartPole-v0, action=0 is left and action=1 is right
        action = agent.act(state)
        next_state, reward, done, _ = env.step(action)
        # in CartPole-v0:
        # state = [pos, vel, theta, angular speed]
        next_state = np.reshape(next_state, [1, state_size])
```

```
        # store every experience unit in replay buffer
        agent.remember(state, action, reward, next_state, done)
        state = next_state
        total_reward += reward


    # call experience relay
    if len(agent.memory) >= batch_size:
        agent.replay(batch_size)


    scores.append(total_reward)
    mean_score = np.mean(scores)
    if mean_score >= win_reward[args.env_id] and episode >= win_
trials:
        print("Solved in episode %d: Mean survival = %0.2lf in %d
episodes"
                % (episode, mean_score, win_trials))
        print("Epsilon: ", agent.epsilon)
        agent.save_weights()
        break
    if episode % win_trials == 0:
        print("Episode %d: Mean survival = %0.2lf in %d episodes" %
            (episode, mean_score, win_trials))
```

Double Q-Learning (DDQN)

In DQN, the target Q-Network selects and evaluates every action resulting in an overestimation of Q value. To resolve this issue, DDQN [3] proposes to use the Q-Network to choose the action and use the target Q-Network to evaluate the action.

In DQN as summarized by *Algorithm 9.6.1*, the estimate of the Q value in line *10* is:

$$
Q_{max} = \begin{cases} r_{j+1} & \text{if episode terminates at } j+1 \\ r_{j+1} + \gamma \max_{a_{j+1}} Q_{target}\left(s_{j+1}, a_{j+1}; \theta^{-}\right) & \text{otherwise} \end{cases}
$$

Q_{target} chooses and evaluates the action a_{j+1}.

DDQN proposes to change line *10* to:

$$Q_{max} = \begin{cases} r_{j+1} & \text{if episode terminates at } j+1 \\ r_{j+1} + \gamma Q_{target}\left(s_{j+1}, \underset{a_{j+1}}{\operatorname{argmax}} Q\left(s_{j+1}, a_{j+1}; \theta\right); \theta^-\right) & \text{otherwise} \end{cases}$$

The term $\underset{a_{j+1}}{\operatorname{argmax}} Q\left(s_{j+1}, a_{j+1}; \theta\right)$ lets Q to choose the action. Then this action is evaluated by Q_{target}.

In Listing 9.6.1, both DQN and DDQN are implemented. Specifically, for DDQN, the modification on the Q value computation performed by `get_target_q_value()` function is highlighted:

```
# compute Q_max
# use of target Q Network solves the non-stationarity problem
def get_target_q_value(self, next_state):
    # max Q value among next state's actions
    if self.ddqn:
        # DDQN
        # current Q Network selects the action
        # a'_max = argmax_a' Q(s', a')
        action = np.argmax(self.q_model.predict(next_state)[0])
        # target Q Network evaluates the action
        # Q_max = Q_target(s', a'_max)
        q_value = self.target_q_model.predict(next_state)[0][action]
    else:
        # DQN chooses the max Q value among next actions
        # selection and evaluation of action is on the target Q
Network
        # Q_max = max_a' Q_target(s', a')
        q_value = np.amax(self.target_q_model.predict(next_state)[0])

    # Q_max = reward + gamma * Q_max
    q_value *= self.gamma
    q_value += reward
    return q_value
```

For comparison, on the average of 10 runs, the `CartPole-v0` is solved by DDQN within 971 episodes. To use DDQN, run:

```
$ python3 dqn-cartpole-9.6.1.py -d
```

Conclusion

In this chapter, we've been introduced to DRL. A powerful technique believed by many researchers as the most promising lead towards artificial intelligence. Together, we've gone over the principles of RL. RL is able to solve many toy problems, but the Q-Table is unable to scale to more complex real-world problems. The solution is to learn the Q-Table using a deep neural network. However, training deep neural networks on RL is highly unstable due to sample correlation and non-stationarity of the target Q-Network.

DQN proposed a solution to these problems using experience replay and separating the target network from the Q-Network under training. DDQN suggested further improvement of the algorithm by separating the action selection from action evaluation to minimize the overestimation of Q value. There are other improvements proposed for the DQN. Prioritized experience replay [6] argues that that experience buffer should not be sampled uniformly. Instead, experiences that are more important based on TD errors should be sampled more frequently to accomplish more efficient training. [7] proposes a dueling network architecture to estimate the state value function and the advantage function. Both functions are used to estimate the Q value for faster learning.

The approach presented in this chapter is value iteration/fitting. The policy is learned indirectly by finding an optimal value function. In the next chapter, the approach will be to learn the optimal policy directly by using a family of algorithms called policy gradient methods. Learning the policy has many advantages. In particular, policy gradient methods can deal with both discrete and continuous action spaces.

References

1. Sutton and Barto. *Reinforcement Learning: An Introduction*, 2017 (http://incompleteideas.net/book/bookdraft2017nov5.pdf).

2. Volodymyr Mnih and others, *Human-level control through deep reinforcement learning*. Nature 518.7540, 2015: 529 (http://www.davidqiu.com:8888/research/nature14236.pdf)

3. Hado Van Hasselt, Arthur Guez, and David Silver *Deep Reinforcement Learning with Double Q-Learning*. AAAI. Vol. 16, 2016 (http://www.aaai.org/ocs/index.php/AAAI/AAAI16/paper/download/12389/11847).

4. Kai Arulkumaran and others *A Brief Survey of Deep Reinforcement Learning*. arXiv preprint arXiv:1708.05866, 2017 (https://arxiv.org/pdf/1708.05866.pdf).

5. David Silver *Lecture Notes on Reinforcement Learning*, (http://www0.cs.ucl.ac.uk/staff/d.silver/web/Teaching.html).

6. Tom Schaul and others. *Prioritized experience replay*. arXiv preprint arXiv:1511.05952, 2015 (https://arxiv.org/pdf/1511.05952.pdf).

7. Ziyu Wang and others. *Dueling Network Architectures for Deep Reinforcement Learning*. arXiv preprint arXiv:1511.06581, 2015 (https://arxiv.org/pdf/1511.06581.pdf).

10
Policy Gradient Methods

In the final chapter of this book, we're going to introduce algorithms that directly optimize the policy network in reinforcement learning. These algorithms are collectively referred to as *policy gradient methods*. Since the policy network is directly optimized during training, the policy gradient methods belong to the family of *on-policy* reinforcement learning algorithms. Like value-based methods that we discussed in *Chapter 9, Deep Reinforcement Learning*, policy gradient methods can also be implemented as deep reinforcement learning algorithms.

A fundamental motivation in studying the policy gradient methods is addressing the limitations of Q-Learning. We'll recall that Q-Learning is about selecting the action that maximizes the value of the state. With Q function, we're able to determine the policy that enables the agent to decide on which action to take for a given state. The chosen action is simply the one that gives the agent the maximum value. In this respect, Q-Learning is limited to a finite number of discrete actions. It's not able to deal with continuous action space environments. Furthermore, Q-Learning is not directly optimizing the policy. In the end, reinforcement learning is about finding that optimal policy that the agent will be able to use to decide on which action it should take in order to maximize the return.

In contrast, policy gradient methods are applicable to environments with discrete or continuous action spaces. In addition, the four policy gradient methods that we will be presenting in this chapter are directly optimizing the performance measure of the policy network. This results in a trained policy network that the agent can use to act in its environment optimally.

In summary, the goal of this chapter is to present:

- The policy gradient theorem
- Four policy gradient methods: **REINFORCE**, **REINFORCE with baseline**, **Actor-Critic**, and **Advantage Actor-Critic (A2C)**
- A guide on how to implement the policy gradient methods in Keras in a continuous action space environment

Policy gradient theorem

As discussed in *Chapter 9, Deep Reinforcement Learning*, in Reinforcement Learning the agent is situated in an environment that is in state s_t, an element of state space $\mathcal{S}$. The state space $\mathcal{S}$ may be discrete or continuous. The agent takes an action a_t from the action space $\mathcal{A}$ by obeying the policy, $\pi(a_t|s_t)$. $\mathcal{A}$ may be discrete or continuous. Because of executing the action a_t, the agent receives a reward r_{t+1} and the environment transitions to a new state s_{t+1}. The new state is dependent only on the current state and action. The goal of the agent is to learn an optimal policy π^* that maximizes the *return* from all the states:

$$\pi^* = argmax_\pi R_t \quad \text{(Equation 9.1.1)}$$

The return, R_t, is defined as the discounted cumulative reward from time t until the end of the episode or when the terminal state is reached:

$$V^\pi(s_t) = R_t = \sum_{k=0}^{T} \gamma^k r_{t+k} \quad \text{(Equation 9.1.2)}$$

From *Equation 9.1.2*, the return can also be interpreted as a value of a given state by following the policy π. It can be observed from *Equation 9.1.1* that future rewards have lower weights compared to immediate rewards since generally $\gamma^k < 1.0$ where $\gamma \in [0,1]$.

So far, we have only considered learning the policy by optimizing a value based function, $Q(s,a)$. Our goal in this chapter is to directly learn the policy by parameterizing $\pi(a_t|s_t) \rightarrow \pi(a_t|s_t,\theta)$. By parameterization, we can use a neural network to learn the policy function. Learning the policy means that we are going to maximize a certain objective function, $\mathcal{J}(\theta)$ which is a performance measure with respect to parameter θ. In episodic reinforcement learning, the performance measure is the value of the start state. In the continuous case, the objective function is the average reward rate.

Maximizing the objective function $\mathcal{J}(\theta)$ is achieved by performing *gradient ascent*. In gradient ascent, the gradient update is in the direction of the derivative of the function being optimized. So far, all our loss functions are optimized by minimization or by performing *gradient descent*. Later, in the Keras implementation, we're able to see that the gradient ascent can be performed by simply negating the objective function and performing gradient descent.

The advantage of learning the policy directly is that it can be applied to both discrete and continuous action spaces. For discrete action spaces:

$$\pi\left(a_i \mid s_t, \theta\right) = softmax\left(a_i\right) \; for \; a_i \in A \qquad \text{(Equation 10.1.1)}$$

In that formula, a_i is the i-th action. a_i can be the prediction of a neural network or a linear function of state-action features:

$$a_i = \phi\left(s_t, a_i\right)^T \theta \qquad \text{(Equation 10.1.2)}$$

$\phi\left(s_t, a_i\right)$ is any function such as an encoder that converts the state-action to features.

$\pi\left(a_i \mid s_t, \theta\right)$ determines the probability of each a_i. For example, in the cartpole balancing problem in the previous chapter, the goal is to keep the pole upright by moving the cart along the 2D axis to the left or to the right. In this case, a_0 and a_1 are the probabilities of the left and right movements respectively. In general, the agent takes the action with the highest probability, $a_t = \max_i \pi\left(a_i \mid s_t, \theta\right)$.

For continuous action spaces, $\pi\left(a_t \mid s_t, \theta\right)$ samples an action from a probability distribution given the state. For example, if the continuous action space is the range $a_t \in [-1.0, 1.0]$, then $\pi^* = argmax_\pi R_t$ is usually a Gaussian distribution whose mean and standard deviation are predicted by the policy network. The predicted action is a sample from this Gaussian distribution. To ensure that no invalid prediction is generated, the action is clipped between -1.0 and 1.0.

Formally, for continuous action spaces, the policy is a sample from a Gaussian distribution:

$$\pi\left(a_t \mid s_t, \theta\right) = a_t \sim \mathcal{N}\left(\mu\left(s_t\right), \sigma\left(s_t\right)\right) \qquad \text{(Equation 10.1.3)}$$

The mean, μ, and standard deviation, σ, are both functions of the state features:

$$\mu\left(s_t\right) = \phi\left(s_t\right)^T \theta_\mu \qquad \text{(Equation 10.1.4)}$$

$$\sigma\left(s_t\right) = \varsigma\left(\phi\left(s_t\right)^T \theta_\sigma\right) \qquad \text{(Equation 10.1.5)}$$

$\phi(s_t)$ is any function that converts the state to its features. $\varsigma(x) = \log(1 + e^x)$ is the *softplus* function that ensures positive values of standard deviation. One way of implementing the state feature function, $\phi(s_t)$, is using the encoder of an autoencoder network. At the end of this chapter, we will train an autoencoder and use the encoder part as the state feature function. Training a policy network is therefore a matter of optimizing the parameters $\theta = \left[\theta_\mu \; \theta_\sigma\right]$.

Given a continuously differentiable policy function, $\pi\left(a_t \middle| s_t, \theta\right)$, the policy gradient can be computed as:

$$\nabla\mathcal{J}\left(\theta\right) = \mathbb{E}_\pi\left[\frac{\nabla_\theta\pi\left(a_t \middle| s_t, \theta\right)}{\pi\left(a_t \middle| s_t, \theta\right)}Q^\pi\left(s_t, a_t\right)\right] = \mathbb{E}_\pi\left[\nabla_\theta ln\pi\left(a_t \middle| s_t, \theta\right)Q^\pi\left(s_t, a_t\right)\right] \quad \text{(Equation 10.1.6)}$$

Equation 10.1.6 is also known as the *policy gradient theorem*. It is applicable to both discrete and continuous action spaces. The gradient with respect to the parameter θ is computed from the natural logarithm of the policy action sampling scaled by the Q value. *Equation 10.1.6* takes advantage of the property of the natural logarithm, $\frac{\nabla x}{x} = \nabla \ln x$.

Policy gradient theorem is intuitive in the sense that the performance gradient is estimated from the target policy samples and proportional to the policy gradient. The policy gradient is scaled by the Q value to encourage actions that positively contribute to the state value. The gradient is also inversely proportional to the action probability to penalize frequently occurring actions that do not contribute to the increase of performance measure.

In the next section, we will demonstrate the different methods of estimating the policy gradient.

For the proof of policy gradient theorem, please see [2] and lecture notes from David Silver on Reinforcement Learning, http://www0.cs.ucl.ac.uk/staff/d.silver/web/Teaching_files/pg.pdf

There are subtle advantages of policy gradient methods. For example, in some card-based games, value-based methods have no straightforward procedure in handling stochasticity, unlike policy-based methods. In policy-based methods, the action probability changes smoothly with the parameters. Meanwhile, value-based actions may suffer from drastic changes with respect to small changes in parameters. Lastly, the dependence of policy-based methods on parameters leads us to different formulations on how to perform gradient ascent on the performance measure. These are the four policy gradient methods to be presented in the succeeding sections.

Policy-based methods have their own disadvantages as well. They are generally harder to train because of the tendency to converge on a local optimum instead of the global optimum. In the experiments to be presented at the end of this chapter, it is easy for an agent to become comfortable and to choose actions that do not necessarily give the highest value. Policy gradient is also characterized by high variance.

The gradient updates are frequently overestimated. Furthermore, training policy-based methods are time-consuming. The training requires thousands of episodes (that is, not sample efficient). Each episode only provides a small number of samples. Typical training in the implementation provided at the end of the chapter would take about an hour for 1,000 episodes on a GTX 1060 GPU.

In the following sections, we discuss the four policy gradient methods. While the discussion focuses on continuous action spaces, the concept is generally applicable to discrete action spaces. Due to similarities in the implementation of the policy and value networks of the four policy gradient methods, we will wait until the end of this chapter to illustrate the implementation into Keras.

Monte Carlo policy gradient (REINFORCE) method

The simplest policy gradient method is called REINFORCE [5], this is a Monte Carlo policy gradient method:

$$\nabla \mathcal{J}(\theta) = \mathbb{E}_{\pi}\left[R_t \nabla_\theta ln\pi\left(a_t | s_t, \theta\right)\right] \quad \text{(Equation 10.2.1)}$$

where R_t is the return as defined in *Equation 9.1.2*. R_t is an unbiased sample of $Q^\pi\left(s_t, a_t\right)$ in the policy gradient theorem.

Algorithm 10.2.1 summarizes the REINFORCE algorithm [2]. REINFORCE is a Monte Carlo algorithm. It does not require knowledge of the dynamics of the environment (that is, model-free). Only experience samples, $\langle s_i a_i r_{i+1} s_{i+1}\rangle$, are needed to optimally tune the parameters of the policy network, $\pi(a_t|s_t,\theta)$. The discount factor, γ, takes into consideration that rewards decrease in value as the number of steps increases. The gradient is discounted by γ^t. Gradients taken at later steps have smaller contributions. The learning rate, α, is a scaling factor of the gradient update.

The parameters are updated by performing gradient ascent using the discounted gradient and learning rate. As a Monte Carlo algorithm, REINFORCE requires that the agent completes an episode before processing the gradient updates. Due to its Monte Carlo nature, the gradient update of REINFORCE is characterized by high variance. At the end of this chapter, we will implement the REINFORCE algorithm into Keras.

Algorithm 10.2.1 REINFORCE

Require: A differentiable parameterized target policy network, $\pi(a_t|s_t,\theta)$.

Require: Discount factor, $\gamma \in [0,1]$ and learning rate α. For example, $\gamma = 0.99$ and $\alpha = 1e - 3$.

Require: θ_0, initial policy network parameters (for example, $\theta_0 \to 0$).

1. Repeat

2.   Generate an episode $\left(s_0 a_0 r_1 s_1, s_1 a_1 r_2 s_2, \ldots, s_{T-1} a_{T-1} r_T s_T\right)$ by following $\pi\left(a_t | s_t, \theta\right)$

3.   for steps $t = 0, \ldots, T-1$ do

4.   Compute return, $R_t = \sum_{k=0}^{T} \gamma^k r_{t+k}$

5.   Compute discounted performance gradient, $\nabla \mathcal{J}(\theta) = \gamma^t R_t \nabla_\theta \ln \pi\left(a_t | s_t, \theta\right)$

6.   Perform gradient ascent, $\theta = \theta + \alpha \nabla \mathcal{J}(\theta)$

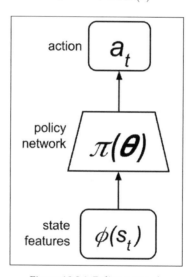

Figure 10.2.1: Policy network

In REINFORCE, the parameterized policy can be modeled by a neural network as shown in *Figure 10.2.1*. As discussed in the previous section, for the case of continuous action spaces, the state input is converted into features. The state features are the inputs of the policy network. The Gaussian distribution representing the policy function has a mean and standard deviation that are both functions of the state features. The policy network, $\pi(\theta)$, could be an MLP, CNN, or an RNN depending on the nature of the state inputs. The predicted action is simply a sample from the policy function.

REINFORCE with baseline method

The REINFORCE algorithm can be generalized by subtracting a baseline from the return, $\delta = R_t - B(s_t)$. The baseline function, $B(s_t)$ can be any function as long as it does not depend on a_t. The baseline does not alter the expectation of the performance gradient:

$$\nabla \mathcal{J}(\theta) = \mathbb{E}_\pi \left[\left(R_t - B(s_t) \right) \nabla_\theta ln\pi \left(a_t \left| s_t, \theta \right. \right) \right] = \mathbb{E}_\pi \left[R_t \nabla_\theta ln\pi \left(a_t \left| s_t, \theta \right. \right) \right] \quad \text{(Equation 10.3.1)}$$

Equation 10.3.1 implies that $\mathbb{E}_\pi \left[B(s_t) \nabla_\theta ln\pi \left(a_t \left| s_t, \theta \right. \right) \right] = 0$ since $B(s_t)$ is not a function of a_t.

While the introduction of baseline does not change the expectation, it reduces the variance of the gradient updates. The reduction in variance generally accelerates learning. In most cases, we use the value function, $B(s_t) = V(s_t)$ as the baseline. If the return is overestimated, the scaling factor is proportionally reduced by the value function resulting to a lower variance. The value function is also parameterized, $V(s_t) \rightarrow V(s_t, \theta_v)$ and is jointly trained with the policy network. In continuous action spaces, the state value can be a linear function of state features:

$$v_t = V\left(s_t, \theta_v \right) = \phi\left(s_t \right)^T \theta_v \quad \text{(Equation 10.3.2)}$$

Algorithm 10.3.1 summarizes the REINFORCE with baseline method [1]. This is similar to REINFORCE except that the return is replaced by s. The difference is we are now training two neural networks. As shown in *Figure 10.3.1*, in addition to the policy network, $\pi(\theta)$, the value network, $V(\theta)$, is also trained at the same time. The policy network parameters are updated by the performance gradient, $\nabla \mathcal{J}(\theta)$, while the value network parameters are adjusted by the value gradient, $\nabla V(\theta_v)$. Since REINFORCE is a Monte Carlo algorithm, it follows that the value function training is also a Monte Carlo algorithm.

The learning rates are not necessarily the same. Note that the value network is also performing gradient ascent. We illustrate how to implement REINFORCE with baseline using Keras at the end of this chapter.

Algorithm 10.3.1 REINFORCE with baseline

Require: A differentiable parameterized target policy network, $\pi\left(a_t \left| s_t, \theta \right. \right)$.

Require: A differentiable parameterized value network, $V\left(s_t, \theta_v \right)$.

Require: Discount factor, $\gamma \in [0,1]$, the learning rate α for the performance gradient and learning rate for the value gradient, α_v.

Require: θ_0, initial policy network parameters (for example, $\theta_0 \rightarrow 0$). θ_{v0}, initial value network parameters (for example, $\theta_{v0} \rightarrow 0$).

1. Repeat

2. Generate an episode $\langle s_0 a_0 r_1 s_1, s_1 a_1 r_2 s_2, \ldots, s_{T-1} a_{T-1} r_T s_T \rangle$ by following $\pi\left(a_t | s_t, \theta\right)$

3. for steps $t = 0, \ldots, T-1$ do

4. Compute return, $R_t = \sum_{k=0}^{T} \gamma^k r_{t+k}$

5. Subtract baseline, $\delta = R_t - V\left(s_t, \theta_v\right)$

6. Compute discounted value gradient, $\nabla V\left(\theta_v\right) = \gamma^t \delta \nabla_{\theta_v} V\left(s_t, \theta_v\right)$

7. Perform gradient ascent, $\theta_v = \theta_v + \alpha_v \nabla V\left(\theta_v\right)$

8. Compute discounted performance gradient,
$\nabla \mathcal{J}\left(\theta\right) = \gamma^t \delta \nabla_\theta ln\pi\left(a_t | s_t, \theta\right)$

9. Perform gradient ascent, $\theta = \theta + \alpha \nabla \mathcal{J}\left(\theta\right)$

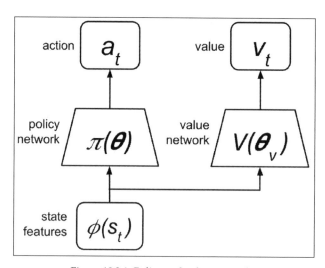

Figure 10.3.1: Policy and value networks

Actor-Critic method

In REINFORCE with baseline method, the value is used as a baseline. It is not used to train the value function. In this section, we'll introduce a variation of REINFORCE with baseline called the Actor-Critic method. The policy and value networks played the roles of actor and critic networks. The policy network is the actor deciding which action to take given the state. Meanwhile, the value network evaluates the decision made by the actor or the policy network. The value network acts as a critic which quantifies how good or bad the chosen action made by the actor is. The value network evaluates the state value, $V(s, \theta_v)$, by comparing it with the sum of the received reward, r, and the discounted value of the observed next state, $\gamma V(s', \theta_v)$. The difference, δ, is expressed as:

$$\delta = r_{t+1} + \gamma V\left(s_{t+1}, \theta_v\right) - V\left(s_t, \theta_v\right) = r + \gamma V\left(s', \theta_v\right) - V\left(s, \theta_v\right) \quad \text{(Equation 10.4.1)}$$

where we dropped the subscripts of r and s for simplicity. *Equation 10.4.1* is similar to the temporal differencing in Q-Learning discussed in *Chapter 9, Deep Reinforcement Learning*. The next state value is discounted by $\gamma \in [0,1]$ Estimating distant future rewards is difficult. Therefore, our estimate is based only on the immediate future, $r + \gamma V\left(s', \theta_v\right)$. This has been known as *bootstrapping* technique. The bootstrapping technique and the dependence on state representation in *Equation 10.4.1* often accelerates learning and reduces variance. From *Equation 10.4.1*, we notice that the value network evaluates the current state, $s = s_t$, which is due to the previous action, a_{t-1}, of the policy network. Meanwhile, the policy gradient is based on the current action, a_t. In a sense, the evaluation is delayed by one step.

Algorithm 10.4.1 summarizes the Actor-Critic method [1]. Apart from the evaluation of the state value which is used to train both the policy and value networks, the training is done online. At every step, both networks are trained. This is unlike REINFORCE and REINFORCE with baseline where the agent completes an episode before the training is performed. The value network is consulted twice. Firstly, during the value estimate of the current state and secondly for the value of the next state. Both values are used in the computation of gradients. *Figure 10.4.1* shows the Actor-Critic network. We will implement the Actor-Critic method in Keras at the end of this chapter.

Algorithm 10.4.1 Actor-Critic

Require: A differentiable parameterized target policy network, $\pi\left(a|s, \theta\right)$.

Require: A differentiable parameterized value network, $V\left(s, \theta_v\right)$.

Require: Discount factor, $\gamma \in [0,1]$, the learning rate α for the performance gradient, and the learning rate for the value gradient, α_v.

Require: θ_0, initial policy network parameters (for example, $\theta_0 \rightarrow 0$). θ_{v0}, initial value network parameters (for example, $\theta_{v0} \rightarrow 0$).

1.   Repeat

2.   for steps $t = 0,...,T-1$ do

3.   Sample an action $a \sim \pi(a|s,\theta)$

4.   Execute the action and observe reward r and next state s'

5.   Evaluate state value estimate, $\delta = r + \gamma V(s',\theta_v) - V(s,\theta_v)$

6.   Compute discounted value gradient, $\nabla V(\theta_v) = \gamma'\delta \nabla_{\theta_v} V(s,\theta_v)$

7.   Perform gradient ascent, $\theta_v = \theta_v + \alpha_v \nabla V(\theta_v)$

8.   Compute discounted performance gradient, $\nabla J(\theta) = \gamma'\delta \nabla_\theta ln\pi(a|s,\theta)$

9.   Perform gradient ascent, $\theta = \theta + \alpha \nabla J(\theta)$

10. $s = s'$

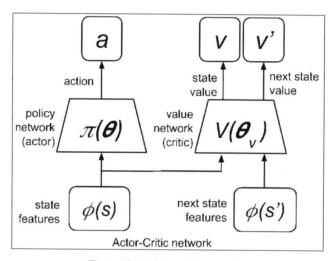

Figure 10.4.1: Actor-critic network

Advantage Actor-Critic (A2C) method

In the Actor-Critic method from the previous section, the objective is for the value function to evaluate the state value correctly. There are other techniques to train the value network. One obvious method is to use **MSE (mean squared error)** in the value function optimization, similar to the algorithm in Q-Learning. The new value gradient is equal to the partial derivative of the MSE between the return, R_t, and the state value:

$$\nabla V\left(\theta_v\right) = \frac{\delta\left(R_t - V\left(s,\theta_v\right)\right)^2}{\delta\theta_v} \qquad \text{(Equation 10.5.1)}$$

As $\left(R_t - V\left(s,\theta_v\right)\right) \to 0$, the value network prediction gets more accurate. We call this variation of the Actor-Critic algorithm as A2C. A2C is a single threaded or synchronous version of the **Asynchronous Advantage Actor-Critic (A3C)** by [2]. The quantity $\left(R_t - V\left(s,\theta_v\right)\right)$ is called *Advantage*.

Algorithm 10.5.1 summarizes the A2C method. There are some differences between A2C and Actor-Critic. Actor-Critic is online or is trained on per experience sample. A2C is similar to Monte Carlo algorithms REINFORCE and REINFORCE with baseline. It is trained after one episode has been completed. Actor-Critic is trained from the first state to the last state. A2C training starts from the last state and ends on the first state. In addition, the A2C policy and value gradients are no longer discounted by γ'.

The corresponding network for A2C is similar to *Figure 10.4.1* since we only changed the method of gradient computation. To encourage agent exploration during training, A3C algorithm [2] suggests that the gradient of the weighted entropy value of the policy function is added to the gradient function, $\beta\nabla_\theta H\left(\pi\left(a_t \mid s_t,\theta\right)\right)$. Recall that entropy is a measure of information or uncertainty of an event.

Algorithm 10.5.1 Advantage Actor-Critic (A2C)

Require: A differentiable parameterized target policy network, $\pi\left(a_t \mid s_t,\theta\right)$.

Require: A differentiable parameterized value network, $V\left(s_t,\theta_v\right)$.

Require: Discount factor, $\gamma \in [0,1]$, the learning rate α for the performance gradient, the learning rate for the value gradient, α_v and entropy weight, β.

Require: θ_0, initial policy network parameters (for example, $\theta_0 \rightarrow 0$). θ_{v0}, initial value network parameters (for example, $\theta_{v0} \rightarrow 0$).

1. Repeat

2.   Generate an episode $\langle s_0 a_0 r_1 s_1, s_1 a_1 r_2 s_2, \ldots, s_{T-1} a_{T-1} r_T s_T \rangle$ by following $\pi(a_t | s_t, \theta)$

3. $R_t = \begin{cases} 0 & \text{if } s_T \text{ is terminal} \\ V(s_T, \theta_v) & \text{for non-terminal}, s_T, \text{bootstrap from last state} \end{cases}$

4.   for steps $t = T-1, \ldots, 0$ do

5.   Compute return, $R_t = r_t + \gamma R_t$

6.   Compute value gradient, $\nabla V(\theta_v) = \dfrac{\partial \left(R_t - V(s, \theta_v) \right)^2}{\partial \theta_v}$

7.   Accumulate gradient, $\theta_v = \theta_v + a_v \nabla V(\theta_v)$

8.   Compute performance gradient,
$\nabla \mathcal{J}(\theta) = \nabla_\theta \ln\pi(a_t | s_t, \theta)\left(R_t - V(s, \theta_v)\right) + \beta\nabla_\theta H\left(\pi(a_t | s_t, \theta)\right)$

9.   Perform gradient ascent, $\theta = \theta + a\nabla \mathcal{J}(\theta)$

Policy Gradient methods with Keras

The four policy gradient methods (*Algorithms 10.2.1 to 10.5.1*) discussed in the previous sections use identical policy and value network models. The policy and value networks in *Figures 10.2.1 to 10.4.1* have the same configurations. The four policy gradient methods differ only in:

- Performance and value gradients formula
- Training strategy

In this section, we discuss the implementation in Keras of *Algorithms 10.2.1 to 10.5.1* in one code, since they share many common routines.

 The complete code can be found on https://github.com/
PacktPublishing/Advanced-Deep-Learning-with-Keras.

But before discussing the implementation, let's briefly explore the training environment.

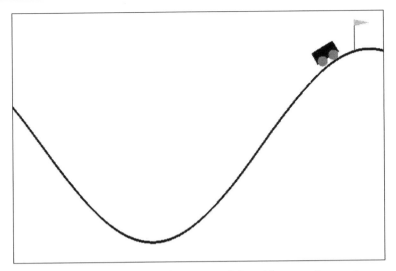

Figure 10.6.1 MountainCarContinuous-v0 OpenAI gym environment

Unlike Q-Learning, policy gradient methods are applicable to both discrete and continuous action spaces. In our example, we'll demonstrate the four policy gradient methods on a continuous action space case example, MountainCarContinuous-v0 of OpenAI gym, https://gym.openai.com. In case you are not familiar with OpenAI gym, please see *Chapter 9, Deep Reinforcement Learning.*

A snapshot of MountainCarContinuous-v0 2D environment is shown in *Figure 10.6.1.* In this 2D environment, a car with a not too powerful engine is between two mountains. In order to reach the yellow flag on top of the mountain on the right, it must drive back and forth to gain enough momentum. The more energy (that is, the greater the absolute value of action) that is applied to the car, the smaller (or, the more negative) is the reward. The reward is always negative, and it is only positive upon reaching the flag. In that case, the car receives a reward of +100. However, every action is penalized by the following code:

```
reward-= math.pow(action[0],2)*0.1
```

The continuous range of valid action values is [-1.0, 1.0]. Beyond the range, the action is clipped to its minimum or maximum value. Therefore, it makes no sense to apply an action value that is greater than 1.0 or less than -1.0. The MountainCarContinuous-v0 environment state has two elements:

- Car position
- Car velocity

The state is converted to state features by an encoder. The predicted action is the output of the policy model given the state. The output of the value function is the predicted value of the state:

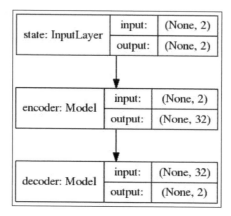

Figure 10.6.2 Autoencoder model

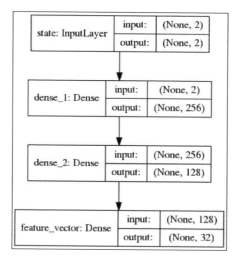

Figure 10.6.3 Encoder model

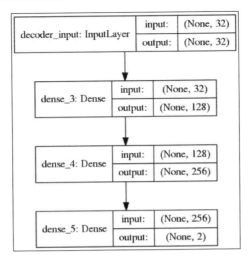

Figure 10.6.4 Decoder model

As shown in *Figures 10.2.1* to *10.4.1*, before building the policy and value networks, we must first create a function that converts the state to features. This function is implemented by an encoder of an autoencoder similar to the ones implemented in *Chapter 3, Autoencoders. Figure 10.6.2* shows an autoencoder made of an encoder and a decoder. In *Figure 10.6.3*, the encoder is an MLP made of `Input(2)-Dense(256, activation='relu')-Dense(128, activation='relu')-Dense(32)`. Every state is converted into a 32-dim feature vector. In *Figure 10.6.4*, the decoder is also an MLP but made of `Input(32)-Dense(128, activation='relu')-Dense(256, activation='relu')-Dense(2)`. The autoencoder is trained for 10 epochs with an **MSE**, loss function, and Keras default Adam optimizer. We sampled 220,000 random states for the train and test dataset and applied 200k/20k train-test split. After training, the encoder weights are saved for future use in the policy and value networks training. *Listing 10.6.1* shows the methods for building and training the autoencoder.

Listing 10.6.1, `policygradient-car-10.1.1.py` shows us the methods for building and training the autoencoder:

```
# autoencoder to convert states into features
def build_autoencoder(self):
    # first build the encoder model
    inputs = Input(shape=(self.state_dim, ), name='state')
    feature_size = 32
    x = Dense(256, activation='relu')(inputs)
    x = Dense(128, activation='relu')(x)
    feature = Dense(feature_size, name='feature_vector')(x)

    # instantiate encoder model
```

```
    self.encoder = Model(inputs, feature, name='encoder')
    self.encoder.summary()
    plot_model(self.encoder, to_file='encoder.png',
show_shapes=True)


    # build the decoder model
    feature_inputs = Input(shape=(feature_size,),
name='decoder_input')
    x = Dense(128, activation='relu')(feature_inputs)
    x = Dense(256, activation='relu')(x)
    outputs = Dense(self.state_dim, activation='linear')(x)

    # instantiate decoder model
    self.decoder = Model(feature_inputs, outputs, name='decoder')
    self.decoder.summary()
    plot_model(self.decoder, to_file='decoder.png',
show_shapes=True)


    # autoencoder = encoder + decoder
    # instantiate autoencoder model
    self.autoencoder = Model(inputs,
self.decoder(self.encoder(inputs)), name='autoencoder')
    self.autoencoder.summary()
    plot_model(self.autoencoder, to_file='autoencoder.png',
show_shapes=True)


    # Mean Square Error (MSE) loss function, Adam optimizer
    self.autoencoder.compile(loss='mse', optimizer='adam')


# training the autoencoder using randomly sampled
# states from the environment
def train_autoencoder(self, x_train, x_test):
    # train the autoencoder
    batch_size = 32
    self.autoencoder.fit(x_train,
                         x_train,
                         validation_data=(x_test, x_test),
                         epochs=10,
                         batch_size=batch_size)
```

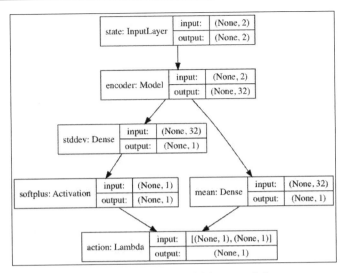

Figure 10.6.5: Policy model (actor model)

Given the `MountainCarContinuous-v0` environment, the policy (or actor) model predicts the action that must be applied on the car. As discussed in the first section of this chapter on policy gradient methods, for continuous action spaces the policy model samples an action from a Gaussian distribution, $\pi(a_t|s_t,\theta) = a_t \sim \mathcal{N}(\mu(s_t),\sigma(s_t))$. In Keras, this is implemented as:

```
# given mean and stddev, sample an action, clip and return
# we assume Gaussian distribution of probability of selecting an
# action given a state
def action(self, args):
    mean, stddev = args
    dist = tf.distributions.Normal(loc=mean, scale=stddev)
    action = dist.sample(1)
    action = K.clip(action,
                    self.env.action_space.low[0],
                    self.env.action_space.high[0])
    return action
```

The action is clipped between its minimum and maximum possible values.

The role of the policy network is to predict the mean and standard deviation of the Gaussian distribution. *Figure 10.6.5* shows the policy network to model $\pi(a_t|s_t,\theta)$. It's worth noting that the encoder model has pretrained weights that are frozen. Only the mean and standard deviation weights receive the performance gradient updates.

The policy network is basically the implementation of *Equations 10.1.4* and *10.1.5* that are repeated here for convenience:

$$\mu(s_t) = \phi(s_t)^T \theta_\mu \qquad \text{(Equation 10.1.4)}$$

$$\sigma(s_t) = \varsigma\left(\phi(s_t)^T \theta_\sigma\right) \qquad \text{(Equation 10.1.5)}$$

where $\phi(s_t)$ is the encoder, θ_μ are the weights of the mean's Dense (1) layer, and θ_σ are the weights of the standard deviation's Dense (1) layer. We used a modified *softplus* function, $\varsigma(\cdot)$, to avoid zero standard deviation:

```
# some implementations use a modified softplus to ensure that
# the stddev is never zero
def softplusk(x):
    return K.softplus(x) + 1e-10
```

The policy model builder is shown in the following listing. Also included in this listing are the log probability, entropy, and value models which we will discuss next.

Listing 10.6.2, `policygradient-car-10.1.1.py` shows us the method for building the policy (actor), `logp`, entropy, and value models from the encoded state features:

```
def build_actor_critic(self):
    inputs = Input(shape=(self.state_dim, ), name='state')
    self.encoder.trainable = False
    x = self.encoder(inputs)
    mean = Dense(1,
                 activation='linear',
                 kernel_initializer='zero',
                 name='mean')(x)
    stddev = Dense(1,
                   kernel_initializer='zero',
                   name='stddev')(x)
    # use of softplusk avoids stddev = 0
    stddev = Activation('softplusk', name='softplus')(stddev)
    action = Lambda(self.action,
                    output_shape=(1,),
                    name='action')([mean, stddev])
    self.actor_model = Model(inputs, action, name='action')
    self.actor_model.summary()
    plot_model(self.actor_model, to_file='actor_model.png',
show_shapes=True)
```

```
    logp = Lambda(self.logp,
                  output_shape=(1,),
                  name='logp')([mean, stddev, action])
    self.logp_model = Model(inputs, logp, name='logp')
    self.logp_model.summary()
    plot_model(self.logp_model, to_file='logp_model.png', show_
shapes=True)

    entropy = Lambda(self.entropy,
                     output_shape=(1,),
                     name='entropy')([mean, stddev])
    self.entropy_model = Model(inputs, entropy, name='entropy')
    self.entropy_model.summary()
    plot_model(self.entropy_model, to_file='entropy_model.png', show_
shapes=True)
    value = Dense(1,
                  activation='linear',
                  kernel_initializer='zero',
                  name='value')(x)
    self.value_model = Model(inputs, value, name='value')
    self.value_model.summary()
```

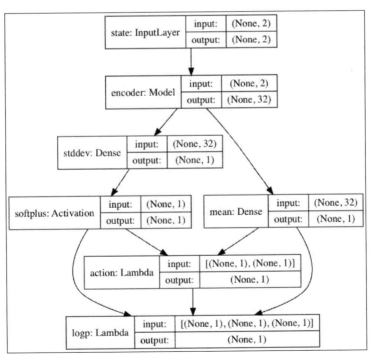

Figure 10.6.6: Gaussian log probability model of the policy

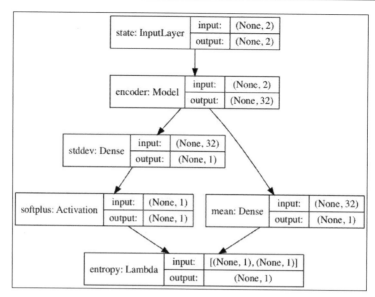

Figure 10.6.7: Entropy model

Apart from the policy network, $\pi(a_t|s_t,\theta)$, we must also have the action log probability (`logp`) network $\ln \pi(a_t|s_t,\theta)$ since this is actually what calculates the gradient. As shown in *Figure 10.6.6*, the `logp` network is simply the policy network where an additional `Lambda(1)` layer computes the log probability of the Gaussian distribution given action, mean, and standard deviation. The `logp` network and actor (policy) model share the same set of parameters. The `Lambda` layer does not have any parameter. It is implemented by the following function:

```
# given mean, stddev, and action compute
# the log probability of the Gaussian distribution
def logp(self, args):
    mean, stddev, action = args
    dist = tf.distributions.Normal(loc=mean, scale=stddev)
    logp = dist.log_prob(action)
    return logp
```

Training the `logp` network trains the actor model as well. In the training methods that are discussed in this section, only the `logp` network is trained.

As shown in *Figure 10.6.7*, the entropy model also shares parameters with the policy network. The output `Lambda(1)` layer computes the entropy of the Gaussian distribution given the mean and standard deviation using the following function:

```
# given the mean and stddev compute the Gaussian dist entropy
def entropy(self, args):
```

```
mean, stddev = args
dist = tf.distributions.Normal(loc=mean, scale=stddev)
entropy = dist.entropy()
return entropy
```

The entropy model is only used by the A2C method:

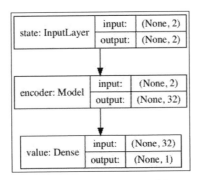

Figure 10.6.8: A value model

Preceding figure shows the value model. The model also uses the pre-trained encoder with frozen weights to implement following equation which is repeated here for convenience:

$$v_t = V\left(s_t, \theta_v\right) = \phi\left(s_t\right)^T \theta_v \qquad \text{(Equation 10.3.2)}$$

θ_v are the weights of the Dense(1) layer, the only layer that receives value gradient updates. *Figure 10.6.8* represents $V(s_t, \theta_v)$ in *Algorithms 10.3.1* to *10.5.1*. The value model can be built in a few lines:

```
inputs = Input(shape=(self.state_dim, ), name='state')
self.encoder.trainable = False
x = self.encoder(inputs)

value = Dense(1,
              activation='linear',
              kernel_initializer='zero',
              name='value')(x)
self.value_model = Model(inputs, value, name='value')
```

These lines are also implemented in method `build_actor_critic()`, which is shown in *Listing 10.6.2*.

After building the network models, the next step is training. In *Algorithms 10.2.1 to 10.5.1*, we perform objective function maximization by gradient ascent. In Keras, we perform loss function minimization by gradient descent. The loss function is simply the negative of the objective function being maximized. The gradient descent is the negative of gradient ascent. *Listing 10.6.3* shows the `logp` and value loss functions.

We can take advantage of the common structure of the loss functions to unify the loss functions in *Algorithms 10.2.1 to 10.5.1*. The performance and value gradients differ only in their constant factors. All performance gradients have the common term, $\nabla_{\theta} \ln \pi \left(a_{t} \mid s_{t}, \theta \right)$. This is represented by y_pred in the policy log probability loss function, `logp_loss()`. The factor to the common term, $\nabla_{\theta} \ln \pi \left(a_{t} \mid s_{t}, \theta \right)$, depends on which algorithm and is implemented as y_true. Table 10.6.1 shows the values of y_true. The remaining term is the weighted gradient of entropy, $\beta \nabla_{\theta} H \left(\pi \left(a_{t} \mid s_{t}, \theta \right) \right)$. It is implemented as the product of `beta` and `entropy` in the `logp_loss()` function. Only A2C uses this term, so by default, `beta=0.0`. For A2C, `beta=0.9`.

Listing 10.6.3, `policygradient-car-10.1.1.py`: The loss functions of `logp` and value networks.

```
# logp loss, the 3rd and 4th variables (entropy and beta) are needed
# by A2C so we have a different loss function structure
def logp_loss(self, entropy, beta=0.0):
    def loss(y_true, y_pred):
        return -K.mean((y_pred * y_true) + (beta * entropy), ax
is=-1)

    return loss


# typical loss function structure that accepts 2 arguments only
# this will be used by value loss of all methods except A2C
def value_loss(self, y_true, y_pred):
    return -K.mean(y_pred * y_true, axis=-1)
```

Algorithm	y_true of logp_loss	y_true of value_loss
10.2.1 REINFORCE	$\gamma^{t} R_{t}$	Not applicable
10.3.1 REINFORCE with baseline	$\gamma^{t} \delta$	$\gamma^{t} \delta$
10.4.1 Actor-Critic	$\gamma^{t} \delta$	$\gamma^{t} \delta$
10.5.1 A2C	$\left(R_{t} - V \left(s, \theta_{v} \right) \right)$	R_{t}

Table 10.6.1: y_true value of logp_loss and value_loss

Similarly, the value loss functions of *Algorithms 10.3.1* and *10.4.1* have the same structure. The value loss functions are implemented in Keras as value_loss() as shown in *Listing 10.6.3*. The common gradient factor $\nabla_{\theta_v} V(s_t, \theta_v)$ is represented by the tensor y_pred. The remaining factor is represented by y_true. The y_true values are also shown in *Table 10.6.1*. REINFORCE does not use a value function. A2C uses the MSE loss function to learn the value function. In A2C, y_true represents the target value or ground truth.

Listing 10.6.4, policygradient-car-10.1.1.py shows us, REINFORCE, REINFORCE with baseline, and A2C are trained by episode. The appropriate return is computed first before calling the main train routine in *Listing 10.6.5*:

```
# train by episode (REINFORCE, REINFORCE with baseline
# and A2C use this routine to prepare the dataset before
# the step by step training)
def train_by_episode(self, last_value=0):
    if self.args.actor_critic:
        print("Actor-Critic must be trained per step")
        return
    elif self.args.a2c:
        # implements A2C training from the last state
        # to the first state
        # discount factor
        gamma = 0.95
        r = last_value
        # the memory is visited in reverse as shown
        # in Algorithm 10.5.1
        for item in self.memory[::-1]:
            [step, state, next_state, reward, done] = item
            # compute the return
            r = reward + gamma*r
            item = [step, state, next_state, r, done]
            # train per step
            # a2c reward has been discounted
            self.train(item)

        return

    # only REINFORCE and REINFORCE with baseline
    # use the ff codes
    # convert the rewards to returns
    rewards = []
    gamma = 0.99
    for item in self.memory:
```

```
        [_, _, _, reward, _] = item
        rewards.append(reward)

    # compute return per step
    # return is the sum of rewards from t til end of episode
    # return replaces reward in the list
    for i in range(len(rewards)):
        reward = rewards[i:]
        horizon = len(reward)
        discount = [math.pow(gamma, t) for t in range(horizon)]
        return_ = np.dot(reward, discount)
        self.memory[i][3] = return_

    # train every step
    for item in self.memory:
        self.train(item, gamma=gamma)
```

Listing 10.6.5, `policygradient-car-10.1.1.py` shows us the main `train` routine
used by all the policy gradient algorithms. Actor-critic calls this every experience
sample while the rest call this during train per episode routine in *Listing 10.6.4*:

```
# main routine for training as used by all 4 policy gradient
# methods
def train(self, item, gamma=1.0):
    [step, state, next_state, reward, done] = item

    # must save state for entropy computation
    self.state = state

    discount_factor = gamma**step

    # reinforce-baseline: delta = return - value
    # actor-critic: delta = reward - value + discounted_next_value
    # a2c: delta = discounted_reward - value
    delta = reward - self.value(state)[0]

    # only REINFORCE does not use a critic (value network)
    critic = False
    if self.args.baseline:
        critic = True
    elif self.args.actor_critic:
        # since this function is called by Actor-Critic
        # directly, evaluate the value function here
        critic = True
        if not done:
```

```
            next_value = self.value(next_state)[0]
            # add  the discounted next value
            delta += gamma*next_value
    elif self.args.a2c:
        critic = True
    else:
        delta = reward

    # apply the discount factor as shown in Algortihms
    # 10.2.1, 10.3.1 and 10.4.1
    discounted_delta = delta * discount_factor
    discounted_delta = np.reshape(discounted_delta, [-1, 1])
    verbose = 1 if done else 0

    # train the logp model (implies training of actor model
    # as well) since they share exactly the same set of
    # parameters
    self.logp_model.fit(np.array(state),
                        discounted_delta,
                        batch_size=1,
                        epochs=1,
                        verbose=verbose)

    # in A2C, the target value is the return (reward
    # replaced by return in the train_by_episode function)
    if self.args.a2c:
        discounted_delta = reward
        discounted_delta = np.reshape(discounted_delta, [-1, 1])

    # train the value network (critic)
    if critic:
        self.value_model.fit(np.array(state),
                            discounted_delta,
                            batch_size=1,
                            epochs=1,
                            verbose=verbose)
```

With all network models and loss functions in place, the last part is the training strategy, which is different for each algorithm. Two train functions are used as shown in *Listings 10.6.4* and *10.6.5*. *Algorithms 10.2.1, 10.3.1*, and *10.5.1* wait for a complete episode to finish before training, so it runs both `train_by_episode()` and `train()`. The complete episode is saved in `self.memory`. Actor-Critic *Algorithm 10.4.1* trains per step and only runs `train()`.

Each algorithm processes its episode trajectory in a different way.

Algorithm	y_true **formula**	y_true **in Keras**
10.2.1 REINFORCE	$\gamma^t R_t$	`reward * discount_factor`
10.3.1 REINFORCE with baseline	$\gamma^t \delta$	`(reward - self.value(state)[0]) * discount_factor`
10.4.1 Actor-Critic	$\gamma^t \delta$	`(reward - self.value(state)[0] + gamma*next_value) * discount_factor`
10.5.1 A2C	$\left(R_t - V\left(s, \theta_v\right)\right)$ and R_t	`(reward - self.value(state)[0])` and `reward`

Table 10.6.2: y_true value in Table 10.6.1

For REINFORCE methods and A2C, the `reward` is actually the return as computed in `train_by_episode()`. `discount_factor = gamma**step`.

Both REINFORCE methods compute the return, $R_t = \sum_{k=0}^{T} \gamma^k r_{t+k}$, by replacing the reward value in the memory as:

```
# only REINFORCE and REINFORCE with baseline
# use the ff codes
# convert the rewards to returns
rewards = []
gamma = 0.99
for item in self.memory:
    [_, _, _, reward, _] = item
    rewards.append(reward)

# compute return per step
# return is the sum of rewards from t til end of episode
# return replaces reward in the list
for i in range(len(rewards)):
    reward = rewards[i:]
    horizon = len(reward)
    discount = [math.pow(gamma, t) for t in range(horizon)]
    return_ = np.dot(reward, discount)
    self.memory[i][3] = return_
```

This then trains the policy (actor) and value models (with baseline only) for each step beginning with the first step.

The training strategy of A2C is different in the sense that it computes gradients from the last step to the first step. Hence, the return accumulates beginning from the last step reward or the last next state value:

```
# the memory is visited in reverse as shown
# in Algorithm 10.5.1
for item in self.memory[::-1]:
    [step, state, next_state, reward, done] = item
    # compute the return
    r = reward + gamma*r
    item = [step, state, next_state, r, done]
    # train per step
    # a2c reward has been discounted
    self.train(item)
```

The `reward` variable in the list is also replaced by return. It is initialized by `reward` if the terminal state is reached (that is, the car touches the flag) or the next state value for non-terminal states:

```
v = 0 if reward > 0 else agent.value(next_state)[0]
```

In the Keras implementation, all the routines that we mentioned are implemented as methods in the `PolicyAgent` class. The role of the `PolicyAgent` is to represent the agent implementing policy gradient methods including building and training the network models and predicting the action, log probability, entropy, and state value.

Following listing shows how one episode unfolds when the agent executes and trains the policy and value models. The `for` loop is executed for 1000 episodes. An episode terminates upon reaching 1000 steps or when the car touches the flag. The agent executes the action predicted by the policy at every step. After each episode or step, the training routine is called.

Listing 10.6.6, `policygradient-car-10.1.1.py`: The agent runs for 1000 episodes to execute the action predicted by the policy at every step and perform training:

```
# sampling and fitting
for episode in range(episode_count):
    state = env.reset()
    # state is car [position, speed]
    state = np.reshape(state, [1, state_dim])
    # reset all variables and memory before the start of
    # every episode
    step = 0
    total_reward = 0
    done = False
    agent.reset_memory()
```

```
while not done:
    # [min, max] action = [-1.0, 1.0]
    # for baseline, random choice of action will not move
    # the car pass the flag pole
    if args.random:
        action = env.action_space.sample()
    else:
        action = agent.act(state)
    env.render()
    # after executing the action, get s', r, done
    next_state, reward, done, _ = env.step(action)
    next_state = np.reshape(next_state, [1, state_dim])
    # save the experience unit in memory for training
    # Actor-Critic does not need this but we keep it anyway.
    item = [step, state, next_state, reward, done]
    agent.remember(item)

    if args.actor_critic and train:
        # only actor-critic performs online training
        # train at every step as it happens
        agent.train(item, gamma=0.99)
    elif not args.random and done and train:
        # for REINFORCE, REINFORCE with baseline, and A2C
        # we wait for the completion of the episode before
        # training the network(s)
        # last value as used by A2C
        v = 0 if reward > 0 else agent.value(next_state)[0]
        agent.train_by_episode(last_value=v)

    # accumulate reward
    total_reward += reward
    # next state is the new state
    state = next_state
    step += 1
```

Performance evaluation of policy gradient methods

The four policy gradients methods were evaluated by training the agent for 1,000 episodes. We define 1 training session as 1,000 episodes of training. The first performance metric is measured by accumulating the number of times the car reached the flag in 1,000 episodes. *Figures 10.7.1 to 10.7.4* shows five training sessions per method.

In this metric, A2C reached the flag with the greatest number of times followed by REINFORCE with baseline, Actor-Critic, and REINFORCE. The use of baseline or critic accelerates the learning. Note that these are training sessions with the agent continuously improving its performance. There were cases in the experiments where the agent's performance did not improve with time.

The second performance metric is based on the requirement that the `MountainCarContinuous-v0` is considered solved if the total reward per episode is at least 90.0. From the five training sessions per method, we selected one training session with the highest total reward for the last 100 episodes (episodes 900 to 999). *Figures 10.7.5 to 10.7.8* show the results of the four policy gradient methods. REINFORCE with baseline is the only method that was able to consistently achieve a total reward of about 90 after 1,000 episodes of training. A2C has the second-best performance but could not consistently reach at least 90 for the total rewards.

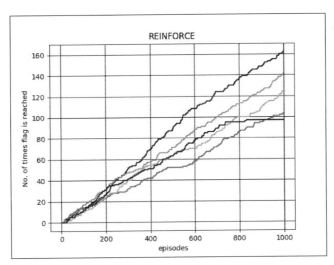

Figure 10.7.1: The number of times the mountain car reached the flag using REINFORCE method

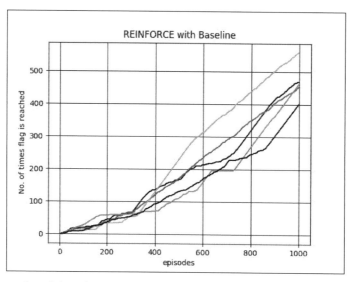

Figure 10.7.2: The number of times the mountain car reached the flag using REINFORCE with baseline method

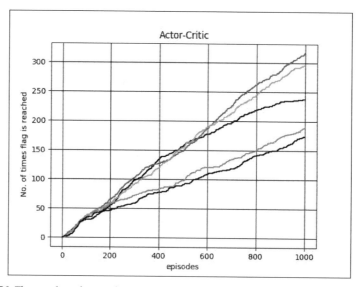

Figure 10.7.3: The number of times the mountain car reached the flag using the Actor-Critic method

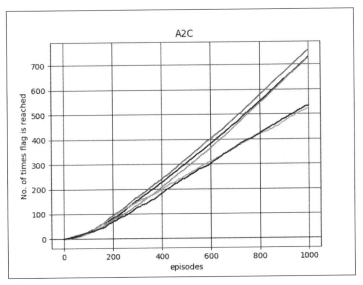

Figure 10.7.4: The number of times the mountain car reached the flag using the A2C method

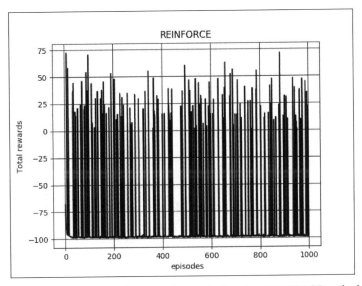

Figure 10.7.5: Total rewards received per episode using REINFORCE method

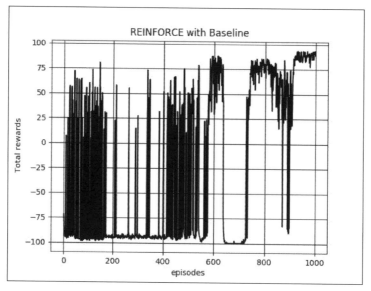

Figure 10.7.6: Total rewards received per episode using REINFORCE with baseline method.

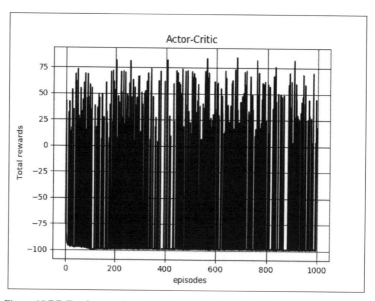

Figure 10.7.7: Total rewards received per episode using the Actor-Critic method

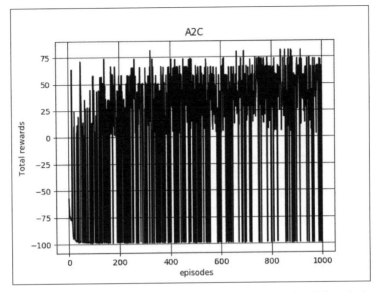

Figure 10.7.8: The total rewards received per episode using the A2C method

In the experiments conducted, we used the same learning rate, `1e-3`, for log probability and value networks optimization. The discount factor is set to 0.99, except for A2C which is easier to train at a 0.95 discount factor.

The reader is encouraged to run the trained network by executing:

```
$ python3 policygradient-car-10.1.1.py
--encoder_weights=encoder_weights.h5 --actor_weights=actor_weights.h5
```

Following table shows other modes of running `policygradient-car-10.1.1.py`. The weights file (that is, `*.h5`) can be replaced by your own pre-trained weights file. Please consult the code to see the other potential options:

Purpose	Run
Train REINFORCE from scratch	`python3 policygradient-car-10.1.1.py` `--encoder_weights=encoder_weights.h5`
Train REINFORCE with baseline from scratch	`python3 policygradient-car-10.1.1.py` `--encoder_weights=encoder_weights.h5 -b`
Train Actor-Critic from scratch	`python3 policygradient-car-10.1.1.py` `--encoder_weights=encoder_weights.h5 -a`
Train A2C from scratch	`python3 policygradient-car-10.1.1.py` `--encoder_weights=encoder_weights.h5 -c`

Train REINFORCE from previously saved weights	```python3 policygradient-car-10.1.1.py```
	```--encoder_weights=encoder_weights.h5```
	```--actor_weights=actor_weights.h5 --train```

Train REINFORCE with baseline from previously saved weights	```python3 policygradient-car-10.1.1.py```
	```--encoder_weights=encoder_weights.h5```
	```--actor_weights=actor_weights.h5```
	```--value_weights=value_weights.h5 -b --train```

Train Actor-Critic from previously saved weights	```python3 policygradient-car-10.1.1.py```
	```--encoder_weights=encoder_weights.h5```
	```--actor_weights=actor_weights.h5```
	```--value_weights=value_weights.h5 -a --train```

Train A2C from previously saved weights	```python3 policygradient-car-10.1.1.py```
	```--encoder_weights=encoder_weights.h5```
	```--actor_weights=actor_weights.h5```
	```--value_weights=value_weights.h5 -c --train```

Table 10.7.1: Different options in running policygradient-car-10.1.1.py

As a final note, the implementation of the policy gradient methods in Keras has some limitations. For example, training the actor model requires resampling the action. The action is first sampled and applied to the environment to observe the reward and next state. Then, another sample is taken for training the log probability model. The second sample is not necessarily the same as the first one, but the reward that is used for training comes from the first sampled action, which can introduce stochastic error in the computation of gradients.

The good news is Keras is gaining a lot of support from TensorFlow in the form of `tf.keras`. Transitioning from Keras to a more flexible and powerful machine learning library, like TensorFlow, has been made a lot easier. If you started with Keras and wanted to build low-level custom machine learning routines, the APIs of Keras and `tf.keras` share strong similarities.

There is a small learning curve in using Keras in TensorFlow. Furthermore, in `tf.keras`, you're able to take advantage of the new easy to use Dataset and Estimators APIs of TensorFlow. This simplifies a lot of the code and model reuse that ends up with a clean pipeline. With the new eager execution mode of TensorFlow, it becomes even easier to implement and debug Python codes in `tf.keras` and TensorFlow. Eager execution allows the execution of codes without building a computational graph as we did in this book. It also allows code structures similar to a typical Python program.

Conclusion

In this chapter, we've covered the policy gradient methods. Starting with the policy gradient theorem, we formulated four methods to train the policy network. The four methods, REINFORCE, REINFORCE with baseline, Actor-Critic, and A2C algorithms were discussed in detail. We explored how the four methods could be implemented in Keras. We then validated the algorithms by examining the number of times the agent successfully reached its goal and in terms of the total rewards received per episode.

Similar to Deep Q-Network [2] that we discussed in the previous chapter, there are several improvements that can be done on the fundamental policy gradient algorithms. For example, the most prominent one is the A3C [3] which is a multi-threaded version of A2C. This enables the agent to get exposed to different experiences simultaneously and to optimize the policy and value networks asynchronously. However, in the experiments conducted by OpenAI, `https://blog.openai.com/baselines-acktr-a2c/`, there is no strong advantage of A3C over A2C since the former could not take advantage of the strong GPUs available nowadays.

Given that this is the end of the book, it's worth noting that the area of deep learning is huge, and to cover all the advances in one book like this is impossible. What we've done is carefully selected the advanced topics that I believe will be useful in a wide range of applications and that you, the reader will be able to easily build on. The implementations in Keras that have been illustrated throughout this book will allow you to carry on and apply the techniques in your own work and research.

References

1. Sutton and Barto. *Reinforcement Learning: An Introduction*, `http://incompleteideas.net/book/bookdraft2017nov5.pdf`, (2017).

2. Mnih, Volodymyr, and others. *Human-level control through deep reinforcement learning*, Nature 518.7540 (2015): 529.

3. Mnih, Volodymyr, and others. *Asynchronous methods for deep reinforcement learning*, International conference on machine learning, 2016.

4. Williams and Ronald J. *Simple statistical gradient-following algorithms for connectionist reinforcement learning*, Machine learning 8.3-4 (1992): 229-256.

Other Books You May Enjoy

If you enjoyed this book, you may be interested in these other books by Packt:

Deep Reinforcement Learning Hands-On

Maxim Lapan

ISBN: 978-1-78883-424-7

- Understand the DL context of RL and implement complex DL models
- Learn the foundation of RL: Markov decision processes
- Evaluate RL methods including Cross-entropy, DQN, Actor-Critic, TRPO, PPO, DDPG, D4PG and others
- Discover how to deal with discrete and continuous action spaces in various environments
- Defeat Atari arcade games using the value iteration method
- Create your own OpenAI Gym environment to train a stock trading agent
- Teach your agent to play Connect4 using AlphaGo Zero
- Explore the very latest deep RL research on topics including AI-driven chatbots

Deep Learning with TensorFlow

Giancarlo Zaccone, Md. Rezaul Karim

ISBN: 978-1-78883-110-9

- Apply deep machine intelligence and GPU computing with TensorFlow
- Access public datasets and use TensorFlow to load, process, and transform the data
- Discover how to use the high-level TensorFlow API to build more powerful applications
- Use deep learning for scalable object detection and mobile computing
- Train machines quickly to learn from data by exploring reinforcement learning techniques
- Explore active areas of deep learning research and applications

Leave a review - let other readers know what you think

Please share your thoughts on this book with others by leaving a review on the site that you bought it from. If you purchased the book from Amazon, please leave us an honest review on this book's Amazon page. This is vital so that other potential readers can see and use your unbiased opinion to make purchasing decisions, we can understand what our customers think about our products, and our authors can see your feedback on the title that they have worked with Packt to create. It will only take a few minutes of your time, but is valuable to other potential customers, our authors, and Packt. Thank you!

Index

51320800R00202

Made in the USA
Columbia, SC
16 February 2019